The Pebble in the Shoe

The Diplomatic Struggle for EAST TIMOR

Ali Alatas

The Pebble in the Shoe

The Diplomatic Struggle for EAST TIMOR

aksara karunia

2006

The Pebble in The Shoe:
The Diplomatic Struggle for East Timor

Writer:
Ali Alatas

Photographs:
Reuters, UN/DPI, Antara, *Tempo,* Personal collection

Cover Design & Layout by:
muidmular

First Print 2006; Registered ©Aksara Karunia

Perpustakaan Nasional RI: Katalog Dalam Terbitan (KDT)
Alatas, Ali

The Pebble in The Shoe: The Diplomatic Struggle for East Timor/by Ali Alatas — Jakarta: Aksara Karunia; 2006.

xx + 330 pages, 15 X 23.5 cm

ISBN 979-3851-09-0

1. Timor Timur--Politik dan Pemerintahan.
I. Judul. 959.86

Dedication

To my Colleagues

in the Foreign Service

who waged with me

a long and arduous

struggle for peace

Acknowledgements

WRITING a book is never easy, especially a book on so complex a subject as a diplomatic struggle that lasted for decades and involved many determined and resourceful individuals contending on a myriad intricate issues. Fortunately, in the writing of this book, I had plenty of help.

I wish to thank first of all my companions in that struggle, for without their labours and initiatives, the diplomatic struggle could not have been as ably waged as it had been, and there would have been much less worth remembering and even less to write about. I am grateful, too, to the three United Nations Secretaries-General and their collaborators who provided the field and the arbiters of that struggle, and even to the worthy adversaries with whom we contended over the years.

As always, I owe a special debt to my family for their support and for their sacrifice of some of the time I should have been spending with them in my retirement so that the book could be written. As always, I am especially grateful to my wife, Junisa for her patience.

I also wish to acknowledge the help of my long-time collaborator, Jamil Maidan Flores, in the chapter-by-chapter editing of the text and that of his wife Noreen M. Flores in the supervision of pre-print production and in the collation of the illustrative photographs. I owe a debt of gratitude to *Reuter's* and *Kompas* for the photographs they contributed. For the cover design and for the book design, I thank graphic artists Bharata Kusuma and Muid respectively.

Finally, I am thankful to my publisher, Aristides Katoppo, for the act of faith that he made in ensuring that this book would finally see the light of print.

All the inadvertencies in the book are, of course, all mine.

Ali Alatas

Jakarta

Table of Content

Foreword

THIS is a book that had to wait for its time to be written. Had it been written too soon after the tragic developments in East Timor in 1999, it could have become part of a burning debate, one that had been generating more heat than light. So much passion and so much pride attended that debate and produced so much smoke and dust that a clear-eyed appreciation of what I wanted to tell was probably not possible.

On the other hand, if I had waited too long in writing it, there would have been the problem of memory, for much of the story that I would tell, although substantiated by documents, is for the most part a personal experience. And it must be acknowledged that with the passing of time, memory does not improve.

And there would have been a greater problem of resolve in carrying out a complex and demanding task. There are many things that a person in retirement can do that are easier, more enjoyable, and safer than writing a book about controversial events that not a few of those involved would rather forget.

But it is a necessary task. The book must be written if only for the sake of completeness.

For despite the many books that have already been written about East Timor, the complete story has yet to be told. There are important parts and aspects of it that have yet to be made public.

I have read a good number of books on East Timor, including on the events that led to the political exercise in which the East Timorese opted for separation from Indonesia, and the tragedy that came about in its wake. Here and there in my reading I have come across a few versions and details that do not correspond to what I believe actually transpired, but in any case this book is not meant to refute all of these misrepresentations.

But I have something important to add to what they have written or said. In the first place, most of the existing books on East Timor today were written by foreign observers. There is therefore the need to present the East Timor story from the perspective of an Indonesian who, moreover, has been intimately involved in the East Timor question for almost all of the twenty-five years of its existence.

Another urgent reason this book must be written is that there is an essential aspect of the East Timor story that must be told to the Indonesian public and to the world at large: the arduous and often frustrating negotiations to find a peaceful, just and comprehensive solution to the problem, especially the period from 1983 to 1991, which mostly took place behind closed doors. This book will try to tell that story in greater detail.

It may be worth noting that among the main protagonists in the East Timor negotiations were a succession of three United Nations Secretaries-General—Javier Perez de Cuellar, Boutros Boutros-Ghali and Kofi Annan—and, on the side of Portugal, three successive Foreign Ministers and three Ambassadors. But one and the same person negotiated on the Indonesian side: Ambassador and Permanent Representative of Indonesia to the United Nations and later Minister for Foreign Affairs of Indonesia, Ali Alatas, who was, of course, ably assisted by a number of very proficient and loyal Indonesian diplomats.

The third reason for writing this book is the need to present an introspective and retrospective account of the East Timor problem and the dramatic developments that attended it for over a quarter of a century. These developments have had such a profound impact not only on Indonesia's image abroad but also on its self-consciousness.

Yet another reason for writing this book is that there are basic misconceptions that cry out for rectification. For example, when the story of the East Timor problem is finally told in an essentially complete way, the picture that emerges is an East Timor issue that is not quite as simple as a morality play: good guys versus bad guys.

We will still see the story of the East Timor issue as a story of conflict, but not a simple one between East Timorese who passionately desired independence and those who just as passionately stood for integration—certainly, it was not just a conflict between East Timor and Indonesia, nor just between the former colonial power, Portugal, and Indonesia.

The greatest conflict in that story is the one between the individuals who went on a quest for a peaceful, just and comprehensive political solution to the East Timor issue, a solution that is acceptable to all concerned, and the obstacles that stood in the way of this quest: the passions, the prejudices, the illusions and delusions, the ambitions, the fears and man's inhumanity to man that are the natural enemies of rational decision-making.

The individuals who went on this quest were by no means all Indonesians. Though they stood on the opposite side of debates in the UN General Assembly, or sat across us at the negotiating table, our Portuguese counterparts were in the final analysis not simply our adversaries but fellow seekers of a lasting solution to a very difficult problem. So were the United Nations officials, especially the Secretaries-General and their Personal and Special Representatives who mediated and moderated the negotiations.

The story of this quest is therefore not only worth telling, but also one that must be told if all the precious lessons of our experience with East Timor are to be learned and put to good use in our continuing endeavour to develop our nation. I believe that there are insights that can be drawn from the story that will help the political observer, whatever may be his nationality or his calling, acquire a better understanding of contemporary international affairs as well as national inter-ethnic and inter-cultural dynamics.

In telling that story, I have relied heavily on documents, some of which are being made public for the first time. I have also made use of my notes in the course of my functioning as an Indonesian diplomat working on the East Timor issue, much of the time as the chief negotiator on the Indonesian side. I have also interviewed a number of colleagues who worked closely with me on this issue. And, in those instances, when there is nothing else to rely on, I have had to depend on my memory, with all the risk of its failing.

This is by no means the last word on the East Timor issue. It is probable, maybe even inevitable that someday, when East Timor as a sovereign and independent state has found its niche in the Southeast Asian and West Pacific communities of nations, there may yet be some significant data or insights that may be added to the picture of the East Timor issue. For that is what history is all about: the accumulation of insights from past events, and the growth of understanding of human nature that those insights bring.

Unfortunately, knowledge of history does not prevent us from repeating it. Let us hope it is not repeated in the cases of Aceh and Papua.

Introduction

ON 20 May 2002, Timor Leste, also known as East Timor or Timor Lorosae, became an independent, sovereign state through a process of "popular consultation" that took place on 30 August 1999.

Although it now proudly bears the name the Democratic Republic of Timor Leste, I shall, for purposes of this book, continue to refer to it by the name that became a byword in the annals of the United Nations where debates and negotiations on its political status took place for more than two decades. Thus to me, East Timor is not only the name of a territory that has become a nation-state in its own right but a name that has many associations with the arduous diplomatic struggle that I had to wage for many years, first as Ambassador/Permanent Representative to the UN in Geneva and later to the UN in New York and subsequently as Foreign Minister of Indonesia.

By the time that East Timor became a nation-state, it had gone a long way: from languishing as a Portuguese colony for four hundred years, through a quarter of a century as the twenty-seventh province of the Republic of Indonesia, through a thirty-month tutelage under the United Nations, to becoming the eleventh nation-state in Southeast Asia and the hundred-and-ninetieth Member of the United Nations.

It is a saga that has been told many times and in various ways by historians and journalists. Indonesia, of course, figures as one of the principal characters in that story. Unfortunately for Indonesia, its role as perceived by the overwhelming majority of observers is that of antagonist to the East Timorese struggle toward freedom and independence. The triumph of East Timor is therefore seen by most people, even by most Indonesians, as a defeat for Indonesia.

That is why I was not surprised at all when one afternoon in late April 2001, in the course of a lengthy and frank dialogue with a visiting delegation from the *Centro Nacional de Cultura* of Portugal, one of the delegates asked me whether, as a result of East Timor's act of separating from Indonesia, I suffered a sense of loss.

I told the lady who had asked the question that East Timor's separation from Indonesia did not evoke from me any feeling of loss or having lost. But I did have a sense of regret and of failure for not having been able to secure a more peaceful resolution of the issue of East Timor.

For in 1998, in the course of negotiations between Portugal and Indonesia, under the aegis of the UN Secretary-General, to try to resolve the issue of East Timor by way of a political compromise through the offer of a special status and wide-ranging autonomy within the Republic of Indonesia—it was distinctly possible that the resolution of the issue would not be attended by turmoil and bloodshed.

Over the years, I had on many occasions stressed, both publicly and privately, that it would be risky, even potentially explosive, to put the two rival groups in East Timor, those who were pro-independence and those in favour of integration with Indonesia, in a confrontational situation such as a referendum or a plebiscite, that would instantly force a choice on the political status of the territory.

I feared that whichever party would lose the contest would not accept defeat; it would reject the result. If the losing party were the pro-independence group, they would simply return to the mountains and continue their armed struggle, thereby putting the entire negotiating effort back to square one. If the losing party were the pro-integration group, they would just as certainly reject the result and resort to violence to either vent their frustration or prevent the realization of a political status that was unacceptable to them.

As events turned out, there came about a sudden change in the negotiating position of Indonesia in January 1999. This was the offer by President B. J. Habibie of a "second option" to the East Timorese people. It meant that if they did not accept the offer of wide-ranging autonomy, the Indonesian President would then report and propose to the newly elected Indonesian People's Consultative Assembly that in view of this rejection, Indonesia and East Timor would part ways peacefully and East Timor would revert back to its original status as a non-self-governing territory in the United Nations.

That sudden change made possible the holding of a "popular consultation" on the basis of a direct ballot on 30 August of the same year in which the overwhelming majority of East Timorese voted to reject the option of a special status and wide-ranging autonomy and thus opened the door for President Habibie's second option to be implemented.

In the aftermath of that political exercise, my worst fears became a reality. As might be expected, the losing party, the pro-integration group, was enraged by the result and in the days immediately following the announcement of the results of the ballot, the militia among them went on a rampage that killed scores of East Timorese and burned down large parts of Dili and many other towns.

Although I had been saying for years that such a political contest would probably lead to violence, I did not foresee, nor could anybody else have foreseen (except perhaps the perpetrators themselves) the virulence of the bloodbath, the vandalism and the social upheaval that would ensue.

I was as shocked and horrified as anyone else at the tragedy. It also imbued me with a sense of deep regret for having failed to convince my Government that in addressing such a complex issue as East Timor, there were no easy shortcuts. I was not able to persuade my Government that a peaceful, comprehensive and just solution could only be obtained through negotiation and dialogue that must be relentlessly but patiently pursued until all the parties concerned arrive at a consensus through compromise and harmonization of perceptions.

It is also undeniably true that over the years the East Timor issue has given rise to a number of misconceptions. There is, for instance, the mistaken notion that all throughout the Soeharto's era, Indonesia's position on East Timor was one of intractable rigidity in defending integration and rejecting outright any and all proposals for a compromise. Corollary to this notion is the view that it was only during the tenure of President B.J. Habibie that Indonesia suddenly manifested a willingness to seek a peaceful solution.

The facts show otherwise, for indeed since 1983, when the tripartite dialogue between Portugal and Indonesia under the aegis of the Secretary-General of the United Nations was launched, Indonesian diplomacy was already directed towards finding a "comprehensive, just and internationally acceptable" solution to the problem.

In fact, in 1986-87, Indonesia accepted the compromise plan for settlement of the issue proposed by UN Secretary-General Javier Perez de Cuellar, but Portugal at the last moment rejected the formula. Again in 1991 when the UN Secretary-General, this time Boutros Boutros-Ghali, proposed another compromise plan, Indonesia accepted and Portugal initially indicated agreement only to change its mind on the eve of the implementation of the plan.

Misconceptions such as this are possible because there is an important part of the East Timor saga that is yet to be made public. The untold part of the whole story, as I have pointed out in the foreword, is the diplomatic struggle to "find a peaceful, just and internationally acceptable solution" to the East Timor problem.

It is my hope that this book will serve not only to dispel any misconceptions that may still be circulating about the East Timor issue but also to give the reader a fuller view and better appreciation of an important part of the intertwined history of East Timor and Indonesia.

Glossary

AIETD	: The All-inclusive Intra-East Timorese Dialogue
Aiti	: Associacao Integracao de Timor Indonesia
ALIA	: The Associacao Luso-Indonesia para Amizadee Cooperacao
ANP	: The Accao Nacional Popular
Apodeti	: Associacao Popular Democratica de Timor
ASEM	: The First Asia-Europe Meeting
BAKIN	: National Intelligence Coordinating Agency
CBMs	: Confidence-building measures
Civpols	: Civilian Police
CNECRK	: Commissioner of the National Electoral Commission of the Republic of Korea
CNRT	: The Concelho Nacional da Resistencia Timorense
CPR	: The Council of People's Representatives
DMC	: The District Military Command
DMP	: Dadurus Merah Putih
DPR	: Dewan Perwakilan Rakyat
FCEONI	: Former Chief Electoral Officer for Northern Ireland
FPIF	: Force of Pro-Integration Fighters
FRETILIN	: Frente Revolucionaria de Timor Leste Independente
ICRC	: The International Committee of the Red Cross
IDPs	: The Number of Internally Displaced Persons
IFOR	: International Force
IISS	: International and Strategic Studies
INHRC	: The Indonesian National Human Rights Commission
INTERFET	: The Interim Force for East Timor
KODAM	: Komando Daerah Militer

KODIM	: Komando Distrik Militer
KOLAKOPS	: The Special East Timor Military Operations Command
Komnas HAM	: Komisi Nasional Hak Asasi Manusia
Komnas	: Komisi Nasional
Kopassus	: Commander of the Special Forces
KOTA	: Klibur Oan Timur Aswain
MNF	: Multi-national Force
MNLF	: The Moro National Liberation Front
MOU	: Memorandum of Understanding
MPR	: Majelis Permusyawaratan Rakyat
NGOs	: Non Goverments Organization
PCA	: People's Consultative Assembly
PIFA	: Portuguese-Indonesian Friendship Association
PPI	: Pasukan Pejuang Integrasi
RDC	: Regular regional/district command
Satgas P3TT	: Satgas Pelaksanaan Penentuan Pendapat di Timor Timur
UDT	: Uniao Democratica Timorense
UN	: Unites States
UNAMET	: The United Nations Mission in East Timor
UNDP	: United Nation Development Programe
UNHCR	: The United Nations High Commissioner on Refugees
UNHCR	: United Nations High Commissioner on Refugees
UNICEF	: United Nation for International Children Fund
UNIF	: Front Bersama Pro-Otonomi Timor Timur
UNMISET	: United Nations Mission of Support in East Timor
USA	: United State America
WWF	: World Food Programme

Chapter 1
The Beginnings

ON 25 April 1974 an event took place in Portugal that would forever change the course of history for East Timor and for the East Timorese people. On that day the dictatorial regime of President Tomas and Prime Minister Caetano was overthrown by the Portuguese military under the leadership of General Antonio Spinola.

The new government restored the civil rights of Portuguese citizens, declared its intention to hold elections and announced a new policy on its overseas colonies. On 16 May 1974, General Spinola, now the new president of the country, declared that all Portuguese subjects in the overseas colonies in Africa and Asia, including East Timor, then also known as Portuguese Timor, would equally be accorded democratic rights.

In East Timor itself, the Governor and military commander of the territory, Col. Fernando Alves Aldela, on 28 May 1974 issued a statement that the people of the territory would be given the opportunity to decide their own political future in a referendum to be held on 13 March 1975. For that purpose, they were allowed to form political parties.

In that projected referendum, the people of Portuguese Timor would be offered three options:

1. To become an autonomous territory in federation with Portugal;
2. To become a sovereign and independent country within or outside a Portuguese Commonwealth; or
3. To integrate with the Republic of Indonesia.

Early cooperation

On 21 September 1974, the Foreign Minister of Portugal, Mario Soares, and the Foreign Minister of Indonesia, Adam Malik, met in New York to discuss Portuguese-Indonesian relations, with particular focus on the process of decolonization in Portuguese Timor. They agreed that their countries work closely together during the implementation of that decolonization process. For that purpose, they decided that diplomatic relations be established between their governments as soon as possible and that their respective ambassadors accredited to the United Nations keep in close touch and hold regular consultations on their behalf.

That was the first high-level meeting between Indonesia and a representative of the new Portugal. As secretary to the late Foreign Minister Adam Malik, I was privileged to attend this historic meeting. Throughout the discussions, Foreign Minister Mario Soares struck me as someone quite sympathetic towards Indonesia and open-minded towards the possibility of East Timor eventually integrating with Indonesia. In later years I would therefore often ask myself why the same Mario Soares, by then Prime Minister and subsequently President of Portugal, had become such a harsh and implacable critic of Indonesia.

On 14 October 1974, Lt. Gen. Ali Moertopo[1] arrived in Lisbon as Special Envoy of President Soeharto. He and his delegation were received by President Francisco da Costa Gomes who had in the meantime succeeded President Spinola. During that two-day visit, Gen. Moertopo held consultations with Prime Minister Vasco Goncalves, Foreign Minister Mario Soares, and the Minister for Inter-territorial Co-ordination, Dr. Antonio de Almeida Santos.

The result of these consultations was very heartening to Gen. Moertopo. For example, it was reported that in his remarks President Costa Gomes described full independence for East Timor as an "unrealistic" alternative, while Prime Minister Goncalves reportedly called it "nonsense."

At any rate, these consultations resulted in further understanding on how cooperation between the two governments on the decolonization of Portuguese Timor could be enhanced. The two governments also reaffirmed their intention of opening their respective embassies in Jakarta and Lisbon.

In all the conversations, the Portuguese Government leaders indicated that the integration of East Timor with the Republic of Indonesia was a possibility that it could accept, provided that it was achieved through democratic means and in accordance with the wishes of the people of the territory.

From 16 to 19 October 1974, the Portuguese Minister for Interterritorial Affairs, Dr. Antonio de Almeida Santos, paid a visit to Jakarta for further consultations with the Indonesian Government. At a press interview upon his arrival at the Halim Perdanakusuma Airport, he said that it would be unrealistic to advocate the establishment of an independent state of East Timor, as political freedom and a weak economy would only make it vulnerable to re-colonization by other countries. He added that the decolonization of East Timor would be carried out through an electoral process that would select responsible representatives of the people.

On 18 October Dr. de Almeida met with President Soeharto who assured him that Indonesia had no territorial ambitions in East Timor or anywhere else, being firmly opposed to colonialism in all its forms as laid down in the 1945 Constitution. However, he said, Indonesia could accept Portuguese Timor's integration with the Indonesian unitary state if this was in line with the wishes of the people of the territory and carried out in accordance with the 1945 Constitution.

Seeds of misunderstanding

At this point, the seeds of future misunderstanding between Portugal and Indonesia had been sown. Portugal had clearly indicated in public statements and in private consultations that the eventual integration of Portuguese Timor with the Republic of Indonesia was a possibility it could accept, but each time it added the condition that such integration should be achieved through democratic means.

Lt. Gen. Ali Moertopo and his negotiating team apparently did not pay too much attention to that condition set forth by the Portuguese and when they reported on the results of their meetings with Portuguese leaders, the tone was so optimistic that an impression was engendered in the mind of the Indonesian public that the Portuguese Government had practically committed itself to the eventual integration of Portuguese Timor with the Republic of Indonesia.

When subsequent events proved that this was not the case, there was indignation on the part of the Indonesian Government at what was perceived as Portuguese perfidy. The misunderstanding had unfortunate consequences for both Portugal and Indonesia.

A springtime of democracy

Meanwhile, East Timor bustled with political activity, something that could not have happened during the Caetano regime when only one party, the *Accao Nacional Popular* (ANP), was allowed to exist, as it served as an instrument of the dictatorship. But now the formation of political parties was encouraged by the colonial administration and five political parties promptly sprang up:

1. ***Uniao Democratica Timorense*** (UDT). Formed on 11 May 1974 by a group of 23 East Timorese, three of whom had been members of the ANP, the UDT was at first reluctant to seek immediate independence for East Timor, convinced that the conditions necessary for statehood did not exist at that time. It sought to ensure that Portugal met its responsibility to lead East Timor gradually to independence so that the territory could achieve a sufficient level of socio-economic development before it was left on its own. Later, however, the UDT opted for independence with a privileged relationship with Portugal. Because it had the support of 230 of the 472 *suku*'s or clans in the territory, which represented about half of the entire population, the UDT claimed to be the most popular party in East Timor. Francisco Xavier Lopes da Cruz was its president while its Secretary General was Domingos de Oliveira.

2. ***Frente Revolucionaria de Timor Leste Independente*** (FRETILIN). This party called for immediate independence and for radical social and economic changes in East Timor, although in the past it had never participated in the struggle against Portuguese colonialism. Its membership was a curious mélange of, on the one hand, a small group of young radicals and, on the other, elements of the Portuguese colonial army. FRETILIN was headed by Francisco Xavier do Amaral, a tax and customs officer with links to Portugal's colonial secret police. Its secretary general was Jose Ramos Horta, a former journalist of the Dili newspaper, *A Voz de Timor.*

3. ***Associacao Popular Democratica de Timor*** (APODETI). Originally named Associacao Integracao de Timor Indonesia (AITI), this party from the very beginning aimed at integration with Indonesia. APODETI's view was that the people of East Timor and those of Indonesian West Timor were essentially one, as they shared the same island, the same ancestry and the same culture, and were separated into two peoples only because of the vagaries

of colonialism. Most of the supporters of this party lived in the western part of East Timor, close to the border with Indonesian West Timor. Some of its leaders had taken part in a revolt that flared against the Portuguese colonial government in 1959 in the town of Viqueque. Some 500 East Timorese lost their lives in that failed revolt.

APODETI was chaired by Arnaldo dos Reis Araujo, a former teacher who had been jailed for 29 years by the Portuguese. Its secretary general was Jose Fernandez Osorio Soares, an intellectual and former employee of the Portuguese Timor Social Service.

4. ***Klibur Oan Timur Aswain*** (KOTA). Founded on 10 November 1974, this party, whose name means "Sons of the Warriors," sought to preserve the authority of the *liurai*, the traditional leaders of East Timor, who are elected by popular assemblies following ancient tradition. Later, however, it came out in favour of integration with Indonesia. KOTA was led by Jose Martins, whose father, a former *liurai* of Ermera, was forced into exile because of his opposition to the colonial authorities.

5. ***Partido Trabalhista*** (Labour Party). When it was founded in October 1974, this party's main goal was independence for East Timor, while retaining some association with Portugal, somewhat along the lines of the commonwealth system. As such it was closely associated with the UDT. Later, it decided to stand for integration with Indonesia.

The leaders of these political parties soon began to visit Jakarta to meet with Indonesian leaders on the future of East Timor. During a visit by FRETILIN leaders in June 1974, Foreign Minister Adam Malik said that Indonesia would strictly observe a policy of non-interference in the decolonization process. APODETI leaders visited Jakarta the following August and September. On that occasion, the APODETI chairman announced that the party's goal was integration with Indonesia as its 27th province.

A new colonial Governor

On 14 November 1974, Col. Mario Lemos Pires replaced Fernando Alvez Aldela as colonial Governor of East Timor. On his arrival the new Governor stated that conditions in the territory favoured decolonization but that did not necessarily mean a complete break between East Timor and Portugal.

On 22 January 1975, the UDT agreed to form a coalition with FRETILIN. At that time reports were rife in the Australian press that Portugal had agreed to hand over the government of the territory to these two parties. Whether or not this alliance was formed with Portuguese complicity, it was apparently prompted by a rapid growth of popular support for the APODETI, which stood consistently for integration with Indonesia. In a joint communiqué, the coalition strongly criticized APODETI's stand.

The coalition, however, would prove to be short-lived. There were, of course, differences in ideology and policy between the two parties, but one particularly thorny issue was FRETILIN's resort to blackmail and intimidation in its efforts to enlarge its membership and support. In early 1975, FRETILIN cadres who had served in the colonial army launched a campaign of intimidation against the other political parties, especially targeting the leaders of the APODETI, many of whom had to flee for their lives, often across the border into Indonesian West Timor.

All the while the colonial Governor of East Timor was issuing public statements that Portugal was firmly committed to a free exercise of self-determination by the people of East Timor. On a visit to Jakarta on 17 March 1975, he denied reports that Portuguese troops had killed APODETI members in the border areas and asserted that these had died "while crossing a swollen river."

Reiterating his assurances of Portugal's commitment to decolonization, he also said that any problems that might arise in the course of decolonization, particularly those concerning relations with Indonesia, could be solved through consultations between the two governments. As to the possibility of integration with Indonesia, the Governor stated to the press that: "If the majority of the people wish to do so, this will not cause any problems."

In Kupang, the capital of Indonesian West Timor, on the way back to Dili on 30 March 1975, the Governor of East Timor said that the leftist trend, then very much evident in Portugal itself, would not in any way affect East Timor. He also expressed confidence that Indonesia would neither attack nor invade the territory.

The London meeting

As tension continued to rise in the territory, the Portuguese Government sought a meeting with the Indonesian Government to discuss the situation. The meeting took place in London on 9 March 1975 with Major Victor Alves, Minister for Decolonization, leading the Portuguese delegation, and Lt. Gen. Ali Moertopo leading the Indonesian side. Compared to the meeting in Lisbon the previous year, the atmosphere at the London meeting was decidedly different. The Portuguese side conveyed to the Indonesian side that it intended to implement the decolonization of East Timor through the establishment of either a Provisional Government or a Consultative Body, comprising the three major political parties and the Portuguese colonial government.

Towards this end and in order to restore calm to East Timor, the two sides agreed that the Portuguese Government would meet with the various political parties of the territory to thresh out ways of carrying out the decolonization process in a peaceful and orderly manner. The conference would be held from 26 to 28 June 1975 in the Portuguese colony of Macau.

At the same time, in recognition of its interests in the process, it was agreed that Indonesia could extend assistance to APODETI in advancing that party's aim of integrating with Indonesia—provided the assistance was not carried out too overtly. Indonesia was also requested to persuade APODETI not to boycott the projected meeting between Portugal and the political parties.

On future developments in East Timor, Indonesia was assured that it would always be consulted, its opinions sought and taken into consideration. For this reason, Indonesia was requested to have a delegation on standby in Hong Kong while Portugal would be meeting with the political parties in the nearby colony of Macau.

In May 1975, Francisco Lopes da Cruz, chairman of the UDT, came to Jakarta and presented his party's programme. He said that if the majority of the East Timorese electorate decided to integrate with Indonesia, his party would abide by that decision.

In the middle of the same month, the coalition between the UDT and FRETILIN began to break up. Having learned that some of the Portuguese colonial military officers were using their position to give undue advantage to FRETILIN, UDT requested that FRETILIN remove former informants of the colonial secret police from its roster of leaders. FRETILIN ignored this request and the coalition ceased to be viable.

The Macau conference

On 9 June 1975, a member of APODETI, Casimiro Ascancao de Araujo, who had arrived in Jakarta two days earlier on his way to the conference in Macau, told the press that his party's goal in that conference was to work for East Timor's integration with Indonesia.

FRETILIN, on the other hand, refused to attend the Macau conference on decolonization. It did so on various pretexts. Since no consensus was possible in the absence of FRETILIN, separate hearings were held instead between the Portuguese delegation and the representatives of the UDT and APODETI. No binding conclusions were reached on the date of the implementation of the act of free choice or on the type of government that would replace the Portuguese administration in East Timor.

The UDT and APODETTI lambasted FRETILIN's boycott of the Macau conference as undemocratic and a travesty of the fundamental rights of the people. They urged Portugal to carry out its own declared policy to take stern measures against any party that boycotted or obstructed the process of decolonization, which in this case was FRETILIN.

Soon after the Macau conference, the Portuguese Government promulgated Constitutional Law 7/75, which laid down the regulations on the decolonization process in East Timor. It provided for the formation of a Transitional Government that would prepare for and conduct the election of a Popular Assembly in October 1976.

The Transitional Government would be headed by a High Commissioner appointed by the Government of Portugal. It would have five members, two of whom would be appointed by the Government of Portugal, while the other three would be chosen from among the representatives of the political parties.

The law also provided for the establishment of a Transitional Government Council, an advisory body composed of members elected by the regional councils and those nominated by the political parties.

The Popular Assembly would finally determine the future status of East Timor. Portuguese sovereignty would be terminated in October 1978, unless otherwise agreed between the Government of Portugal and the Popular Assembly.

The FRETILIN continued to obstruct the process, reiterating its demand that the Portuguese Government immediately declare its intention to grant full independence to East Timor. It refused to appoint representatives to the Transitional Government. At the same time, it intensified its campaign of intimidation and terror in the interior as the October 1976 election drew near.

Ominous developments

Soon after Col. Lemos Pires was installed as Governor of East Timor in November 1974, two members of his cabinet, Major Mota and Jonatas, promptly went into action in support of the FRETILIN. They recruited some 75 men drawn from the ranks of the colonial army and formed it into a Commission for the Dynamization of Timor Armed Forces, which they utilized as an instrument to manipulate political developments in the territory and to unleash a campaign of intimidation and physical violence and even assassination, especially against members of the APODETI and their families. Through this Commission, they were also able to coordinate FRETILIN's activities with those of the still intact colonial armed forces.

While the FRETILIN was growing in strength as a result of its military backing, the head of the political department of the Lemos Pires cabinet ordered that the *chefes de posto* (district officers) and the district council administrators be replaced by members of the military and FRETILIN supporters.

From the point of view of the other political parties, this move could only mean that the FRETILIN and its supporters in the colonial administration were ousting all non-FRETILIN supporters from positions in the government in preparation for an outright seizure of power. The UDT, in particular, was convinced by evidence it had gathered that the FRETILIN would stage a *coup d'etat* on 15 August 1975.

To forestall that anticipated coup, the UDT staged a mass demonstration in Dili, demanding the expulsion of Majors Mota and Jonatas, blaming them for the rise in tension in the territory, the persecution of Timorese leaders fighting for independence, and obstructing the decolonization process.

A preemptive strike

On 7 August, a UDT delegation presented the demand for the expulsion of the two majors to Governor Lemos Pires. The Governor was non-committal and told the delegation that he would not act under pressure. The delegation then warned him that in view of his attitude, they could not be held responsible for what might happen afterwards.

The following day, 8 August, the UDT masses went on strike. Government offices, shops and commercial establishments were closed and Dili came to a standstill. Again, a UDT delegation went to see the Governor to resume talks but was told that he had gone to Los Palos in the eastern part of the territory.

The UDT Central Committee then planned further moves to counter the threat of a coup by FRETILIN. It organized another demonstration on Sunday, 10 August. Four thousand UDT members and supporters took part in this demonstration. On the evening of the same day, the Dili police chief, Lt. Maggiolo Buoveia, was persuaded to visit the UDT headquarters, where he was seized and held prisoner.

That was when UDT operatives, although virtually unarmed, launched a surprise attack on the police headquarters. Having armed themselves with captured weapons, they went on to occupy the harbour, the radio station, the airport and other vital public installations. In the early hours of Monday, 11 August, the UDT announced over Dili radio that it had taken control of the territory.

The UDT once again called on the Governor to expel the two majors from the territory. It also proposed talks on the future of East Timor, to which FRETILIN was invited to join. The FRETILIN leadership, however, insisted on a number of conditions for its participation, which the UDT could not accept. During the talks, the commander of the UDT operation, Joao Carrascalao, announced that the party was motivated by "Unity, Self-determination and Anti-communism."

The main result of the talks was the expulsion of the two majors. They were taken out of Dili on a plane that took them first to Darwin and then to Lisbon. When the plane returned to Dili, it brought along a letter from Ramos Horta, who was then in Darwin, addressed to the UDT commander, assuring him that he totally rejected the FRETILIN position and that he intended to join the UDT.

The counter-strike

In Darwin, however, Horta was telling journalists that FRETILIN's well-trained brigades, manned by former *Tropas* (colonial troops) would in no time wipe out the UDT fighters.

In fact, while the Governor and representatives of the Portuguese military were engaged in talks with the UDT, some Portuguese officers together with a FRETILIN field commander, Rogerio Lobato, who was also a Timorese warrant officer, were preparing a counterstrike.

Having got wind of the imminent attack a day before it took place, the UDT fighters in Dili dug in. On 20 August 1975, FRETILIN forces descended from the surrounding hills and entered Dili, using heavy mortar, machine guns and artillery. The UDT fighters were forced to abandon the city but carried on the fight in various other towns.

The other political parties—APODETI, KOTA and *Trabalhista*—which had remained neutral for some time, now decided to join with the UDT and civil war raged through all of East Timor.

The violence of the fighting drove tens of thousands of East Timorese to the safety of Indonesian territory. Unprepared for such a massive flood of people, the authorities in Indonesian West Timor could barely cope with the task of feeding and sheltering such a large number of refugees. The social and economic life of West Timor was severely disrupted, raising the concern of the Indonesian Government. In spite of the efforts of the Indonesian Government to help them, the refugees lived in a state of great privation.

The abandonment

Meanwhile the Portuguese Government made no effort to restore peace and order in the territory. Worse, the Governor and other Portuguese officials precipitously abandoned the capital on 26 August 1975 and evacuated to the island of Atauro, about 20 miles outside the harbour of Dili.

In a few weeks, they would abandon even this outpost, leaving all of East Timor in an administrative power vacuum.

The Portuguese military left the bulk of its arsenal in the hands of the FRETILIN, which thus enjoyed an enormous advantage in the raging civil war. The other forces ranged against FRETILIN took heavy casualties. By October 1975, some 3.000 East Timorese had lost their lives in the internecine conflict.

As the situation in East Timor rapidly deteriorated, the Portuguese Government sent the former Minister for Inter-territorial Affairs, Dr. Almeida Santos, as a special envoy on a mission to Indonesia, Australia and

Atauro Island to discuss possible ways of restoring order in the territory. When he arrived in Jakarta on 28 August 1975, Dr. Almeida Santos stated that the civil war in East Timor "must be stopped." His talks with Indonesian officials were held in two stages, the first on 29 August and the second on 11 September 1975, after his return from his visit to Australia.

After the initial talks with Dr. Almeida Santos, the *ad interim* Foreign Minister of Indonesia, Dr. Mochtar Kusumaatmadja[2], told a press conference on 30 August that Indonesia was approaching the question of East Timor with great caution and was determined to take a "correct attitude" in the search for a solution. He stressed again that Indonesia harboured no territorial ambitions on East Timor and that it supported decolonization. However, Indonesia hoped that the process of decolonization would be carried out in an orderly manner and that no single political group would be allowed to impose its will on the people.

He also revealed that in the course of the talks of the previous day, Portugal and Indonesia had reached an understanding on the following points:

1. Indonesia recognized the Portuguese Government and its representative, the Governor of East Timor, as the sole authority in that territory.
2. Portugal and Indonesia firmly upheld the principle of an orderly decolonization process in East Timor, which would enable the people of the territory to freely decide their own political future.
3. The worsening situation, the result of the raging civil war, required measures to restore peace and order as well as humanitarian action such as the evacuation of non-combatants, the provision of emergency food supplies, all of which would help make it possible for the decolonization process to be carried out in a peaceful manner.

A proposed multi-lateral approach

With regard to the civil war in East Timor and the humanitarian problems that it had brought about, the Foreign Minister *ad interim* of Indonesia presented to the Portuguese delegation a proposal for a multilateral approach to the problem, in view of Portugal's inability to meet its obligations in the territory. This would entail the establishment of a Joint Authority composed of Australia, Indonesia, Portugal and Malaysia.

The Joint Authority would serve as the highest administering body in

East Timor, pending re-establishment of Portuguese authority. The Joint Authority and a joint task force for the restoration for peace and order would create the necessary conditions for the return of Portuguese authority. The task force commander would be particularly responsible for the restoration of peace and order during that time. After Portuguese authority had been reestablished, the Joint Authority would focus on preparing for the orderly implementation of the decolonization process. During this phase, the task force commander would be under the supervision of the Joint Authority.

This attempt to establish a temporary multilateral authority in fact once again demonstrated that Indonesia had no territorial claim over East Timor and that it remained of the view that the decolonization of East Timor had to be carried out peacefully and reflect the wish of the majority of the people in the territory.

Unfortunately, the Portuguese delegation rejected the proposal. On 30 August, Dr. Almeida Santos left Jakarta for Australia to hold talks with that country's leaders.

The Australian view

Commenting on the anticipated visit of the Portuguese envoy, the Australian Prime Minister, Mr. Gough Whitlam, informed Parliament that the Government had turned down Portugal's request for the dispatch of Australian troops to East Timor. He further said, "Portugal's appeal for international aid can only be carried out if and when security and order has been restored in that area."

Furthermore, he said, the Timorese security problems were the "sole responsibility of the Portuguese Government" while the political destiny of the territory should be decided by Portugal, the East Timorese people themselves and Indonesia.

Australia was aware, he said, of Indonesia's concern that East Timor might become a threat to the stability and security of the region. East Timor, he stressed, was a Portuguese colony and Portugal must accept responsibility for developments there.

At about the same time, a spokesman for the Foreign Office stated that Australia believed it would not be proper for Portugal to hand power over to one group in East Timor at the expense of the other groups.

Dr. Almeida Santos must have been told as much when he got to Australia. When he returned to Jakarta, he once again pledged that his

Government would carry out its decolonization policy and would allow full and free participation of all groups in the process. He categorically denied that Portugal had any plan to hand over power to FRETILIN. The whole process, he stressed, would have to be in accordance with Constitutional Law 7/75, which was promulgated right after the Macau conference.

Even as Dr. Almeida Santos was holding talks with Indonesian officials, in Lisbon itself, the President of Portugal, Gen. General Francisco da Costa Gomes, issued a statement assuring Indonesia that Portugal would not impose a one-sided settlement of the question of East Timor's decolonization. He also said that in the search for a solution, Portugal would always take into consideration the views of the Government of Indonesia.

Dr. Almeida Santos's mission led to no concrete measure that would restore peace and order in East Timor. The situation continued to deteriorate as the FRETILIN intensified its armed offensive as well as its propaganda campaign abroad. Obviously confident that it now had the upper hand over its rivals, the FRETILIN refused all proposals for dialogue.

The Batugade Petition

In early September 1975, a major development took place: the UDT, previously known for its pro-Portuguese political sentiments, now joined two other parties, KOTA and *Trabalhista*, in declaring their desire for the integration of East Timor with Indonesia.

At a meeting in Batugade, on the western part of East Timor, on 7 September 1975, leaders of the UDT, KOTA and the *Trabalhista* parties signed a petition addressed to the President of the Republic of Indonesia seeking integration of East Timor with the Republic.

In that petition they pointed out that Portugal had failed to promote the process of decolonization and that the deteriorating situation in the territory was due to the inability of the administering power to prevent civil strife, which in turn led to the killing of a large number of people. They also stressed that the people of East Timor had strong ethnic and cultural links with the people of Indonesia. To prevent further bloodshed and complete the decolonization process, they said, they therefore sought integration with Indonesia.

On 16 September 1975, President Soeharto responded to the petition of the three political parties in Batugade by declaring that while Indonesia welcomed the wishes of the people of East Timor for integration with the Republic, such an eventuality should be the result of the exercise of the right to self-determination by the people of East Timor. He added that should this happen, those who joined Indonesia would be guaranteed the same rights and would bear the same duties as those of all Indonesians throughout the country.

Civil war rages on

Meanwhile civil war continued to rage in East Timor. In the battle for Batugade, FRETILIN mortar fire fell on the Indonesian border town of Matoain, inflicting civilian casualties. Batugade fell to FRETILIN, but soon after, the combined forces of the four allied parties (UDT, APODETI, KOTA and *Trabalhista*) regrouped and launched a series of counteroffensives that recaptured town after town: first Batugade, then Balibo, Maliana and Bobonaro. Guerilla units harassed FRETILIN outposts in Los Palos in the eastern part of the territory, and in Baucau, the second biggest town.

Alarmed at the shelling of Indonesian territory by FRETILIN, President Soeharto ordered security forces posted along the border to increase their vigilance and strengthen their positions. But according to news reports, FRETILIN units continued to slip across the border in order to steal cattle and food supplies from the villagers.

Villagers on the East Timor side of the border bore the brunt of the fighting. FRETILIN troops commandeered all the food supplies they could get their hands on and those who refused to surrender their foodstuffs were accused of spying for the UDT and the APODETI. The FRETILIN troops raided homes in search of men whom they would forcibly press into service. As the four allied forces continued to advance, the FRETILIN grew more oppressive and resorted to killings and torture to secure compliance with its wishes.

As the number of casualties mounted in the civil war in the colony, the Portuguese Government in early October 1975 once again sought talks with Indonesia in an effort to reach a peaceful solution to the problem of East Timor. Addressing the UN General Assembly on 9 October 1975, Portuguese Foreign Minister Melo Antunes said, "We are ready to accept a wide range of political formulas which would truly consider the interests of the people of East Timor." He added that a settlement could not fail to take into account the interests of the countries in the region.

Back in Lisbon from the United Nations, the Portuguese Foreign Minister acknowledged in public that, aside from Portugal, Indonesia was the only country that had a legitimate interest in the problem of East Timor. He said that Portugal recognized that nothing could be done in East Timor without discussing it first with Indonesia. He then promised that his Government would seek a dialogue with Indonesia on this issue as soon as possible.

He stressed that the territory's future would have to be determined by the will of the people, noting, however, that this could be expressed in various ways. He also gave the assurance that the invitation to the political parties for talks with the Portuguese Government still stood.

The Indonesian response came on 12 October when Foreign Minister Adam Malik announced that his Government welcomed Portugal's proposal for a new dialogue on East Timor. He said that Indonesia was prepared "to help the Portuguese Government realize its policy of decolonization, which has been approved by the former and present Government of Portugal as well as by the political parties in the Portuguese colony."

Talks in Rome

The two Governments agreed to hold the talks in Rome on 1 and 2 November 1975. As he announced this decision, the Indonesian Foreign Minister said that his Government would "try to find a way to prevent bloodshed in Portuguese Timor and solve the crisis there." Commenting on reports from Macau that some citizens of third countries were in Dili helping to rearm FRETILIN, he warned that the introduction of more arms into the already troubled situation would only delay its solution.

The Rome talks began as scheduled on 1 November, with Indonesian Foreign Minister Adam Malik leading a five-member delegation. As secretary to the Foreign Minister, I was part of the delegation. After two days of friendly dialogue in Rome, the two sides issued a Memorandum of Understanding, inter alia covering the following points:

Both sides would continue to adhere to the principles of decolonization as stated in pertinent UN resolutions and to the safeguarding of the principle of respect for the will of the people of East Timor.

They agreed that the fundamental responsibility for the decolonization of East Timor lies with Portugal and that Portugal as the legitimate authority in the territory should work for the speedy and orderly implementation of the act of self-determination by the people of East Timor.

There was an urgent need to restore peace and order in the territory so as to enable its people to decide freely their own future.

They agreed on the need to convene as soon as possible a meeting between Portugal and all political parties in East Timor, which would be aimed at ending the armed strife and bringing about a peaceful and orderly process of decolonization.

They acknowledged the need for a speedy solution to the problem of refugees from East Timor now living in Indonesia and the question of the 23 Portuguese nationals detained by the UDT.

They agreed that in the implementation of the decolonization process, it would also be essential to protect the interests of all the countries in the region, particularly those of Indonesia as the closest neighbouring country. Both sides therefore pledged to work closely together on all aspects and phases of the decolonization process[3].

The Rome meeting again showed that even as late as November 1975, Indonesia itself urged Portugal to exercise its authority and fulfill its responsibility for the conduct of a just and orderly decolonization process.

Declarations of Independence

The result of the Rome meeting drew contradictory responses from the FRETILIN. In Dili, Francisco do Amaral, chairman of FRETILIN, went on the radio to announce that his party opposed the meeting of the Portuguese and Indonesian foreign ministers. At the same time, the foreign press reported that FRETILIN had indicated its willingness to negotiate with the UDT and APODETI.

In early November 1975, Foreign Minister Adam Malik sought to brief the UDT and APODETI on the results of the Rome meeting in Atambua in Indonesian Timor. On 19 November, the Foreign Minister announced that these two parties and the FRETILIN had expressed willingness to discuss matters related to the future of East Timor. APODETI suggested Bali as the venue of the talks; FRETILIN indicated willingness to attend talks in Bali provided there was a guarantee of safe conduct by Indonesia. The Foreign Minister affirmed that although it would not take part in the talks, the Indonesian side was prepared to go anywhere to help the three parties negotiate, in line with its commitments in Rome.

But all of a sudden, on 28 November, FRETILIN unilaterally issued a "Declaration of Independence" of the territory, giving it the name "Democratic Republic of East Timor."

The four other parties promptly denounced that act of the FRETILIN as a clear demonstration of bad faith, which revealed its intention to thwart all efforts at a peaceful decolonization process and to impose its will on the people of East Timor.

And in the town of Balibo in East Timor on 30 November 1975, the four allied parties—the UDT, APODETI, KOTA and *Trabalhista*—proclaimed the independence of East Timor and its simultaneous integration with the Republic of Indonesia. They cited FRETILIN's unilateral action as foreclosing any avenue to a peaceful solution to the problem and appealed to the Government and people of Indonesia to take steps to protect the lives of East Timorese who had declared themselves Indonesian citizens.

On 17 December 1975, the four parties announced the establishment of the "Provisional Government of East Timor" in Dili. Again, they appealed to the Indonesian Government for economic and military aid.

Portuguese and Indonesian responses

The Portuguese Government promptly rejected both FRETILIN's unilateral declaration of independence and the four allied parties' declaration of independence through integration with Indonesia. On 29 November, the Portuguese National Decolonization Commission issued a communiqué stressing Portugal's continuing role as the territory's administering power. Just the previous day, however, the Charge d'Affaires a.i. of the Portuguese Mission to the United Nations had written a letter to the UN Secretary-General admitting that his Government could not deal effectively with the situation in East Timor.

Reacting to these rapid developments, the Indonesian Government issued a statement on 4 December 1975 observing that the decolonization process had not been properly carried out and that FRETILIN's unilateral declaration of independence had made the Rome agreement difficult to implement. The statement also noted Portugal's admission of inability to exercise authority over the territory.

The Indonesian Government also deplored the unilateral action of FRETILIN, as it ignored the wishes of the majority of the East Timorese people who were represented by the four allied parties. Recognizing the right of the members of the four parties to participate in determining the destiny of their homeland, the Indonesian Government expressed understanding and sympathy for their joint declaration of integration with the Republic of Indonesia.

Nevertheless Indonesia appealed to all concerned to earnestly carry out a peaceful and orderly decolonization process. It also acknowledged a moral obligation to help the people of East Timor in going through that process, while taking all steps to secure and safeguard its own sovereignty and territorial integrity.

On 6 December 1975, the Indonesian House of Representatives unanimously adopted a resolution expressing concern for the plight of the people of East Timor, deploring FRETILIN's unilateral declaration of independence as a violation of the Rome agreement, and welcomed the four parties' proclamation of East Timor's independence and integration with Indonesia.

The resolution also called on the Indonesian Government to take steps to restore order in East Timor so that its people could exercise their right to self-determination in a free and orderly manner.

Indonesia enters East Timor

After Portugal's precipitate abandonment of the territory and its failure to fulfill its responsibilities as administering authority, and in the face of the FRETILIN's mounting reign of terror against its own people, the four other political parties considered themselves no longer bound to any decolonization covenant with the erstwhile colonial power.

They intensified their struggle against the FRETILIN forces and, apart from proclaiming on 30 November 1975 the independence of East Timor through integration with the Republic of Indonesia, they established a Provisional Government under the leadership of the head of Apodeti, Arnaldo dos Reis Araujo, and called upon the Government of Indonesia to take the necessary steps to protect the lives of the

East Timorese who had declared themselves to be part of Indonesia.

It was thus at this point, with no action taken by anyone to stop the violence, the killings and atrocities perpetrated against the East Timorese people, that Indonesia became inexorably and militarily involved in the East Timor crisis. On 7 December 1975, Indonesian troops, in response to the request of the Provisional Government, entered East Timor.

The foreign media at that time carried speculative reports that Indonesia was emboldened in its invasion of East Timor because of the explicit or tacit support of US President Gerald Ford who, accompanied by Secretary of State Henry Kissinger, happened to be visiting Jakarta on 5 and 6 December 1975. It was alleged that in their discussions, President Soeharto had informed President Ford of the intention to invade East Timor and asked for the support of the United States for the invasion and that the American President had given it.

This version has been denied by both sides. However, on the basis of US diplomatic cables and memos declassified and released, in 2001 and 2006, it is apparent that a discussion on East Timor did take place on that occasion.

A recently declassified American diplomatic report may present a different set of details about that meeting but the most credible report from Indonesian sources is that in his typically oblique fashion, President Suharto only spoke of the need to establish peace and stability in the territory for the sake of security in the region, and that he hoped for American understanding if quick and decisive action were taken. President Ford reportedly nodded, conveying his understanding, and Kissinger added a warning against the use of US-made arms and reiterated the necessity to solve the problem as quickly as possible.

The declassified diplomatic files show that the United States and Britain had anticipated, as early as October 1975, that Indonesia would invade East Timor.

In any case, it was clear at that time that events were propelling Indonesia to sending a military force into East Timor. But the Department of Foreign Affairs had no information on any firm decision on this matter until that fateful first week of December 1975.

At the request of Portugal, the UN Security Council convened a session in mid-December 1975 to assess the situation in East Timor. The Council heard statements from the representatives of the Portuguese Government and the Indonesian Government as well as representatives of the people of East Timor. This led the Council to adopt Resolution 384 on 22 December 1975, which, while regretting that Portugal did not discharge fully its responsibilities as administering power in East Timor, called on Indonesia to withdraw without delay all its forces from the territory.

The resolution also mandated the UN Secretary-General to send a Special Representative to East Timor to make an on-the-spot assessment of the existing situation and to establish contact with all parties in the territory and all states concerned. On the basis of the report that the Special Representative would submit after fulfilling his mission, the Secretary-General was requested to submit his recommendations to the UN Security Council.

The Guicciardi Mission to East Timor

Accordingly, on 29 December 1975, UN Secretary-General Kurt Waldheim appointed Vittorio Winspeare Guicciardi, Director-General of the UN Office in Geneva, as his Special Representative. By January 1976, I was stationed in Geneva as Ambassador/Permanent Representative to the UN. In that capacity, I was tasked to assist in all the preparations and activities connected with Winspeare Guicciardi's mission.

Two months later, Guicciardi would submit a report recounting his efforts to make an on-the-spot assessment of the situation in East Timor.

He spent much of early January 1976 meeting in New York, Lisbon and Geneva with representatives of the Portuguese and Indonesian Governments, FRETILIN and the International Committee of the Red Cross to obtain background briefings from them. The Provisional Government of East Timor, hesitant at first to receive the visit of the Special Representative, finally agreed at the insistence of Indonesian Foreign Minister Adam Malik. In a cabled message, the FRETILIN office in Australia also indicated its willingness to receive his visit in the Fretilin-controlled parts of East Timor.

Guicciardi arrived in Jakarta on 15 January 1976. On the next several days he had an audience with President Soeharto and met with Foreign Minister Adam Malik and other senior officials of the Indonesian Government. On 19 January, he flew to Kupang, West Timor where he met the provincial government officials and representatives of the Provisional Government of East Timor, who had flown in from Dili.

The following day he flew by chartered light aircraft to the enclave of Oecusse, the island of Atauro and then to Dili. In each place he met with members of the Provisional Government and representatives of the five political parties. Then he flew by helicopter to the towns of Manatuto and Baucau, where he again met with representatives of the Provisional Government and the five political parties. Since, for technical and security reasons, he could not visit any more of the significant population centres, he flew back to Indonesia on 22 January.

There he had more meetings with Foreign Minister Adam Malik and other senior officials. He also received a cabled message from Jose Ramos Horta, who was then in Australia, suggesting that he visit Suai, Same, Viqueque and Com in East Timor by using light aircraft. However, for security reasons, the Australian and Indonesian Governments would not allow the use of their respective aircrafts and crews in such a venture.

The situation was further complicated by the FRETILIN office in Australia having difficulties contacting by radio their operatives in East Timor. The Portuguese Government offered the use of the communication facilities of one of its two naval corvettes stationed in the Timor Sea and also the availability of one of the vessels to bring Guicciardi and his team to East Timor. In spite of this, the FRETILIN representatives in Australia could not make the necessary arrangements for a landing place. On 6 February, they finally announced that they could not guarantee the safety of the UN delegation so long as the Indonesian forces had not been withdrawn from East Timor.

A Fretilin proposal

On 7 February he flew to Sydney where he met with the UN Secretary-General who had flown in from New York. He returned to Geneva on 9 February and, on 10 February, to Lisbon where he met with Portuguese senior officials.

Before flying to Lisbon he had conveyed to the *Charge' d'affaires* of the Indonesian Mission a FRETILIN proposal for an immediate ceasefire; withdrawal of all Indonesian forces and their replacement by an international force composed of Portuguese and West European contingents, preferably Nordic, or of exclusively Nordic contingents if Portugal could not participate; a one-man one-vote referendum after the withdrawal of the Indonesian forces, with a choice between integration with Indonesia and independence under the FRETILIN.

To a large extent, the Portuguese Government was supportive of the proposal, maintaining, however, that should a Portuguese contingent be part of the international force that would replace the Indonesian forces, the command of that international force should be given to a Portuguese officer. As to the referendum, the Portuguese Government suggested that the choice be between integration with Indonesia and independence in consultation with all political forces in East Timor.

The Provisional Government of East Timor turned down the FRETILIN proposal, saying it would go through the process of ratifying the decision of the people of East Timor to integrate with Indonesia, with UN representatives to be invited to witness the process. It refused to recognize the FRETILIN as a valid representative of the East Timorese people and pointed out that as of 30 January, the political parties in East Timor had dissolved themselves to form a united national front. It also invited the Special Representative of the UN Secretary-General to make another visit to East Timor.

Essentially, the position of the Government of Indonesia was to leave the FRETILIN proposal in the hands of the Provisional Government of East Timor, this being now the *de facto* authority in the territory.

In February 1976, Guicciardi submitted his report recounting his efforts to make an on-the-spot assessment of the situation in East Timor.

In that Report, under the heading, "Findings", Guicciardi observed: "Any accurate assessment of the situation as a whole remains elusive. Without doubt it continues to evolve. The terrain and conditions generally are such as to rule out front lines and to favour guerilla warfare. In the places visited ... there were signs of a functioning administration and schools as well as health services were working."

Guicciardi further noted that although the views of the Governments and parties concerned with the future of East Timor were widely divergent, these bore one common element, an affirmation of the need for consultation of the people of East Timor. He then suggested that as a first step, it might be possible to build on that slender common element.

Another try at assessment

On 22 April 1976, after having considered the reports of the UN Secretary-General and Guicciardi on the mission to East Timor, the UN Security Council passed another resolution requesting the

Secretary-General to have his Special Representative continue with his assignment to make an on-the-spot assessment of the situation in East Timor and to pursue consultations with the parties concerned.

Guicciardi immediately held consultations in Geneva with representatives of the Provisional Government in East Timor, the Indonesian Government and the Portuguese Government. A meeting with representatives of FRETILIN could not be arranged but he received letters and cable messages written on behalf of the Government of the "Democratic Republic of East Timor," most of them sent from Australia.

In his meetings with the representatives of the Provisional Government, he was briefed on the mechanics of the exercise of the right of self-determination that would be held in East Timor, including procedures for participation in the exercise by East Timorese in hiding and those that were abroad.

They reiterated their invitation for him to visit East Timor and advised him that similar invitations would also be addressed to the Security Council and to the Special Committee on the Situation with regard to the Implementation of the Declaration on the Granting of Independence to Colonial Countries and Peoples (Committee of 24).

On 12 June, the Indonesian Government sent him an invitation to visit East Timor at a time when a fact-finding mission from Indonesia would be in the territory. He was informed that similar invitations had been sent to the Security Council, the Committee of 24 and the Secretary-General. By then, the act of self-determination had been carried out in East Timor

Because his mandate came from the Security Council, which had already turned down the invitation to visit East Timor, Guicciardi felt that it would not be appropriate for him to respond to the invitation addressed to him.

FRETILIN, on the other hand, had suggested that he go to East Timor from Australia on a vessel sponsored by Australian trade unions. However, FRETILIN did not name any specific landing area, and considering the circumstances that prevented him from visiting FRETILIN-controlled areas earlier in February, he felt he could not accede to the request.

Once more Guicciardi had to report to the Secretary-General that under prevailing circumstances it was not possible to assess accurately the prevailing situation in East Timor.

Invitations turned down

Meanwhile the Provisional Government tried very hard to restore peace and order and to get the government administrative machinery moving again. Several shiploads of relief goods came in from Indonesia. With some normalcy restored, the Provisional Government began preparing in earnest for the exercise of self-determination by the people of East Timor.

Both the Provisional Government of East Timor and the Government of Indonesia sought involvement of the United Nations in the completion of the decolonization process.

On 12 April 1976 Mr. Maria Guilherme Goncalves, representative of the Provisional Government, told the 1908th meeting of the UN Security Council: "If the United Nations, this Council or the Committee of the 24 desires to send a mission to the territory to witness the real situation in East Timor, it is welcome to do so. The Provisional Government will do its utmost to facilitate such a visit."

Two days later, at the 1909th meeting of the Council, the Indonesian Permanent Representative to the UN declared: "It is also the view of the Indonesian Government that the United Nations should be involved during the remaining stage of the decolonization process."

To these invitations, the United Nations gave no response. Nevertheless the Provisional Government continued preparations for the exercise of self-determination by the East Timorese people in the hope that some form of United Nations presence could still be arranged.

As to the mechanics of the political exercise, the Provisional Government chose the medium of a People's Assembly composed of representatives popularly elected at the district level. Two delegates would represent each of the 13 districts in the territory, except the area around Dili, which would be represented by three delegates, considering the density of the population there. In addition to these 27 delegates, the Provisional Government appointed ten prominent citizens from various walks of life as delegates at large, to ensure that representation in the assembly covered as wide a range of political views as possible. The Provisional Government deemed this plan a close parallel to the concept for the decolonization process adopted by Portugal (Law no.7/1975).

The Provisional Government then sent cable messages to the Secretary-General of the United Nations and his Special Representative Winspeare Guicciardi, the President of the UN Security Council, the Chairman of the UN Special Committee on

Decolonization, and the Government of Indonesia, inviting them to witness the electoral process and the act of decolonization to be carried out by the elected delegates.

In addition, the Provisional Government sent delegations to New York and Geneva to meet and invite the pertinent UN officials. The invitations were turned down. As a result the UN denied itself first-hand information so necessary to form an objective assessment of the situation in East Timor. Nevertheless, the Provisional Government constantly reported on every stage of the process to the UN Secretary-General and his Special Representative, to the President of the Security Council and to the Chairman of the Committee on Decolonization.

Formalities of integration

The exercise of the right to self-determination was carried out by the People's Assembly of East Timor on 31 May 1976 in an open session during which it formally requested the Government of Indonesia to accept the decision of the people of East Timor to integrate the territory with the Republic of Indonesia. Members of the diplomatic corps accredited to Jakarta and members of the Indonesian and foreign press observed the proceedings.

Seven days later in Jakarta, a delegation of the People's Assembly and the Provisional Government of East Timor presented the formal request for integration with the Republic of Indonesia to President Soeharto. In response, the Indonesian Government decided to send a fact-finding mission to East Timor to ascertain whether the request accurately reflected the wishes of the majority of the people. The Government of Indonesia then sent invitations to the Secretary-General, the Security Council and the Committee of 24 to send their own observers to East Timor during the visit of the fact-finding mission. This invitation, too, received no positive response.

On its return from East Timor, the fact-finding mission submitted a positive report. On the basis of that report, the Indonesian Parliament passed legislation on integration on 15 July 1976, which the President signed into law on 17 July.

By that act, four centuries of Portuguese colonialism and months of fratricidal strife and suffering among the people of East Timor had come to an end.

President Soeharto would explain the decision in his State Address on 16 August 1976. "Time and again," he said, "we have stated that the East Timor problem is a problem of abolishing colonialism. The fate of the people of East Timor can only be decided by themselves and right there on the soil of East Timor. Not in New York, not in Lisbon and not even in Jakarta. Now the people of East Timor have made the decision about their own future, namely integration with the people and state of the Republic of Indonesia. There is no other way, therefore, but to accept with full responsibility such an integration."

As far as the Government of Indonesia was concerned, East Timor had become in fact and legally the 27th province of the Republic. But not to FRETILIN, which continued to wage guerilla warfare in the hills of East Timor. And not to Portugal, which immediately severed diplomatic relations with Indonesia. And not to the United Nations itself, which continued to recognize Portugal as the administering authority in East Timor.

A sterile debate

After 21 June 1976, when the Security Council turned down the invitation of the Indonesian Government to visit East Timor, the question of East Timor was addressed exclusively in the General Assembly. The first resolution of the General Assembly on East Timor was adopted on 1 December 1976, with 68 member states voting in favour, 20 against and 49 abstaining.

Towards the end of every year after that, the General Assembly would pass a resolution on East Timor. From 1976 to 1978, each of these resolutions contained an operative paragraph that drew the attention of the Security Council to "the critical situation in the Territory of East Timor and recommends that it take all effective steps for the implementation of its resolutions 384 (1975) and 389 (1976) with a view to securing the full exercise by the people of East Timor of their right to self-determination and independence."

However, starting with the General Assembly Resolution of 21 November 1979, this series of resolutions no longer contained such an operative paragraph that refers to the Security Council resolutions on East Timor. The Indonesian Government cited two reasons for this change: 1) a better understanding of the international community of the question of East Timor and Indonesia's position on the matter;

and 2) the fact that since 1976 the Security Council had not taken any action on the question of East Timor.

Also worthy of note was the fact that every year, the votes cast for the resolution against Indonesia diminished in number. In 1976, the recorded vote was 68 against Indonesia, 20 with Indonesia and 49 abstentions. In 1980, the figures had become: 58 against Indonesia, 35 for Indonesia, with 46 abstentions. In 1982, when the last of this series of annual resolutions was passed, 50 votes were cast against Indonesia, 46 for Indonesia, with 50 abstentions. Yemen and St. Vincent and Grenadine, which were absent during the vote, each sent a letter to the UN Secretary-General after the vote, informing him that had they been present, they would have voted against the resolution (i.e. for Indonesia).

The resolution adopted by the General Assembly on 28 November 1982 reflected an even more significant departure from previous General Assembly resolutions: it did not contain an operative paragraph that "reaffirms the inalienable rights of the people of East Timor to self-determination and independence, and the legitimacy of their struggle to achieve that right."

Instead, in that resolution, the General Assembly requested the Secretary-General "to initiate consultations with all parties directly concerned, with a view to exploring avenues for achieving a comprehensive settlement of the problem and to report thereon to the General Assembly at the 38th Session."

These developments signified that the Security Council resolutions on East Timor had been superseded by General Assembly resolutions that had been gradually watered down, presumably with the consent of Portugal, since it was Portugal that tabled these resolutions. And the reason that Portugal allowed the resolutions to be watered down could only be that it was becoming more and more difficult to gather support for too strongly worded resolutions—a fact that was reflected in the trend of the annual vote.

Being then already Ambassador/Permanent Representative to the UN, I told the 37th session of the UN General Assembly: "This trend, which has been apparent for several years now, that is: growing support for Indonesia's position and waning support for the sponsors of the resolution, is viewed by my delegation as gratifying indeed. And we are confident that Indonesia's support will grow.

"The unmistakable conclusion that can be drawn from this year's vote, together with the voting trend as earlier noted, is that the time has come to view East Timor on the basis of facts and realism rather than on baseless accusations and wishful thinking. Therefore it is high time for this Assembly to dispense with the sterile debate that has been going on for seven years on an issue that should not have been on its agenda in the first place."

The "sterile debate" would indeed come to an end. But another process—more challenging but nevertheless more promising—was about to begin.

Footnotes

[1] Lt. Gen. Ali Moertopo was deputy head of BAKIN, the National Intelligence Coordinating Agency. But he was much better known as Special Assistant and close confidante of President Suharto. In 1978 he became Minister of Information.

[2] At that time, Prof. Dr. Mochtar Kusuma-Atmadja was Minister of Justice. It is Indonesian state practice to designate another minister as Foreign Minister *ad interim* when the incumbent is out of the country.

[3] For the full text of the Memorandum, see Annexes.

Chapter 2
The Tripartite Talks

IN December 1982, the Secretary-General of the United Nations, Mr. Javier Perez de Cuellar, asked me to see him. It was about the November 1982 General Assembly Resolution (Res 37/30), which had as one of its operative paragraphs an injunction requesting the Secretary-General "to initiate consultations with all parties directly concerned, with a view to exploring avenues for achieving a comprehensive settlement of the problem …."

Apparently he had sent a similar invitation to my colleague the Ambassador/Permanent Representative of Portugal to the United Nations, Mr. Rui E. Barbosa de Medina.

During my meeting with the UN Secretary-General, he asked me whether Indonesia would be willing to accept his good offices in the search for a solution to the East Timor question, in accordance with the operative paragraph of that resolution.

My first response was to ask him why, with all due respect to the UN Secretary-General personally, Indonesia should accept his intermediation, given the result of the vote on the latest resolution and the voting pattern over the last eight years, which showed steadily declining support for Portugal's position and continuously growing support for Indonesia's position.

"Would it not be logical," I asked the Secretary-General, "for Indonesia to just wait to see whether next year's vote would finally defeat the Portuguese-sponsored draft resolution?"

The Secretary-General expressed understanding for Indonesia's attitude, especially in the light of the last vote in the General Assembly, but he reminded me that the defeat of the Portuguese draft resolution could only be assumed if the Portuguese side would come up with the same or a similar text of a draft resolution the following year. This, he said, he doubted very much that they would do.

They could come up with a much softer text that would be more difficult to object to, or they could initiate an entirely different approach. He also pointed out, and I agreed with him, that even if a Portuguese resolution were defeated the following year, it would still not automatically mean that the East Timor issue would be stricken off the UN agenda.

For that to happen, Indonesia needed to move its own draft resolution, explicitly proposing that the item on East Timor be deleted from the agenda of the General Assembly and from the list of issues upon which the Security Council had reached an impasse. That proposal would, of course, have to be supported by the appropriate considerations and arguments. But this move would undoubtedly require time and additional efforts in order to acquire the necessary majority of votes from the UN membership.

At any rate, he asked me to convey the proposal to the Indonesian Government, which I agreed to do.

Indonesia decides to negotiate

In January 1983, I flew home to Jakarta on what was to become annual consultations during which I would report to the President of Indonesia the results of the just-concluded UN General Assembly session and to receive new directives for any pending problems.

In Jakarta, I first consulted with the Minister for Foreign Affairs, Prof. Dr. Mochtar Kusuma-Atmadja. He was an old friend from the Law Faculty days at the University of Indonesia where he was two years my senior. We always cooperated well together during his tenure as Minister (1978-1988).

When I reported the Secretary-General's proposal, Mochtar's first reaction was the same as mine: Why should we accept it? Were we not riding a winning horse? But after some discussion, he agreed with me that I should present the Secretary-General's proposal, with all his considerations and arguments, to the President.

The next day, I called on President Soeharto and reported to him the new developments on the East Timor issue, including the proposal of the Secretary-General.

To my surprise, the President responded favourably to the proposal. "The Secretary-General is right," he said. "We aim to have a comprehensive and thorough solution to the problem and for this it may be good to try dialogue and negotiations." He then quoted to me a Javanese saying, which essentially meant that the best way to win is to make the other side feel it is not the loser.

On my return to the United Nations in New York City, I conveyed to the Secretary-General the Indonesian Government's willingness to accept his offer of good offices. He told me that Portugal had also accepted it. I stressed, however, that Indonesia's acceptance would have to be: (1) outside the context of Resolution 37/30 of 1982 as this Resolution (like similar Resolutions of previous years) had been firmly rejected by Indonesia, and (2) without prejudice to its consistently maintained position that the decolonization process of the people of East Timor had already taken place in 1976.

The Secretary-General posed no objections and assured me that the talks could very well be held in the context of his own general mandate.

Eventually, the Secretary-General, Portugal and Indonesia would agree on a neutrally phrased statement of objectives for the tripartite talks: "to achieve a comprehensive, just and internationally acceptable solution."

On the basis of these understandings, preliminary contacts and discussions were made in the following months between the Permanent Representatives of Portugal and Indonesia in New York, under the auspices of the Secretary-General. For purposes of the talks, the Secretary-General appointed one of his very able deputies, Under Secretary-General Rafeeuddin Ahmed, as his Special Representative, who thereafter regularly attended the tripartite talks in that capacity.

Formal talks begin

These preliminary contacts and discussions became more formal and structured after a meeting and exchange of views between Foreign Minister Jaime Gama of Portugal and Foreign Mochtar Kusuma-Atmadja of Indonesia, which took place on 1 October 1984 while the United Nations General Assembly was in session.

The manner in which the two Foreign Ministers met is worth recounting. Due to the absence of diplomatic relations between the two sides and the great sensitivities this created, no formal meeting could be contemplated as this would have drawn the premature attention of the press in both countries. Instead, Ambassador Rui Medina and I, assisted by USG Rafee Ahmed, devised a carefully timed "chance encounter" between the two Foreign Ministers in one of the corridors of the UN General Assembly building, whereupon they both moved to a small room nearby to conduct their talks.

On that occasion, the two Foreign Ministers welcomed the discussions that had taken place and agreed that the dialogue should continue, focusing initially on humanitarian questions and the clarification of each side's position with regard to the actual situation and current developments in East Timor, so as to enlarge mutual understanding and mutual confidence between them.

Specifically, it was agreed to take up the question of the repatriation of Portuguese former civil servants still residing in East Timor but who wanted to return to Portugal.

It was also agreed to discuss the repatriation of a number of East Timorese, who had taken part in a revolt against the colonial authority in East Timor in 1959. After the revolt was brutally suppressed, these people had been exiled to Angola and after the 1974 "carnation revolution" had settled in Portugal. Subsequently, a group of them, under the leadership of Jose Manuel Duarte, expressed the wish to return to East Timor, which would eventually be realized in November 1986.

Thus from 1983 to 1991, the first series of tripartite talks were held under the auspices of then UN Secretary-General Perez de Cuellar. And ever since 1983, every year the debates on the item "Situation in East Timor" would be deferred to the following year, through a procedural mechanism before the General Committee of the UN General Assembly as agreed upon by both sides.

By the end of 1985, the tripartite talks had resulted in an enhancement of understanding of each other's position and the solution of several humanitarian issues. Also, an in-depth analysis of the economic, social, cultural, religious and political life in the province had been conducted to the satisfaction of both sides.

Under the repatriation programme for former Portuguese civil servants, which was implemented with the help of the International Committee of the Red Cross (ICRC) and the United Nations High Commissioner on Refugees (UNHCR), 54 families or a total of 397 persons had been repatriated to Portugal by the end of 1987. In this process, it was the Portuguese Government that determined who were eligible for repatriation.

In his 11 September 1985 progress report to the General Assembly, the Secretary-General observed that:

"The substantive talks between Indonesia and Portugal have

proceeded in a constructive atmosphere. Both sides have reiterated their willingness to continue the present process. It is therefore my sincere hope that, in the coming months, the next phase of the talks will build upon the measure of understanding already reached and that the consideration of the political, civil and other aspects of the problem will prepare the ground for a just, comprehensive and internationally acceptable settlement of the question of East Timor."

Following up on this progress report, the representatives of Portugal and Indonesia continued their consultations in New York with the active participation and guidance of the UN Secretary-General and Under Secretary-General Rafeeuddin Ahmed.

At an informal working luncheon on 23 September 1985, hosted by Secretary-General Perez de Cuellar for the Foreign Ministers of Indonesia and Portugal, the two sides agreed to pursue their substantive talks, building upon the measure of understanding already achieved during the first phase of talks and tackling the much more difficult and sensitive aspect of finding and agreeing upon a viable blueprint or plan that could provide a just, comprehensive and internationally acceptable solution to the East Timor question.

By the end of 1986, as a result of intensive rounds of talks, such a plan had taken concrete shape.

A solution in sight

Under that plan, it was basically envisaged that, with the concurrence of both Portugal and Indonesia, the Secretary-General would dispatch a United Nations observation team to Indonesia to observe the April 1987 General Elections, including East Timor. The composition of the observer team, to be agreed upon by both sides, would include representatives of around five Member States of the UN, selected in a balanced way.

The Secretary-General would submit a report of the team's findings to the resumed forty-first session or the forty-second session of the General Assembly (1987). It was understood that the report would be factual in nature and not contain any recommendations.

The report would then be freely debated upon by the entire membership of the General Assembly. Portugal would be at liberty to concur with or reject the team's findings. Indonesia was hopeful, however, that once the team could observe the real and actual conditions in the province, it would submit a favourable and positive assessment.

On the basis of the Secretary-General's report on the team's findings, one or more member states would then be expected to propose in the General Assembly the deletion of the East Timor question from the agenda. In view of the findings, the member states would give their verdict, which Indonesia expected to be one of support for the proposal, thus providing for a solution acceptable to the international community and an honourable way out for both Portugal and Indonesia.

If indeed such a resolution would be adopted by the General Assembly, then Portugal would request that the item, "The Situation in East Timor," be deleted from the list of matters upon which the Security Council could not agree, and the two countries would subsequently take appropriate steps to normalize their relations.

In addition, under the plan, Indonesia would also give explicit, written assurances on the traditional rights and special characteristics of particular territories as applicable to East Timor under its Constitution. Indonesia would also give assurances on religious freedom, the preservation and promotion of East Timor's cultural heritage and of specific aspects of humanitarian, socioeconomic, political and civil rights conditions in East Timor.

Indonesian assurances

Specifically, during the substantive talks, Indonesia agreed to give firm assurances that, like all its other citizens, the East Timorese would be free to profess and practice any religion of their choice, including the Catholic faith. Like other humanitarian organizations, the Catholic Church would be allowed to participate in the provision of humanitarian assistance to the population.

Members of the clergy would have complete freedom of movement to carry out their apostolic duties and foreign-born missionaries would have free access to the territory, in accordance with immigration regulations. The Catholic Church would have full authority over the parish schools in East Timor.

Indonesia also assured the preservation and protection of the cultural heritage of the people of East Timor, including the Portuguese part of this heritage. All aspects of the culture of the people of East Timor, including their ethnic and linguistic heritage, their traditional and religious ceremonies, customs and ways of artistic expression, including music, dance, painting, folklore and handicrafts would be fully respected and exercised freely. Indonesia would continue to identify, restore and preserve East Timor's historical monuments.

Indonesia gave detailed information on activities being carried out in East Timor that were consistent with these assurances. In particular, the Government was pursuing programmes to develop the educational infrastructure in East Timor and to ensure that all East Timorese had access to all levels of education, especially primary education.

Many East Timorese were being trained as teachers so that the schools in the territory would eventually be staffed by East Timorese. The Catholic teachers-training school in East Timor had been given government assistance and programmes had been developed to promote the teaching of religion in the schools.

Tetum, the most widely spoken language in East Timor was being used as the language of instruction in the schools up to the third grade, and courses were being developed to teach Tetum as a separate linguistic subject in the higher grades. In some parish schools, Portuguese was the medium of instruction.

Mass communication infrastructures were also being developed. Radio and television programmes were being produced and broadcast in the local languages. Indonesia also gave assurances that in the formulation of development projects for the territory, the ethnic and cultural identity of the East Timorese would be respected.

Also taken up during the substantive talks were the concerns of the international community about the humanitarian and human rights situation of the East Timorese people. On this, Indonesia pledged to continue cooperation with international humanitarian organizations engaged in providing assistance and protection to the people of East Timor. Indonesia also assured that these organizations, as well as foreign journalists and diplomats, would have access to the territory for purposes of assessing and verifying the prevailing conditions.

The work of the International Committee of the Red Cross (ICRC) was also discussed, particularly the question of displaced persons on Atauro island and their return to the main island, the repatriation of former Portuguese civil servants, and the repatriation of East Timorese then residing in Portugal who wanted to return to the territory.

Indonesia gave information on its policies to promote the living conditions of the people of East Timor. It reiterated its determination to ensure increased production and adequate distribution of food in the territory and stated the measures it had taken to stimulate local economic activity and industrial development.

Indonesia cited health and medical facilities being made available to the population, including hospitals, clinics, rural public health centres, as well as the launching of preventive health care programmes and the increase in the number of doctors and medical personnel. Indonesia's policy of staffing all levels of the civil service with East Timorese, as far as possible, was also noted.

Like all citizens of Indonesia, the East Timorese were guaranteed equal protection under the Constitution and laws of the country. In particular, the East Timorese were assured of equal status and rights of citizenship as well as civil rights and freedoms without any distinction or discrimination. They also had equal rights of representation and participation at all levels of government and in the conduct of all public affairs through freely-elected representatives. They could vote and be elected in elections, which were by universal and equal suffrage and by secret ballot.

East Timorese would have freedom of movement all over Indonesia, like all other citizens. They had the right to an effective remedy for any violation of their fundamental rights under the Indonesian Constitution and the law of the land. They were guaranteed due process of law, including the right to public trial, in full conformity with the Universal Declaration of Human Rights, and the right of appeal to a higher court. Those who fought on the side of the FRETILIN during the civil war who now renounced subversion were guaranteed amnesty.

Accordingly, the text of a memorandum of understanding (MOU) was drafted containing all the main elements of the proposed plan as well as Indonesia's assurances, for endorsement by the two Governments. A formal letter would also be sent by the Indonesian Foreign Minister inviting the UN Secretary-General to send the observation team. Prospects for a mutually acceptable solution thus appeared quite promising at that stage.

Portugal reverses its position

However, by January 1987 the situation suddenly and unexpectedly took an adverse turn. For in the course of 1986 and early 1987, the President, Prime Minister and Foreign Minister of Portugal made statements that were clearly incompatible with the letter and spirit of the agreed plan advanced by the Secretary-General.

In particular, the address by President Mario Soares to the European Parliament on 9 July 1986 made reference to East Timor that was couched in language totally unacceptable to the Government and people of Indonesia. On that occasion, President Soares stated:

"In this context, we are obliged to recall, with indignation and disgust, the dramatic situation which exists in East Timor, an offence to the most elementary rules of coexistence between nations as well as to the fundamental rights of man. Portugal is not disposed to abandon East Timor to its fate and Portugal expects the Community institutions, particularly this Parliament, to demonstrate the attention and interest that a problem of this gravity requires."

The same ambivalent behaviour was shown by the representative of Portugal who addressed the UN Commission on Human Rights in February 1987, saying:

"... we cannot accept elections, which, besides being called 'administrative' (sic) and which will also take place in East Timor solely because of military occupation, to be considered as the exercise of the right of the people of East Timor to choose their own destiny."

The elections to which the Portuguese representative alluded were the General Parliamentary Elections that were to be held in Indonesia in 1987, which in their imagination were not "administrative" elections.

The tripartite talks in limbo

During the 13th round of talks in February 1987, it became increasingly clear that Portugal intended to renege on the provisions of the agreed plan on the pretext that the Portuguese Parliament would be unable to accept such a solution.

In order to break the impasse caused by the ambiguity of Portugal's response to the proposed MOU, Indonesia agreed to negotiate the contents of the draft invitation of the Indonesian Foreign Minister to the UN Secretary-General to send the observer team to the Indonesian general elections. Had the Portuguese side agreed, the relevant part of the letter would have read:

"In this connection, I wish to inform you that the Indonesian General Elections, including in East Timor, will be held in April 1987. I also wish, on behalf of my Government, to invite you to send a team to observe this event. An opportunity will thus be provided to the international community to further ascertain that the people of East Timor are participating fully and freely in the political life of the country in the same way as other citizens of Indonesia and that, through their participation, they have faithfully reflected their wishes regarding their future.

To this end, it is contemplated that the observation process would encompass all phases of the organization and conduct of the elections, similar to the manner in which UN visiting missions have observed other elections in the past. The modalities for observation remain a matter for further discussion . . . ."

Although Portugal had broadly indicated a reversal of its position in other forums, such as the European Parliament and the UN Commission on Human Rights, it was not until the 14th round of the tripartite dialogue held in March 1987 that the Portuguese side officially confirmed that the Government of Portugal could not accept the terms of the Secretary-General's plan as contained in the draft MOU.

Cited as unacceptable were those provisions dealing with the Indonesian General Elections as the vehicle leading to the solution of the East Timor issue. Portugal added that since the Indonesian elections were getting closer, it appeared that at this stage the dialogue, within the framework of the Secretary-General's plan, could not proceed any further.

New proposals

Instead, Portugal at first proposed that Jose Ramos Horta, of FRETILINM, be permitted to visit East Timor to observe the situation and to meet the FRETILIN guerilla leaders so as to contribute towards a settlement. Indonesia rejected that proposal as unacceptable and unproductive and made a counterproposal to have one or two members of the Portuguese Parliament visit East Timor instead to see for themselves the real situation in the province.

For its part, Portugal proposed to send a full parliamentary mission, representing all political parties in the Portuguese Parliament to visit East Timor for what amounted to an investigative mission, with the possibility of establishing contact with "elements of the armed opposition." Advanced without any indication whether it would conform to the goals set out in the draft MOU, this proposal was clearly unacceptable to Indonesia.

Indonesia's formal response to this proposal was to reiterate that: (1) the Secretary-General's proposed plan remained the best possible solution; (2) the Indonesian proposal to have one or two members of the Portuguese Parliament visit East Timor still stood; and (3) Indonesia would continue to cooperate with the Secretary-General.

The efforts of Indonesia to "go the extra mile" to salvage the MOU were thus to no avail. The UN Secretary-General's proposed plan could not be implemented and a golden opportunity to achieve an internationally acceptable settlement and a face-saving way out for both sides was irretrievably lost.

Through informal sources I subsequently learned that one of the reasons the Portuguese Government reneged on the proposed plan, earlier agreed upon at the Ambassadorial level, was that Ambassador Rui de Medina was considered "to have gone beyond his brief." If true, I thought such an accusation to be quite unfair to the Ambassador, whom I had come to know as a serious and conscientious counterpart in the negotiations, faithfully reporting every development of the process to his Government, as I also did to mine.

From 27 to 29 April 1987, the Secretary-General visited Lisbon and held discussions with President Mario Soares, Prime Minister Anibal Cavaco Silva and Foreign Minister Pires de Miranda. After the return of the Secretary-General to New York, Under Secretary-General Rafeeuddin Ahmed briefed the Indonesian side on the results of the talks between the Secretary-General and the Portuguese Government leaders.

From that briefing it was evident that the Portuguese position remained ambiguous and even contradictory. Essentially, Portugal had conveyed the view that:

(1) The Secretary-General should continue his efforts.
(2) It was interested in pursuing the Indonesian proposal concerning a visit by members of the Portuguese Parliament to East Timor.
(3) It continued to have concerns about the right to self-

determination of the East Timorese, while maintaining that its chief concern was the human rights situation and the preservation of the cultural heritage of the East Timorese, which were aspects that had been previously thoroughly covered to the satisfaction of both sides during the dialogue.

(4) The political situation in Portugal was in a state of flux since a new government would not be formed before August 1987.

In response, the Secretary-General told Portugal that although he was ready to continue his efforts, he needed clear indication from the parties concerned on the direction that such efforts should take. He also told them that he concurred with Indonesia's view that since it was Portugal and not Indonesia that could not continue to work under the agreed plan, namely making use of the Indonesian elections as a vehicle towards a solution, it was up to Portugal to come up with a new proposal.

The dialogue is continued

Both sides readily accepted the Secretary-General's offer of his continued good offices in the search of a mutually acceptable solution. As the Secretary-General had to make a report to the UN General Assembly on the results of the dialogue so far, they now had to agree on the timing of the report and to make a choice of two options, with the choice to be reflected in the Secretary-General's report.

The first choice was to simply admit that the tripartite dialogue had failed to find a comprehensive and mutually acceptable solution and that therefore the dialogue would be discontinued; the other was to admit that the dialogue had hit a temporary snag but also affirm the intention to continue the dialogue with the same objective and under the same conditions as before.

After some discussions, both sides chose the second option and agreed that the Secretary-General would submit his report before the start of the 42nd session of the General Assembly, in September 1987.

After some further discussions and negotiations, whereby the two sides also agreed to consider the possibility of a visit by a Portuguese parliamentary mission, the final text of the 1987 Secretary-General's Report was agreed to read as follows:

"…In my 1986 progress report, I had expressed the hope that the substantive talks between Indonesia and Portugal would lead to a settlement to the question of East Timor. It is a matter of deep regret that this goal has not yet been achieved. Nonetheless, the talks have enabled both sides to establish a useful dialogue and to make a serious attempt to bridge the differences in their respective positions. In this connection the two sides are considering the possibility of a Portuguese parliamentary delegation undertaking a visit to East Timor, with a view to obtaining first-hand information on the situation.

"The two countries have reaffirmed their commitment to cooperate, under my auspices, in the search for a comprehensive and internationally acceptable solution.."

And thus some hope was retained that the East Timor issue could still be solved peacefully through the tripartite dialogue.

Footnotes

[1] The saying, taken from a letter of the Indonesian national heroine Kartini to her brother, runs as follows: "Digdoyo tanpo aji/ Nglurug tanpo bolo/ Menang tanpo ngasorake/ Wani ngalah duwur wekasane."

Chapter 3
Yet Another Missed Opportunity

BY the middle of 1987, after a hiatus of several months, the tripartite talks at the ambassadorial level were resumed, this time mainly focused on discussing the proposed Portuguese parliamentary visit to East Timor.

Taking into account Portugal's insistence on its proposal to send a parliamentary mission to East Timor, the Indonesian Government finally gave me the "green light" to negotiate on this matter.

Accordingly, I told Mr. Rafeeuddin Ahmed that in principle Indonesia could accept a visit by a Portuguese parliamentary delegation to East Timor but first there would have to be some basic common understandings with Portugal. There would have to be explicit concurrence by the Portuguese side that the visit would not be an "investigation" but an "observation" mission, and its purpose would have to be linked to the basic objective of the tripartite dialogue: it should be in the context of finding a comprehensive, just and internationally acceptable solution to the East Timor issue.

The mission would have to be accompanied by representatives of the UN Secretary-General. This was important, as Indonesia expected that the representatives of the Secretary-General would present a more objective and unbiased report. Moreover, before any formal steps would be taken toward the visit, the modalities and timing of the visit would have to be worked out in advance. Mr. Ahmed said that it was his impression that Portugal would concur with such an approach. Hence, the dialogue was resumed, but progress turned out to be frustratingly slow and marred by many delays.

Initially, the Portuguese were reluctant to agree to having representatives of the UN Secretary-General accompany the projected parliamentary mission to East Timor, but after further negotiations, finally accepted the idea. As to the timing of such a mission, both sides agreed that it could only take place after the general elections and the formation of a new Parliament and Cabinet in Portugal, which were all scheduled for late 1987.

Contrary to earlier understandings, in October 1987, the Minister of Foreign Affairs of Portugal, in a message to the Secretary-General, conveyed the request, in the context of the proposed visit, for a letter of invitation from the Indonesian Parliament addressed to the Portuguese Parliament. He added that only upon receipt of such an official invitation would the Portuguese side be in a position to discuss the terms of reference and modalities of the visit.

The Indonesian response was to point out that this was inconsistent with the already informally agreed procedure. Extending a letter of invitation before agreeing on the terms of reference and modalities of the visit would prove embarrassing to both sides if in the end no agreement could be reached on these details and the visit would have to be cancelled.

Nonetheless, I used much of my time during my annual consultation visit in January 1988 in Jakarta lobbying with the Department of Foreign Affairs and the leadership of the Indonesian Parliament for Indonesia's agreement to issue the invitation. Finally, in its desire to proceed expeditiously and as a reflection of its respect for the Secretary-General, the Indonesian Government agreed to issue the invitation. However, I was instructed to make it very clear that the visit could only take place after agreement had been reached on the terms of reference, modalities and timing of the visit.

The letter of invitation from the Chairman of the Indonesian House of Representatives, Mr. Kharis Suhud, was duly presented to the Secretary-General on 4 February 1988 for transmittal to the President of the Assembly of Portugal, Mr. Victor Pereira Crespo. The relevant parts of the letter stated:

"In the course of these (tripartite) talks the possibility of an observation visit to East Timor by a Portuguese Parliamentary Delegation was recently considered.

In pursuance of this idea and on behalf of the leadership and members of the Indonesian House of Representatives, it gives me great pleasure to extend an invitation to Your Excellency and to the honourable members of the Portuguese Parliament to send a delegation to visit Indonesia. With regard to the proposed visit to East Timor, it can only be effected after the Permanent Representatives of Indonesia and Portugal in New York have reached agreement on the terms, modalities and timing of the visit.

I believe that such a visit will provide the delegation with the opportunity to obtain objective and first-hand information on the actual situation and conditions in East Timor and I can assure Your Excellency that the delegation will be accorded the necessary facilities to enable it to do so."

After being so insistent that this invitation be issued, the Portuguese Parliament took six months to accept it—on 28 July 1988. Consequently two meetings were held in August 1988 in which the two sides agreed in principle that a Portuguese Parliamentary Delegation would visit East Timor with a view to obtaining first-hand information on the situation, subject to the elaboration of mutually agreed terms of reference.

After that, the Permanent Representatives of Portugal and Indonesia resumed their substantive talks and starting from 9 May 1989 discussed a Non-Paper prepared by Mr. Rafeeuddin Ahmed on the terms of reference and modalities concerning the visit of the Portuguese Parliamentary Delegation to East Timor.

By that time, I had already left New York, having been recalled to Jakarta in March 1988 to assume the post of Minister for Foreign Affairs, succeeding Dr. Mochtar Kusuma-Atmadja. At the UN, I was succeeded by Ambassador Nana Sutresna Sastradijaya, who continued the tripartite dialogue at the ambassadorial level. From Jakarta, however, I continued to closely engage myself in the process and maintained contact with my Portuguese counterpart at the ministerial level.

A breakthrough in sight

From the beginning, there were three controversial issues blocking quick agreement on the text of the Non-Paper, namely the question of visas for the members of the Portuguese Parliamentary Delegation, the question of transit through Jakarta en route to Dili by the Delegation, and the question of foreign journalists who would accompany the Parliamentary Delegation. Only after difficult and lengthy negotiations could these three issues be resolved through an agreed "package deal."

On the question of visas, the Portuguese side refused to have Indonesian visas stamped on their passports, on grounds that there were no diplomatic relations between the two countries and acceptance of Indonesian visas could also be construed as Portugal's implicit recognition of Indonesian sovereignty over East Timor.

This question was in the end resolved by Indonesia waiving

visa requirements for the Portuguese Parliamentary Delegation members and those accompanying them. Instead, it was agreed that Indonesia would issue a unilateral declaration, to be attached as an annex to the agreement, explaining Indonesia's position on this question.

On the question of transit through Jakarta, the Portuguese side at first insisted on flying directly to Dili, East Timor, either from Singapore or Darwin, Australia, thus bypassing Jakarta altogether. On the other hand, Indonesia insisted that the Delegation would first make a stopover in Jakarta and pay a courtesy call at least on the Chairman of the Indonesian House of Representatives as the person, who after all, had issued the invitation to the Portuguese Delegation.

Finally, this question was resolved by Portugal agreeing to make a brief stopover at Jakarta's international airport, whereupon the leader of the Portuguese Parliamentary Delegation, accompanied by the representatives of the United Nations Secretary-General, would pay a courtesy call on the Chairman of the Indonesian House of Representatives. The rest of the Delegation would remain at the airport and after the courtesy call the Delegation would immediately depart for Dili.

On this issue, it was further agreed that Portugal likewise would issue a unilateral declaration, as an annex to the agreement, explaining Portugal's position on the Jakarta stopover.

On the question of foreign journalists, Indonesia at first questioned the appropriateness and necessity of having foreign journalists formally joining the Delegation. Indonesia argued that it was already agreed to have ten Portuguese journalists accompany the delegation and ten Indonesian journalists joining the visit in Dili. Foreign journalists would normally be issued visas to cover the event and they usually would come at their own initiative rather than join the Delegation. Portugal, however, insisted on this arrangement, offering each side the right to nominate an equal number of journalists.

In the end, Indonesia gave in and it was agreed that 12 international journalists, six selected by each side, would join the Delegation. Each side would communicate its list of international journalists to the other at least three weeks prior to the commencement of the visit. However, it was further agreed that prior to such communication the names of the international journalists would be discussed at the substantive tripartite talks. The clear understanding was that each side would have the right of agreeing or not agreeing to any journalist proposed by the other side.

After these three issues were resolved in a compromise package deal as earlier described, the text of the terms of reference and modalities of the visit as contained in the Non-Paper was agreed *ad referendum* by the two Ambassadors/ Permanent Representatives. But obtaining the formal agreement of the two Governments, especially of the Portuguese Government, turned out to be an excruciatingly slow and tortuous process.

A new issue

On 14 September 1990, the Indonesian Government expressed its agreement to the Non-Paper regarding the terms of reference and modalities of the visit. The Portuguese side assured Mr. Ahmed that its response would be conveyed during the forty-fifth session of the General Assembly, some time in October 1990, when Portugal's Prime Minister would attend the general debate.

Regrettably, more than eight months elapsed since the latest round of talks held in September 1990 and the Portuguese did not give any response to the compromise package concerning the terms of reference and modalities of the visit. Neither did Portugal give any reason for not responding to the proposal other than that presidential elections were to be held in that country.

Finally, Portugal on 23 May 1991 responded to the proposed compromise. However, its response was not acceptable to the Indonesian side because, while expressing its readiness to accept the package deal, the Portuguese ambassador brought up an entirely new issue. He proposed that Portugal issue an additional unilateral interpretative statement, to be annexed to the agreement on the position with regard to the question of "freedom of movement and contacts."

In that proposed statement, Portugal would demand that the provision enjoining Indonesian authorities against taking any action that might prejudice potential contacts with the Delegation, including security measures, should enter into force immediately after any agreement was signed and not wait until the Delegation arrived in East Timor. The Portuguese also expressed the view that the United Nations should henceforth be present in the territory of East Timor and that all armed action be suspended in East Timor during the Secretary-

General's efforts at finding a comprehensive solution.

The Portuguese side tried to explain that this proposal was the result of difficult negotiations between the President of Portugal, the Cabinet and Parliament and since it was a unilateral interpretative statement it did not require Indonesia's agreement nor did it bind any other party.

The Indonesian side firmly rejected the proposal, arguing that this purported interpretative statement departed so drastically from the relevant paragraph of the Non-Paper that it actually constituted an entirely new idea. Such a unilateral interpretative statement, if allowed to stand, would undermine and indeed invalidate the entire agreement as contained in the Non-Paper and as agreed upon. And bringing up this new issue at such a late stage of the negotiations really raised the question of Portugal's sincerity in trying to reach agreement on a comprehensive solution.

The tripartite meeting on 23 May 1991 ended inconclusively and it was only during the next meeting, on 27 June 1991, which was personally chaired by Secretary-General Perez de Cuellar, that Portugal withdrew its proposal to issue an additional unilateral interpretative statement. As a result, the Non-Paper was *ad-referendum* agreed upon at the ambassadorial level and reported to the respective Governments.

Agreement at last

The Portuguese Government gave its consent on 19 July 1991 and the Indonesian Government agreed on 1 August 1991. The next stage, as earlier agreed upon, would be to discuss the practical arrangements of the visit, including the sending of an Advance Team. These discussions were held at the level of Deputy Permanent Representatives of both sides, under the chairmanship of Rafeeuddin Ahmed.

The agreed Non-Paper, which would now be transformed into a formal agreement, contained, among others, the following understandings:

In the preamble, the two sides agreed that the realization of the Portuguese Parliamentary Delegation's visit, in all its aspects, would in no way be construed as prejudicing the respective positions of principle of the parties with regard to the substance of the question.

As regards the objective of the visit, it was clearly stated that it was to obtain first-hand information on the situation in the territory, on the understanding that the visit would not be investigative in nature.

As to the composition of the Delegation, the agreement was that it would comprise 13 Portuguese parliamentarians, accompanied by 13 Portuguese officials and 10 Portuguese journalists. The Portuguese Delegation would be joined by a delegation of the United Nations Secretary-General, the composition and size of which would be left to the discretion of the Secretary-General and for further tripartite discussion.

On the question of participation by journalists, apart from the ten Portuguese journalists who would form an integral part of the Portuguese Delegation, Indonesia on its part would designate ten Indonesian journalists to cover the visit starting from Dili.

In addition, the Portuguese Delegation would be joined by 12 international journalists, six to be selected by each side. In this regard, the understanding was that each side would communicate its list of international journalists to the other at least three weeks prior to the commencement of the visit. Before such communication would be sent, however, the names of the international journalists would be discussed informally at the substantive talks. The purpose of such an arrangement was clear: so that the composition of the contingent of international journalists would be agreed upon by both sides.

On the issue of visa facilities, as earlier explained, it was agreed that Indonesia would issue a unilateral declaration, which in essence would state that: "In order to facilitate the visit and out of respect for the noble efforts of the Secretary-General… to promote the reaching of an agreement between Indonesia and Portugal… the Government of Indonesia—in the exercise of its sovereignty—has decided to waive visa requirements for the members of the Portuguese Parliamentary Delegation and those accompanying it."

Likewise, on the question of a stopover at the Jakarta airport, it was agreed that Portugal would issue a unilateral declaration, which in essence would state that: "The stopover in Jakarta and the visit of the leader of the Portuguese Parliamentary Delegation to the Indonesian House of Representatives… to pay a courtesy call on the Speaker, constitute only a gesture of goodwill testifying to the continuing availability of Portugal to achieve.. a just, comprehensive and internationally acceptable settlement to the question of East Timor."

With regard to freedom of movement and of contacts, the agreement stipulated that the Delegation would have "individual access to all parts of the territory, within the context of the agreed objective of the visit, in conditions of peace and security."

It further stated that the Delegation would be "free to meet whomever it wishes and anyone who wishes to meet the Portuguese Delegation will be allowed to do so. No action, including of a security nature, may be taken by the Indonesian authorities which could prejudice any potential or actual contacts. Individuals who meet the Portuguese Parliamentary Delegation shall not be made to suffer any adverse consequences as a result of those contacts."

As to the timing and duration, it was envisaged that the visit would take place during the dry season and last for 10 to 12 days. Subsequently, it was agreed that the visit would start during the first week of November 1991.

Finally it was decided that an Advance Team would travel to East Timor to prepare the practical arrangements for the visit of the Delegation. The Advance Team would be led by a representative of the Secretary-General and include two representatives each from Portugal and Indonesia.

Dispatch of an Advance Team

Starting from 12 August 1991, a series of meetings was held at the level of Deputy Permanent Representatives of both sides, in order to negotiate the practical arrangements for the visit of the Portuguese Parliamentary Delegation as well as that of the Advance Team.

The talks on the Advance Team went reasonably well and the team, led by a staff member of the United Nations Secretariat representing the Secretary-General, and comprising two members each representing the Portuguese and the Indonesian sides, actually visited East Timor from 30 September to 4 October 1991. The Team went to all the places that would be visited by the Parliamentary Delegation, observing the conditions relating to all the technical and logistical aspects of the Parliamentary Delegation's visit.

The discussions on the practical arrangements for the visit of the Parliamentary Delegation itself, however, including follow-up discussions on the findings of the Advance Team, were more difficult and dragged on till the third week of October 1991. But by that time practically all the arrangements for the visit, including such questions as its commencement and duration (from 3 November to 14 November 1991), the itinerary and programme, accommodations, transportation and telecommunication facilities were agreed upon.

Apart from building temporary accommodation facilities at some of the small villages to be visited, Indonesia even transported by air from the city of Bandung in Java to Dili and Baucau, special sophisticated telecommunication equipment in order to enable the Portuguese and international journalists to conveniently file their reports in text and photographic form.

Portugal drops a bombshell

It therefore came as a shock and painful surprise to the Indonesian side when the negotiations came to a deadlock on a question related to the list of international journalists.

As earlier agreed, the Portuguese Parliamentary Delegation would be joined by 12 international journalists, six to be selected by each side. In this regard, there was an agreed understanding that the names of these journalists would first be discussed informally at the substantive talks, for the obvious purpose of ensuring that the composition of the contingent of international journalists would carry the approval of both sides.

On 16 October 1991, the two sides informally exchanged their respective proposed lists of international journalists and it was understood that both sides needed to forward the names submitted by the other side to their respective Governments for clearance.

When subsequently Indonesia registered its objection to the inclusion of one particular person on the Portuguese list, namely Ms. Jill Joliffe, and requested that she be replaced by someone else, Indonesia was clearly acting in conformity with the earlier agreed understanding. In opposing the inclusion of Ms. Joliffe, Indonesia argued that since way back, she had established herself more like an ardent pro-FRETILIN and anti-Indonesian propagandist rather than a "real" journalist. Her participation, therefore, would not be helpful to the visit, which was, after all, to be an objective observation visit, designed to contribute to a comprehensive and internationally acceptable solution to the East Timor question.

Portugal did not only reject Indonesia's request but it did so in a surprisingly rigid and harsh fashion. It claimed that the list of journalists had already been agreed upon at the highest levels of the Portuguese

Government and Parliament and there was no way that it could be changed. Portugal was not even prepared to enter into informal discussions as stipulated by the agreed understanding and instead threatened that if by a certain deadline Indonesia did not give its agreement, then the visit would be off. Efforts by the United Nations Secretary-General to mediate a compromise were also to no avail.

The media as battleground

After a few days of mounting uncertainty and tension, the Portuguese Government on 26 October 1991 announced to the press in Lisbon its unilateral decision to suspend the visit while blaming Indonesia for the impasse and accusing Indonesia of committing "a serious violation of the fundamental principles of the right to inform and be informed."

In going straight to the media, Portugal did not even have the courtesy of informing the UN Secretary-General of its decision.

In view of the serious accusation that Portugal was making against Indonesia in the court of international public opinion, I felt that as Foreign Minister of Indonesia, I had no choice but go to the press myself and disabuse the public of the impression being created by Portugal that Indonesia was curtailing the right of the international press to inform and be informed. I called for a press briefing on 28 October 1991 and gave the media people a detailed view of all that had taken place in the negotiations between Portugal and Indonesia.

I emphasized that our objection to Ms Jill Joliffe being brought into the delegation by the Portuguese side as a foreign journalist had nothing to do with blocking information. For if we had wanted to block information, we should not have agreed to Portugal bringing in ten of its own journalists and the five other foreign journalists that it had selected.

Making full use of that occasion to give Indonesia's side of the story, I pointed out that it was indeed astonishing to see Portugal attaching greater importance to the inclusion of one journalist than the need to respect previously agreed understandings and even to the planned Portuguese Parliamentary visit itself, on which so much effort, time and resources had been spent.

It would later occur to me that apart from raising serious questions as to Portugal's good faith and commitment in its conduct throughout the tripartite talks, that episode also strengthened the suspicion of many international and even some Portuguese observers that the Portuguese Government had gratefully seized the Jill Joliffe imbroglio as a pretext to suspend the visit and thus extricate itself from what had always been a highly sensitive and controversial issue within Portugal's political establishment, notably between the President, the Prime Minister and his Cabinet, and Parliament.

This was not the first time that Portugal at the last minute aborted an agreement in the context of finding a solution to the East Timor question. In 1987, in almost similar circumstances, Portugal suddenly withdrew its support for an earlier informally agreed MOU so painstakingly negotiated during the tripartite talks under the auspices of the UN Secretary-General.

It is a matter of public record, therefore, that on two occasions in the course of the tripartite talks Portugal caused the loss of a realistic opportunity to achieve a solution on the issue of East Timor.

On 29 October 1991, three days after it had announced to the press that it was suspending the parliamentary visit to East Timor, Portugal finally gave the UN Secretary-General the courtesy of a letter informing him of that decision.

Chapter 4
The Santa Cruz Incident and Its Aftermath

THE UNEXPECTED last-minute cancellation of the projected visit of the Portuguese Parliamentary Delegation to East Timor did not only cause bewilderment on the part of the United Nations Secretary-General and of Indonesia, but also evoked feelings of deep disappointment and frustration, especially among the pro-independence elements in East Timor. They had hoped to take full advantage of the visit by organizing demonstrations and other events that would dramatize their cause to the outside world.

The cancellation of the visit therefore left them with an acute sense of a lost opportunity. In the days immediately following the announcement of the indefinite "postponement" of the visit, a sharp rise in tension and friction could be observed among pro-independence and pro-integration youths.

The tension culminated in a clash between these two groups on the evening of 28 October 1991 in front of the Sao Antonio Church, in the Motael district of Dili. In the melee, two persons died, one of them Sebastiao Gomes, a pro-independence youth.

On 12 November, a large crowd had gathered at the Motael church to hear a memorial mass for Sebastiao. After the service, and according to the programme, to which the authorities had earlier agreed, the congregation walked in a procession to the Santa Cruz cemetery to place flowers on Sebastiao's grave.

Peaceful procession turns violent

Unfortunately, however, the intended peaceful procession, which started from the Motael church and moved along the main streets of Dili to the cemetery, a distance of about three kilometers, was from the outset taken over by a small group of agitators and pro-independence youth. The procession quickly turned into a wild, disorderly and at times destructive demonstration.

According to eyewitness and documentary accounts, the demonstration was also marked by deliberate acts of provocation, such as the display of FRETILIN flags and banners, the shouting of anti-integration slogans and insults and taunts hurled at security personnel. At one point along the route, an Indonesian Army officer, Major Andi Gerhan-Lentara, deputy commander of Battalion 700, which was stationed in Dili, tried to persuade the crowd to calm down but he was stabbed for his efforts. An enlisted man, Private Domingus, who tried to help him, was also wounded.

It was also established that a number of foreign nationals, mostly journalists and NGO activists, took part in the demonstration. In fact, the journalists were seen to be actively directing the demonstrators for the purpose of taking still photographs and videotapes of the action.

This aggressive attitude displayed by certain groups within the crowd continued at the Santa Cruz cemetery, where a number of Indonesian Army units had been posted beforehand. It was in that riotous situation, with its atmosphere of rising tensions, tumult and confusion that, most unfortunately, the troops began to shoot at the crowd.

The National Commission of Inquiry, which the Government quickly established on 18 November, would later report that:

"... a spontaneous reaction took place among the security personnel... without command, resulting in excessive shooting at the demonstrators... At the same time, another group of unorganized security personnel, acting outside any control or command, also fired shots and committed beatings ...."

It was clear that the tragic event that took place on 12 November 1991 was not a deliberate act ordered by or reflecting the policy of the Government or of the Armed Forces, whether emanating from the capital or conceived locally. This has also been corroborated by the findings of the National Commission of Inquiry.

It was essentially a tragedy, where things somehow went horribly wrong; a fatal incident to be deeply regretted and this, indeed, was immediately and repeatedly expressed by President Soeharto and by the Government of Indonesia. In fact, President Soeharto, on three separate public occasions conveyed his condolences to the bereaved families.

Witnessed and recorded by media

It cannot be denied that this tragic development constituted a serious setback to all the efforts that had been expended so far to achieve a peacefully negotiated solution to the East Timor issue. The fact that the entire incident was witnessed by a number of foreign journalists and that the shootings at the cemetery had been filmed by a British photo-journalist, Max Stahl, also contributed to the thorough tarnishing of Indonesia's image, especially that of its military, in the eyes of the world.

Coincidentally, at the time of the incident, the UN Special Rapporteur on Torture, Mr. Peter H. Kooymans, also happened to be visiting Dili, on an earlier arranged ten-day tour of East Timor. His eyewitness account and report to the UN Secretary-General added to the adverse publicity that Indonesia suffered as result of the incident.

When the incident occurred, I was in Seoul, Republic of Korea attending the Third APEC Conference. I was deeply shocked when the news of the incident was conveyed to me by telephone by my Foreign Ministry staff in Jakarta. In Seoul, I issued a press statement deploring the incident and calling for a full inquiry and I issued a similar statement upon my return to Jakarta on 15 November.

Swift Government response

In facing this tragedy, the Indonesian Government acted quite firmly and swiftly. On 14 November 1991, two days after the event, an investigating team was sent to East Timor under the leadership of the then Deputy Chief of BAKIN (National Intelligence Coordinating Agency), Arie Sudewo.

On 18 November 1991, the National Commission of Inquiry was established, comprising seven members and headed by a Supreme Court Judge, Mr. M. Jaelani. It was tasked to "independently, meticulously, fairly and comprehensively investigate all aspects of the incident."

The Commission began its work on 21 November 1991. It interviewed scores of people both in East Timor and in Jakarta, and conducted on-the-spot surveys and forensic analyses. It submitted its Advance Report, containing its main findings and conclusions, to the

President on 26 December and published the Report the following day. Its full Report, elaborating all materials, interviews and evidence in support of those conclusions was published on 13 April 1992.

Reading the Report, one gets the impression that the Commission had tried to acquit itself of its task in a serious and responsible way. Apart from detailing its method of work and scope of activities and providing an analysis of events that took place, the Commission used unambiguous and even blunt language in apportioning blame.

For example, it spoke of "actions of a number of security personnel which exceeded acceptable norms and led to the casualties, be it in terms of deaths, gunshot wounds, stabbing wounds, or wounds by blunt instruments.." and referred to ". . . excessive shooting at the demonstrators, causing deaths and wounded . . . ."

It criticized the "lack of proper implementation of riot control procedures, the careless handling of casualties and of identification of the deceased." The Commission also refuted earlier casualty estimates (initially claimed by the Army leadership to be 19 dead and 91 wounded), stating that there were sufficiently strong grounds to conclude that about 50 were killed, while the wounded exceeded 91, with approximately 90 still missing.

In concluding the Report, the National Commission of Inquiry recommended that "in order to uphold justice, action must be taken against all who were involved in the 12th of November incident in Dili and suspected of having violated the law, and they must be brought to trial in accordance with the Rule of Law, *Pancasila* and the 1945 Constitution upon which the Republic of Indonesia is based."

Presidential directives

After receiving the Advance Report of the National Commission of Inquiry, the President promptly responded to it. On 28 December 1991, two days after the Commission's Report was submitted to him, the President called the Vice-President, several Cabinet Ministers and other officials to an extraordinary meeting in his office at the Palace. Those present were: Vice President Sudharmono, Home Affairs Minister Rudini, Defence Minister Benny Murdani, Commander of the Armed Forces Try Sutrisno, Army Chief of Staff Edi Sudrajat, Attorney General Singgih, State Secretary Moerdiono and myself.

At that meeting, after first demanding progress reports from the military commanders present as well as from the Ministers of Home Affairs and Foreign Affairs, the President issued the following directives:

- Replacement of the Commander of Military Region IX/Udayana, which covers East Timor; the Operational Commander of East Timor and other officers down the local command echelons in East Timor, who were all held responsible for the incident;
- The Chief of Staff of the Army to set up a Military Council of Honour that would conduct a thorough investigation into the policies and actions of the regional/local security officials in handling the incident and to recommend steps to be taken on the basis of its findings;
- The Commander of the Armed Forces to take every possible measure in order to find those listed as missing and to clarify the discrepancies in reports on the number of casualties. Also to continue and to step up territorial (civic action) operations, which in the past had earned for the Government and the military the goodwill of the people of East Timor;
- The Home Affairs Ministers to improve the civil service apparatus in East Timor, so as to achieve greater coordination and effectiveness in the implementation of the development programmes in the province;
- The Attorney General to initiate legal action/proceedings against all those suspected of having violated the law;
- The Minister for Foreign Affairs to neutralize and set straight the negative and often distorted reports on the Santa Cruz incident by the foreign media.

In the implementation of some of these directives, the Commander of the Armed Forces announced on 31 December 1991 the replacement of Major General Sintong Panjaitan, Commander of Military Region IX/Udayana, by Major General H.B.L. Mantiri and the replacement of Brig. General R.S. Warouw, Chief of the Operational Command in East Timor, by Brig. General Theo Syafei.

On 2 January 1992, the Chief of Staff of the Army announced the establishment of the Military Council of Honour, headed by Major General Feisal Tandjung and comprising nine members. The Council's task was "to investigate and evaluate the Army's command structure and the implementation of its tasks in connection with the incident" and in particular look into the actions taken by Brig. General Warouw and Major General Panjaitan.

Also in pursuance of the President's directives, I undertook a "damage control" mission in February 1992, visiting Washington DC, New York (United Nations), Ottawa, London, Brussels, The Hague, Paris, Madrid, Bonn, Geneva and Vienna, primarily to explain to the governments in those capitals and the international mass media the policies and measures taken by the Indonesian Government in responding to the incident.

The Wako Report

The Government also agreed to the proposal of the United Nations Secretary-General to send Mr. Amos Wako, Attorney General of Kenya and an international authority on human rights, to East Timor as his Personal Envoy to consult with the Government of Indonesia and to obtain clarifications on the Santa Cruz tragedy. Mr. Wako visited Jakarta and East Timor from 9 to 14 February 1992 and submitted his Report to the United Nations Secretary-General on 19 February 1992. Subsequently, the conclusions and recommendations in the Report were transmitted to the Indonesian Government.

The Indonesian Government found the Report in many important aspects to be unbalanced and unsubstantiated by facts. It contained a number of misperceptions and misrepresentations which required a further straightening out.

So on 30 May I conveyed to the Secretary-General the Indonesian Government's response to it, while also providing him with the full Report of the National Commission of Inquiry, the findings of the Military Council of Honour and a progress report on the actions taken against some members of the armed forces in connection with the Santa Cruz incident.

The clarifications and actions taken by the Government in response to the Santa Cruz tragedy managed to repair to some extent the damage inflicted on Indonesia's international image and reputation by the events of 12 November 1991.

Several Western governments expressed their appreciation for President Suharto's prompt response to the Commission Report and the Chairman of the Geneva-based Human Rights Commission, in a consensus statement, welcomed the swift action taken by the

Government including the disciplinary measures and court proceedings to which the implicated members of the armed forces were subjected.

The case of the Lusitania Expresso

A few weeks after the Santa Cruz incident, news broke out that a number of Portuguese and international youth groups and NGOs would sail to East Timor purportedly to show solidarity with and pay tribute to the victims of the Santa Cruz incident by showering their graves with flowers. They proclaimed that they would do so without bothering to ask permission from the Indonesian Government. For this purpose, they chartered a Portuguese ferry ship, the Lusitania Expresso, which was owned by a certain Mr. Carlos A. Rochas Cabecas and captained by Mr. Luis dos Santos.

This highly provocative action drew a lot of media attention in Portugal and Indonesia from the moment the ship set sail for East Timor in early 1992. There were about 125 persons on board, including journalists. Former Portuguese President Antonio Ramalho Eanes was reportedly among them. From the outset, the Indonesian Government reacted by warning that the ship would be prevented, by force if necessary, from entering Indonesian waters.

By the time the ship reached Darwin, Australia on 8 March 1992, greater realism had sunk in among those on board, especially the owner of the ship, as to the enormity of the danger to which they were exposing themselves. To the press in Darwin, Mr. Carlos Rochas Cabecas announced that he had no intention whatsoever of breaking any rule and endangering his ship, its crew and the passengers. If no permission was given to the *Lusitania Expresso*, he said, the ship would head back to Darwin and he had given clear instructions to the captain to do so.

When the Lusitania Expresso arrived at Indonesia's sea border, east of Timor island, on 11 March 1992 at 06:00 local time, it was duly intercepted by three Indonesian warships, the KRI Yos Sudarso, the KRI Ki Hajar Dewantara and the command ship, the KRI Teluk Banten, with the commander of the Indonesian Eastern Fleet, Rear Admiral Tanto Koeswanto, on board.

After a few warnings by bullhorn from the KRI Yos Sudarso on the dire consequences if the *Lusitania Expresso* did not leave Indonesian waters, the ferry ship meekly turned around and headed back for international waters. There was no incident; not a single warning shot was fired. Thus, the ill-conceived and futile venture of the *Lusitania Expresso* came to a pathetic end.

The turning point

However, it cannot be denied that the violent Santa Cruz incident on 12 November 1991 had dealt a severe setback to Indonesia's efforts at peacefully solving the East Timor problem, from which it would never be able to fully recover. In fact, 12 November 1991 constituted a watershed in Indonesian diplomacy on East Timor and since that date, international support for Indonesia's position inexorably declined while that for the independence movement in East Timor markedly increased. For example, the award of the Nobel Peace Prize jointly to Bishop Belo and Jose Ramos Horta in October 1996 was an important symbol of the extent of the growth of international support and sympathy for the cause of East Timorese independence.

Chapter 5
The Tripartite Talks Resume

AFTER his assumption of the office of United Nations Secretary-General in January 1992 (succeeding Mr. Javier Perez de Cuellar), Dr. Boutros Boutros-Ghali engaged in consultations with Indonesia and Portugal in an effort to find an agreed format and modalities for reconvening the tripartite talks, which had gone on since 1983 but were interrupted after the Santa Cruz incident.

A Portuguese proposal

On 13 January 1992, the Minister for Foreign Affairs of Portugal, Mr. Joao de Deus Pinheiro, wrote a letter to the United Nations Secretary-General expressing Portugal's readiness to resume the tripartite dialogue. In that letter, Mr. Pinheiro reiterated his country's basic position and proposed modalities for the dialogue, in the following words:

"Portugal expresses its availability to initiate immediately, without preconditions and under the auspices of the Secretary-General, the dialogue with Indonesia *and with all parties directly concerned*, aiming at reaching a just, comprehensive and internationally acceptable settlement, *with full respect for the legitimate rights of the people*, in conformity with the principles of the United Nations and of international law. The talks could be held at a diplomatic level, *under the mediation of an internationally prestigious and experienced personality acceptable to the parties, to be appointed by the United Nations Secretary-General.* Besides the representatives of Portugal and Indonesia, *representatives of the East Timorese people would also be represented in the talks*" (itals. mine).

The position conveyed by the Portuguese Foreign Minister was subsequently transmitted to the Indonesian Government, and in the following months I had lengthy discussions on it with the United

Nations Secretary-General, in February 1992 in New York, in April in Beijing (on the occasion of a meeting on the Cambodian issue) as well as in September in Jakarta (at the sidelines of the 10th Non-Alligned Summit Meeting hosted by Indonesia). Similar discussions were held between the United Nations Secretary-General and Portuguese Foreign Minister Pinheiro in January in New York and in August in London during the conference on Yugoslavia.

On 30 May 1992, I conveyed Indonesia's formal response in a letter to the Secretary-General in which I reiterated the Indonesian Government's continuing support for his efforts, just as we were committed to his predecessor's efforts, to reach a just and comprehensive solution. However, I pointed out that as before, the dialogue should be held under the general mandate of the United Nations Secretary-General and not on the basis of, or pursuant to, any specific General Assembly resolution.

In my letter, I also stressed that we would not accept resumption of the dialogue if changes were proposed to its modalities, in particular the Portuguese proposal to include participation by "representatives of East Timor" in the dialogue. I recalled that this idea, in fact, was informally broached when the dialogue was started in 1983 but was subsequently dropped, as it was clear that no agreement could be reached between Indonesia and Portugal as to who were the "legitimate representatives of East Timor."

In short, Indonesia's position was that any resumption of the dialogue should remain an effort of and personally led by the Secretary-General of the United Nations or his designated Deputy (USG Rafeeuddin Ahmed fulfilled that role in the past) and not become a "mediation" effort by third parties. The dialogue should also remain tripartite in nature, although Indonesia was willing to conduct it at a higher political level than before.

In a separate Aide Memoire, submitted through the Indonesian Permanent Mission in New York, which repeated the same arguments in greater detail, the Indonesian Government additionally recalled the tacit understanding among the parties of the dialogue when it was started, i.e. to find a just, comprehensive and internationally acceptable solution that is short of a return to the *status quo ante*. Indonesia had from the very beginning emphasized its position that it could not accept a solution that would "turn the clock back."

An agreement to continue

As a result of these discussions with both sides, Secretary-General Boutros-Ghali decided to invite the two Foreign Ministers to hold informal consultations in New York, at the United Nations Headquarters, at the time of the 47th General Assembly session. These consultations took place on 26 September 1992 and resulted in an agreement to continue the tripartite dialogue under the auspices of the United Nations Secretary-General, this time at the level of Foreign Ministers, but otherwise with exactly the same modalities as before.

Preparatory meetings were also to be held at the level of Permanent Representatives/Ambassadors of the two sides. In this respect, Assistant Secretary-General Alvaro de Soto was appointed as the Secretary-General's Senior Political Adviser to coordinate these meetings. (He was later succeeded by Undersecretary-General Ismat Kittani, a former Iraqi diplomat). In addition, it was announced that the Foreign Ministers would hold their first meeting with the Secretary-General in New York in December 1992.

Thus, during the term of office of Secretary-General Boutros Boutros-Ghali, eight rounds of ministerial-level tripartite talks were held: in New York on 17 December 1992; in Rome, Italy on 21 April 1993; in New York again on 17 September 1993; in Geneva on 6 May 1994, on 9 January 1995 and on 8 July 1995; in London on 16 January 1996, and in Geneva again on 27 June 1996.

Unfortunately, until the end of Secretary-General Boutros Boutros-Ghali's tenure, not much progress could be made in the effort to find a just, comprehensive and internationally acceptable solution to the East Timor question.

The first round of trilateral talks was held in New York on 17 December 1992. The Portuguese side was represented by Mr. Jose Durao Barroso, who as a member of the newly elected Social Democratic Government of Prime Minister Cavaco Silva, succeeded Mr. Joao de Deus Pinheiro as Foreign Minister of Portugal.

These talks took place against the backdrop of the detention of the East Timor armed resistance leader, Mr. Jose Alexandre "Xanana" Gusmao, who was apprehended in Dili on 20 November 1992. Mr. Gusmao, in February 1993 was brought to trial and on 31 May 1993 was sentenced to life imprisonment, a sentence subsequently reduced to 20 years through clemency by President Soeharto. Throughout the trial, a representative of the UN Secretary-General as well as members of the foreign press corps and representatives of some diplomatic missions resident in Jakarta were able to observe the proceedings.

During the talks, the two sides concurred with the Secretary-General's view that on the core question of finding a solution to East Timor there remained a wide divergence of views. However, both sides agreed on the need to continue the dialogue. It was therefore decided that at the initial stage, the tripartite talks would focus on the identification and implementation of confidence-building measures that could help pave the way for tackling the core issue.

In the ensuing discussions, Foreign Minister Durao Barroso appeared to carry a rather narrow brief for the talks and showed quite a rigid stance on the issues discussed. For example, on possible ways to achieve a just, comprehensive and internationally acceptable solution, he continued to stick closely to Portugal's basic position that it could only be realized through an act of self-determination or referendum. On the other hand, the Indonesian view was that efforts to find a solution should be directed at ways that did not constitute a "return to the *status quo ante*."

As to possible confidence-building measures, the Portuguese Foreign Minister appeared to perceive them as measures that should be undertaken by Indonesia only rather than by both sides, in mutual fashion. For example, he kept stressing on various measures which Indonesia should do in the human rights field in East Timor, but on the other hand rejected as premature a proposal by the Secretary-General to consider restoring diplomatic relations or at least the reciprocal establishment of interests sections in friendly embassies in Jakarta and Lisbon.

He was also rather reluctant to agree that an exchange of journalists would be a good confidence-building measure that would enhance mutual understanding between Portugal and Indonesia. He emphasized instead that the important thing was to allow Portuguese journalists and (pro-FRETILIN) NGO's free access to East Timor.

An unproductive process

Under these conditions, the results in terms of what could be agreed upon were inevitably minimal. In his report to the United Nations General Assembly, the Secretary-General admitted to being only "moderately encouraged by the substance and tone of the discussions."

I myself, at that first round of talks, had come to the conclusion that we still had a long way to go in finding a compromise solution and that much would depend on developments in East Timor itself and on the international stage in the months ahead.

Meanwhile, as earlier agreed upon, Mr. Amos Wako, Personal Envoy of the United Nations Secretary-General, made a second visit to Indonesia, including East Timor, from 3 to 8 April 1993. Apart from following up on the results of the first visit in February 1992, Mr. Wako held extensive discussions with the Indonesian authorities, both in Jakarta and East Timor, as well as with representatives of a number of NGO's, human rights activists and East Timorese in detention, including with Mr. Xanana Gusmao.

As was done before, Mr. Wako's report containing his conclusions and recommendations was conveyed to me in a letter dated 7 August 1993. I transmitted the reactions of the Indonesian Government to some of the conclusions in the report that it deemed to be based on misperceptions or were unbalanced.

The second round of tripartite talks, held in Rome on 21 April 1993, was equally unproductive despite intensive preparatory talks at ambassadorial level in New York, which were coordinated by Assistant Secretary-General Alvaro de Soto. Initially, it was hoped that this second round would yield more concrete results or at least would proceed in a more congenial atmosphere because of a message I received from Foreign Minister Durao Barroso through his Ambassador/Permanent Representative in New York. In that message Foreign Minister Barroso conveyed to me his Government's real desire to achieve a comprehensive solution to the East Timor problem and not engage in "diplomatic maneuvers."

He was, he said, sincerely intent, together with me, to find a compromise solution that would be acceptable to both sides. However, since East Timor is a very sensitive issue in Portugal, with many political interests that had to be considered, he hoped for Indonesia's understanding of the limitations of his mandate at this stage. Yet, notwithstanding the goodwill on both sides and the efforts at the preparatory level to negotiate a more specific and elaborate draft text of confidence-building measures, the talks failed to achieve a consensus.

In the end, it was agreed that at the conclusion of the talks, the Secretary-General would issue only a brief and factual press communiqué. In it was a reference to the consideration of "possible confidence-building measures," without further elaboration.

One unexpected and undesired side-effect encountered at the Rome meeting was the presence of a small but persistent group of anti-Indonesian East Timorese demonstrators in front of the hotel where the talks were taking place.

Apparently, the proximity of the Rome venue of the talks provided the opportunity for East Timorese youth residing in Portugal to come to Rome to agitate and put pressure on the Indonesian delegation. Partly due to their presence, there was also a heightened interest on the part of the national and international media throughout the talks. And, as I had occasion to observe to the Secretary-General at the conclusion of the talks, this was not going to make it easier to achieve progress in the negotiations.

Some tentative progress

The third round of the ministerial tripartite dialogue, held in New York on 17 September 1993, was again preceded by intensive preparatory talks at the ambassadorial level coordinated by ASG Alvaro de Soto. The preparatory talks this time focused on a text of a statement drafted by the UN Secretariat and designed to be issued by the UN Secretary-General following the 17 September meeting with the Foreign Ministers of Indonesia and Portugal.

Discussions on the draft text at times brought out basic differences of view and led to sharp exchanges. But thanks to the diligence of the negotiators, led on the Indonesian side by Ambassador Nugroho Wisnumurti and on the Portuguese side by Ambassador Pedro Catarino, an acceptable working draft was completed for presentation to the two Ministers.

The ministerial dialogue was also held against the backdrop of a number of positive developments, i.e. the presidential clemency accorded to Xanana Gusmao, which reduced his life sentence to 20 years; the grant of amnesty to two of his deputy commanders, Mauhudu and Mauhunu, who had surrendered not long after the capture of Xanana; the reduction of the sentences of other East Timorese convicted for their part in masterminding and engaging in security disturbances in Dili; the dissolution of the special East Timor Military Operations Command (KOLAKOPS) and its replacement by a regular regional/district command (KOREM) like those in all other Indonesian provinces, with an attendant reduction in the number of troops deployed in the territory; and the establishment of the Indonesian National Commission on Human Rights.

This round of tripartite talks proceeded in a much more conducive atmosphere and yielded better results than the earlier talks. After some further negotiations at the ministerial level meeting, the two sides finally agreed on a statement, which was issued by the Secretary-General. It stipulated a number of confidence-building measures (CBMs). For example, as proposed by Indonesia from the outset, the two sides agreed to create a favourable and non-confrontational atmosphere to make it easier for them to move toward a comprehensive solution. Both sides also agreed to continue to promote a reciprocal exchange of visits between their respective journalists and personalities.

During the ministerial talks, I again raised the need to establish Portuguese and Indonesian "interests sections" in friendly embassies in each other's capital, as an effective form of CBM, short of resuming full-fledged diplomatic relations. I argued that by thus having our diplomats stationed in each other's capital, we would be able to establish direct contacts between the two Governments, and Portugal would be able to obtain first-hand information on developments in East Timor instead of relying on newspaper reports and unsubstantiated rumours.

But, as before, Minister Barosso rejected the idea, apparently on the mistaken and outlandish notion that such a measure would only "favour Indonesia" rather than Portugal or both countries equally.

On the other hand, it is worth noting that Minister Barosso during the talks again mentioned in passing, as he had done before at the Rome meeting, the possibility of granting autonomy status to East Timor. However, as this autonomy in the thinking of Minister Barosso was conceived as a transitional step towards an eventual referendum and not as the end solution, I again had to turn down his proposal.

A consultation mission

The fourth round of the tripartite dialogue, held in Geneva on 6 May 1994, was preceded by the dispatch of a Representative of the United Nations Secretary-General on a consultation mission to Portugal and Indonesia, including East Timor. The Director of the East Asia and the Pacific Division in the Department of Political Affairs, Mr. Francesc Vendrell, was designated to undertake this mission. In particular, the consultations were to discuss with the two Governments what further possible confidence-building measures could be included on the agenda of the forthcoming tripartite dialogue and in East Timor to assess the different trends of opinion within the two main segments of the East Timorese population.

Mr. Vendrell came to Indonesia in January 1994 accompanied by Mr. Tamrat Samuel, Political Affairs Officer in the East Asia and Pacific Division, after a two-day visit to Portugal.

In wide-ranging discussions held at my office in the Department of Foreign Affairs, Mr. Vendrell came up with a number of suggestions, which he hoped Indonesia could consider and agree as additional CBMs at the next tripartite dialogue. However, most of them were either unrealistic or so obviously Portuguese-inspired and, hence, unbalanced that I had to turn them down.

For example, Mr. Vendrell proposed the stationing of a Special Representative of the Secretary-General in East Timor. I pointed out that such a proposition would clearly compromise Indonesia's basic position on East Timor while confirming Portugal's claim. Furthermore, Indonesia had always agreed whenever the United Nations Secretary-General wished to send a special envoy to East Timor and the Secretary-General also could always, whenever deemed necessary, send a staff member of the United Nations Mission in Jakarta, so I really did not see the need for a "special representative" posted in East Timor.

Mr. Vendrell also proposed the freeing of Xanana Gusmao and his subsequent exile from Indonesia as a possible CBM, as well as a number of East Timorese sentenced to varying prison terms for their part in masterminding and participating in violent demonstrations. I had to reject these proposals too, stressing that the law had had its due course and the Government had to be consistent in enforcing it. On the other hand, full amnesty had been extended to Mauhudu and Mauhunu, two deputies of Xanana Gusmao, who had voluntarily surrendered to the authorities.

Mr. Vendrell also explored the possibility of providing greater opportunity for the East Timorese to learn the Portuguese language and culture and at least to reopen the Portuguese language-based school in Dili, which had been closed earlier.

Surprised at his request, I recalled to him that this question of promoting and protecting the Portuguese language and culture had already been brought up in 1983, when the tripartite talks had just begun.

I told Mr. Vendrell what I had told my counterpart then, namely that among all the former colonies of Portugal, perhaps East Timor was the only one where Portuguese statues in parks as well as streets named after Portuguese heroes were allowed to be maintained, even after integration with Indonesia.

I further told him that Indonesia would indeed vigorously promote the language and culture of East Timor, as part of the national policy on culture in all provinces of Indonesia and not those of the former colonial power. I then asked the rhetorical question whether a former colony was duty-bound to continue the promotion of the language and culture of its erstwhile colonial master.

On my part, I tried once again, although without much hope of succeeding, to argue the merits and the particular advantages for Portugal, of mutually establishing "interests sections" in friendly embassies in each other's capital. As expected, Mr. Vendrell only promised to pass this proposal on to the Portuguese side.

In sum, the consultative visit of the Representative of the Secretary-General, alas, did not move the tripartite dialogue process any further forward, although it did provide quite a revealing glimpse of the mindset of the Portuguese and the United Nations interlocutors.

An effort at reconciliation

The fourth round of the tripartite dialogue was also preceded by another significant development, namely of an unprecedented reunion or informal "reconciliation meeting" between East Timorese leading personalities, both those living abroad and those from Indonesia (East Timor). The idea for this meeting was initiated by Dr. Abilio Araujo, former Chairman of FRETILIN who was at that time already residing in Portugal.

When he proposed the meeting in the spring of 1993, it was promptly welcomed by Mr. Francisco X. Lopes da Cruz, who had been appointed Ambassador-at-Large for Special Affairs by the Government of Indonesia. Lopes da Cruz subsequently sponsored the meeting, which was held on 14-16 December 1993 at the Hanbury Manor Hotel near the town of Ware, Hertfordshire, approximately 25 miles from London. It was attended by 12 participants from East Timor and ten from the "diaspora"—East Timorese then living in Lisbon, Macau and Australia.

This meeting was not intended to discuss political issues, such as the political status of East Timor; it was meant to be a first step towards reunion and reconciliation between the two groups of East Timorese who had been at odds with each other since 1975. It was also hoped that the meeting could contribute ideas on how to assist the overall development efforts in East Timor. Thus, while it did not produce any document at its conclusion, it did create a new atmosphere among the participants, later to be known as the "London Spirit."

The first meeting was followed by a second reconciliation meeting, again held near London in the town of Chepstow, from 29 September to 1 October 1994, which this time issued a Joint Declaration.

With the agreement of both Indonesia and Portugal, a representative of the Secretary-General was present at that second meeting, but only as an observer attending the opening and closing sessions.

The proceedings and results of these and subsequent meetings among East Timorese of the two opposing camps, later known as the All-inclusive Intra-East Timorese Dialogue (AIETD), will be taken up in greater detail in a separate chapter.

The usual trilateral talks at the ambassadorial level in preparation for the fourth round was this time chaired by USG Ismat Kittani, who had been an Iraqi ambassador to the United Nations before joining the Secretariat. He was appointed by Secretary-General Boutrous-Ghali to succeed ASG Alvaro de Soto as Special Adviser on East Timor.

New UN proposals

Mr. Kittani came up with what he called "simple and modest suggestions" from the Secretary-General to be considered as possible additional CBMs at the next round of the ministerial dialogue.

Apart from listing a number of measures already mentioned in the Consensus Chairman's Statement of the 50th Human Rights Commission Session in March 1994, he did put forward some new proposals, i.e. a meeting between the Indonesian Foreign Minister and anti-integration East Timorese personalities and conversely between the Portuguese Foreign Minister and pro-integration East Timorese leaders; the establishment of branch offices in Dili of some well-known Indonesian NGOs that were active in the human rights field; and the convening of a meeting on a wider scale between East Timorese from Indonesia and those from abroad, either under United Nations auspices or facilitated and moderated by an NGO, such as the New York-based International Peace Academy.

As a matter of principle, I rejected outright the first suggestion, especially if such meetings were to be conceived as "regular" events, for they would thus become an unacceptable additional track or forum that would be in competition with the existing tripartite dialogue.

With regard to the second suggestion, I expressed the view that such an idea should be left for the NGOs themselves to consider and that therefore it would not be appropriate to list it as a proposed CBM in the context of the tripartite dialogue.

The third suggestion turned out to be one that the Secretary-General had put great store on as an "encouraging" development. Apparently, he had wanted to bring it under the umbrella of the United Nations as part of his CBM efforts. I argued that organizing an intra-East Timorese dialogue, especially under United Nations auspices, would detract from the ongoing process of reconciliation, which was initiated by and among the East Timorese themselves and should therefore be left to them to develop further.

I conceded that so far there was one group of East Timorese who had not yet joined in the "London process," and this was the group of Jose Ramos Horta. We had received reports, however, that Dr. Abilio Araujo was doing his best to bring this group into the process. And finally I argued that if this intra-East Timorese dialogue were also to discuss political issues, it would become an unacceptable parallel track to our common efforts to find a comprehensive solution to the East Timor issue by way of the tripartite dialogue.

Despite our objections, however, the Secretary-General continued to push for a role in an expanded intra-East Timorese dialogue. At the fourth round of the ministerial tripartite dialogue, a prolonged debate occurred on this issue. Finally a compromise wording on this issue in the Statement released after the fourth round only stated that the two Ministers took note of the Secretary-General's initiative "to explore appropriate efforts to be undertaken towards facilitating an all-inclusive intra-East Timorese dialogue." The Secretary-General also assured Indonesia that such an intra-East Timorese dialogue would not discuss political issues.

As to the proposal for the Foreign Ministers of Indonesia and Portugal to meet with leading East Timorese supporters and opponents of integration respectively, I finally consented to it after it was agreed that such an event would be a one-off affair and that I would meet the group of leading East Timorese opponents of integration in their personal capacity and not in any other.

These meetings eventually took place in Luxembourg and in New York City during the 49th Session of the United Nations General Assembly. On the 4th of October 1994, Foreign Minister Durao Barosso met with Ambassador Lopes da Cruz, Mr. Xavier do Amaral and Mrs. Maria Quintao in his hotel in Luxembourg, where he was staying to attend the ASEAN-EU Ministerial Meeting.

On the morning of 6 October 1994, I received Dr. Abilio Araujo, Dr. Jose Belo, Father Constancio Gusmao and Mr. Rogerio Lobato in my hotel room in New York and subsequently, in the afternoon of the same day, I received Mr. Ramos Horta, Mr. Jose Luis Guterres and Mr. Joao Carrascalao, in their private capacities.

The meetings proceeded in a generally relaxed and amicable atmosphere but, as expected, did not yield any new or changed positions on both sides. On 7 October 1994, USG Ismat Kittani met with Ambassador Lopes da Cruz and Dr. Abilio Araujo to receive their report on the result of the second meeting of the so-called "London process".

Meagre results from the talks

In the following years the rounds of tripartite talks under the auspices of Secretary General Boutros-Ghali continued, but unfortunately with meagre results to show for all the efforts expended.

The main achievement of the fifth round of the tripartite dialogue, held in Geneva on 9 January 1995 was the concurrence between the two Foreign Ministers "to note positively the Secretary General's intention... to facilitate and offer the necessary arrangements for the convening of an All-inclusive Intra-East Timorese Dialogue." As the language agreed upon indicated, Indonesia's view was vindicated, namely, that the initiative for this dialogue should remain in the hands of the East Timorese themselves and not be taken over by the United Nations Secretary-General.

As to the objective of the All-inclusive Intra-East Timorese Dialogue (AIETD), it was also clearly stated that it was "*t*o provide a forum for continuing the free and informal exchange of views to explore ideas of a practical nature that might have a positive impact on the situation in East Timor and assist in the establishment of an atmosphere conducive to the achievement of a solution to the question of East Timor."

It was further agreed that "the dialogue will not address the political status of East Timor and will in no way constitute a parallel negotiating track or be a substitute for the Ministerial talks under the auspices of the Secretary General."

Another concrete decision reached during the fifth round of talks was to begin considering, at the next round of talks, substantive issues and possible ways towards achieving a solution to the East Timor question.

At the sixth round of talks, held on 8 July 1995, again in Geneva, the tripartite dialogue finally moved into a substantive phase. After intensive preparatory talks at the Ambassadorial level, discussions began on an agreed confidential "non-paper" attached to the agenda containing "substantive issues identified by the Secretary-General regarding possible avenues towards achieving a just, comprehensive and internationally acceptable solution to the question of East Timor."

In this context, issues were discussed "related to an eventual framework for the achievement of such a solution" and other related issues, *inter alia*, the preservation and promotion of the cultural identity of the East Timorese people and bilateral relations between Indonesia and Portugal.

Not much could be achieved, however, at this first attempt to discuss substantive issues towards a solution, as the position of both sides were still too far apart.

A new involvement for the UN

One concrete decision taken, however, was "to welcome the convening of the All-inclusive Intra-East Timorese Dialogue, held in Burg Schlaining, Austria, from 2 to 5 June 1995 with the assistance of the Secretary-General" and also "to welcome the Secretary-General's view on the need for convening a further meeting or meetings of the All-inclusive Intra-East Timorese Dialogue".

At this first AIETD meeting, the representative of the United Nations Secretary-General attended the proceedings as an observer and not, as earlier suggested by the Secretary- General and by Portugal, as a moderator.

The next round of trilateral ministerial talks was preceded by the installation of a new Government in Portugal following general elections in October 1995, which resulted in a victory for the Socialist Party. Thus, starting from this round, Portugal was represented by

Foreign Minister Jaime Gama at the Ministerial level tripartite dialogue.

Meanwhile, on 20 November 1995, USG Ismat Kittani was replaced by USG Yasushi Akashi as Special Adviser to the Secretary-General on East Timor. USG Ismat Kittani was to succeed USG Kofi Annan in the post of USG for Peacekeeping Operations. Mr. Akashi did not stay long in this position, however, because in March 1996 the United Nations Secretary- General moved him to a new assignment as USG for Humanitarian Affairs and Emergency Relief Coordination, replacing Mr. Peter Hansen. Mr. Ismat Kittani returned to his previous post as Special Adviser to the Secretary General on East Timor.

From 2-7 December 1995, the United Nations High Commissioner for Human Rights, Mr. Jose Ayala Lasso, visited Indonesia including East Timor in the context of implementing the Chairman's Statement, earlier adopted by consensus, at the Human Rights Commission session in Geneva. At the end of his visit, the High Commissioner and I arrived at an agreement in principle to enhance technical cooperation between the Government of Indonesia and the UNHCR. To this end, a "Memorandum of Agreement" was signed to follow up and replace an earlier "Memorandum of Intent."

It was also agreed to look into the possibility of the High Commissioner assigning a Programme Officer at the United Nations Office in Jakarta in the context of implementing the technical cooperation agreement between the two sides. This officer would also have regular access to East Timor.

Another noteworthy development in this period was the fact that, on humanitarian considerations, the Indonesian Government allowed 39 East Timorese youth to leave for Portugal. They had earlier forcibly broken into the Embassies of Japan, Britain, France and the Netherlands seeking asylum, which was however denied them.

At the same time, the Indonesian Government approved the request of three East Timorese leaders, including five members of their families, who had lived in Portugal since the 1960s, to return to Indonesia and East Timor. These persons arrived in Jakarta on 5 January 1996. They belonged to the group of around 68 leading East Timorese freedom fighters who rebelled against the colonial power in 1959 (the "Viqueque Uprising") and struggled for independence through integration with Indonesia. The 1959 rebellion was crushed and these freedom fighters were exiled to Mozambique and Angola and later on some were allowed to settle in Portugal.

A more positive atmosphere

At the seventh round of talks, held in London on 16 January 1996, the new Foreign Minister of Portugal, Mr. Jaime Gama, showed a more constructive and flexible attitude than his predecessor and hence the talks proceeded in a more positive atmosphere. In terms of substance, however, there was no significant movement of the position of both sides, although there were nuance differences to be noted in the attitude of my Portuguese counterpart.

On the idea of interests sections, for example, Mr. Jaime Gama did not raise preconditions any more but rather expressed concern that the presence of Portuguese and Indonesian diplomats in each other's capital at this stage might provoke demonstrations, or in the case of the Portuguese representation in Jakarta, a possible increase in requests for asylum by East Timorese dissidents. He promised, however, to seriously study this proposal and expressed the hope that this question could be discussed in greater detail in future rounds.

Towards the end of the talks, at the suggestion of the Secretary-General, an informal, "heart-to-heart" meeting was held. It was attended only by the two Ministers and the Secretary-General, with no other delegation members present.

At that meeting, the Secretary-General inquired on the possibility of holding additional, secret meetings among the three sides along the lines of the Arab-Israeli talks that had succeeded in reaching agreement on a Declaration of Principles on 13 September 1993. The two Ministers could not immediately respond to this proposal.

The Secretary-General then raised the possibility of Xanana Gusmao being freed from prison as part of an eventual, agreed package of solution. As my personal and preliminary reaction, I told the Secretary-General that I could visualize such a possibility provided it was part of a final, comprehensive package of a solution in which Portugal would accept the reality of East Timor's integration with Indonesia.

Foreign Minister Gama then indicated his desire to visit Indonesia in a personal capacity in order to meet with Xanana Gusmao. I expressed the view that for him to visit Indonesia in a personal capacity for the sole purpose of seeing Xanana Gusmao could not be accepted by Indonesia. However, if such a visit were in the nature of an informal working visit to Indonesia and would include talks with his counterpart, the Foreign Minister of Indonesia, then a meeting with Xanana Gusmao could be considered.

One concrete decision taken at this round was the concurrence of the two Ministers again to take note positively of the Secretary-General's intention to facilitate the convening of another meeting of the AIETD, in Austria in March 1996, on the basis of the same terms of reference as before.

In the run-up to the eighth round of talks, held in Geneva on 27 June 1996, the Government of Indonesia, on humanitarian grounds, again permitted 39 East Timorese youth, who had tried to seek asylum at the Jakarta embassies of Australia, Poland, France, Netherlands and Germany, to leave for Portugal at the end of January and the middle of April 1996.

Another noteworthy event in this period was the agreement of the Indonesian Government to accredit two consultants from Georgetown University (USA) to the University of East Timor as experts on agriculture and the English language. The Indonesian Government also gave its approval for the Indonesian Merpati Nusantara Airlines to hire two Portuguese pilots who applied for the job and subsequently underwent the normal process for the hiring of expatriate employees in Indonesia.

At this eighth round of talks, the Ministers agreed to base their discussions, as they did since the sixth and seventh rounds, on an agenda that contained the generally phrased agenda item: "Possible substantive issues related to an eventual framework for the achievement of a just, comprehensive and internationally acceptable solution to the question of East Timor."

They also agreed to add a confidential Non-paper describing more detailed topics under this agenda item in order to facilitate the discussions. Thus, in this Non-paper it was agreed that the talks would focus on: "Establishing the parameters within which the two parties are prepared to negotiate" which would enable the talks to define the limits on both ends and narrow the field of focus in the search for a solution; the focus would also be on: "Elements for possible arrangements as part of a just, comprehensive and internationally acceptable solution to the question of East Timor and appropriate modalities for their realization."

Discussions at this round of talks were rather heavily influenced by developments and decisions that had taken place outside the tripartite dialogue proper.

The two Ministers held a lengthy discussion on some of the

concrete proposals that had emanated from the second AIETD, held in Burg Schlaining, Austria, on 19-22 March 1996, notably the proposal to establish an East Timorese Cultural Centre in Dili and the development of human resources (through education and training) in East Timor. Both sides agreed in principle to endorse these proposals and to conduct further consultations with regard to their practical implementation.

But Portugal's suggestion to create a "United Nations Trust Fund" for the financing of the Cultural Centre could not be accepted by Indonesia, which preferred to keep it as a bilaterally supported institution. As to the fostering of human resources development in East Timor, Portugal indicated its preparedness to donate books to the University of East Timor.

As it turned out, however, none of these projects could be realized, as they were overtaken by events, in particular by the change in the United Nations Secretary-General, from Boutros Boutros-Ghali to Kofi Annan towards the end of the year.

Finally, the two Ministers again agreed to the Secretary General's intention to facilitate the convening of another meeting of the AIETD, without mentioning any time or place.

A Portuguese proposal

A large part of the discussions was also taken up by debate over the proposal made by the Portuguese Prime Minister, Antonio Guterres, to President Suharto of Indonesia on 29 February 1996, at the margins of the first Asia-Europe Meeting (ASEM Summit) in Bangkok. On that occasion, Prime Minister Guterres proposed that Portuguese and Indonesian "interests sections" be established in friendly embassies in each other's capital city. However, he linked it to the freeing of Xanana Gusmao and other East Timorese prisoners as well as with the establishment of a United Nations presence in East Timor, especially to observe the human rights situation.

What was surprising was the fact that Prime Minister Guterres made it sound as if the proposal to establish interests sections was his or a Portuguese initiative and not, as the facts showed, a proposal first made by Secretary-General Boutros-Ghali at the first round of the tripartite Ministerial talks on 17 December 1992. A proposal, furthermore, that Indonesia had accepted from the outset and Portugal had consistently rejected.

By Portugal again putting pre-conditions or *quid-pro-quo's* to the proposal, it was to be expected that Indonesia would not accept it. It is true that the impromptu request by Prime Minister Guterres for a meeting with President Soeharto, after an informal plenary meeting of all the summit participants, caught the two Foreign Ministers by surprise, as the Ministers were assembled in a different room and only later realized that the two Heads of Government were having an unscheduled *tête-à-tête*. In fact, the two Ministers joined the meeting belatedly. The interests section proposal obviously also caught President Soeharto by surprise and on that occasion he only responded that he would "study and further consult" on the matter.

So it was left to me to explain, first to the assembled press representatives in Bangkok at that time, and once again at the eighth round of talks, why Indonesia could not accept the way in which Portugal linked the proposal of interests sections to certain preconditions that Indonesia first had to fulfill, as Indonesia had always considered the Secretary-General's proposal as a good confidence-building measure (CBM), which would favour the interests of both sides and not only those of Indonesia.

I further explained that Indonesia could favourably consider the release and granting of amnesty to Xanana Gusmao and his followers if it were part of a comprehensive settlement of the question of East Timor, in which Portugal would accept East Timor's integration with Indonesia. The unprecedented meeting between the two leaders attracted wide publicity at that time and, as could be expected, Prime Minister Guterres was praised by the Portuguese media for his "bold initiative" while I was demonized as the "villain" who had wrecked the initiative.

As to the main item on the agenda, "possible substantive issues related to an eventual framework for solution," again no progress was made and the positions of the two sides remained deadlocked. I reminded the meeting that Indonesia had already twice, in 1987 and 1991, accepted a proposed solution by the UN Secretary-General, which could be described as a compromise between the respective basic positions of the two sides. But Portugal twice rejected those proposed solutions.

I therefore wondered aloud whether Portugal indeed remained committed to finding a just, comprehensive and internationally acceptable solution, which in essence meant a mutually acceptable compromise.

Foreign Minister Jaime Gama, however, continued to insist that Portugal could only accept a solution that was based on a "genuine act of self-determination" and other basic principles of the United Nations and a solution that "respected the wishes of the East Timorese people". Of course, these were positions whose interpretation, from the beginning, had been the bone of contention between the two sides. In the meantime, Portugal deemed it important that conditions in East Timor, especially as regards human rights, first be improved.

On one point, however, the two Foreign Ministers could finally agree, namely that the implementation and progress of the tripartite dialogue so far had been ineffective and slow. This was also due to the fact that the talks, held at the Foreign Ministers level and conducted openly, always attracted the attention and scrutiny of the mass media, which in turn forced the two sides to safeguard their public opinions at home and to maintain their respective basic positions.

In this connection, I suggested that perhaps it would be useful to have secret meetings and try to make progress away from the glare of publicity. This suggestion was agreed upon and it was tentatively decided to have the first of such secret meetings in October 1996 in New York, on the occasion of the United Nations General Assembly session. As it turned out, however, this meeting, too, never materialized as it was overtaken by subsequent developments.

Minimal progress - yet again

The eighth round of talks ended with minimal progress. In retrospect, the eight rounds of tripartite talks under the auspices of United Nations Secretary-General Boutros-Ghali did not succeed in moving the process of finding a solution to the East Timor issue any closer to its goal, despite the strenuous and laudable efforts of the Secretary-General and his able collaborators.

Throughout the process, Portugal seemed unable or unwilling to come to grips with the substantive aspect of negotiating an agreed framework and the required modalities to arrive at a just, comprehensive and internationally acceptable solution. Instead, it claimed that what was important was for Indonesia first to take measures to improve conditions in East Timor, especially with regard to human rights. In fact, in the discussions on CBM's during the first stages of the dialogue, the

Portuguese side continued to demand that Indonesia implement those and other measures in pursuit of Portuguese rather than mutual interests, thus rendering the whole idea of CBM's into a one-sided exercise.

In the case of a really mutually beneficial CBM such as the establishment of interests sections, successive Portuguese Foreign Ministers continued to waffle till the end.

As it turned out, this was to be the last round of the tripartite dialogue under the auspices of Secretary-General Boutros Boutros-Ghali. The ninth round, which was agreed to be held on 21 December 1996, never took place. During the second half of 1996, Portugal became engrossed in its lobbying efforts for a non-permanent seat in the United Nations Security Council. The usual preparatory meetings that preceded the Ministerial talks had to be repeatedly postponed and in the end could not take place at all due to Ambassador Catarino's professed preoccupation with these lobbying efforts.

In the meantime, Mr. Kofi Annan, former USG for Peacekeeping Operations, was elected Secretary-General of the United Nations in November 1996 and was to begin his tenure on the 1st of January 1997. Thus, the scheduled ninth round of talks with the outgoing Secretary-General was shelved altogether and from 1997 onwards the tripartite dialogue was conducted under the auspices of Secretary-General Kofi Annan.

Chapter 6
The London Meetings and The All-inclusive Intra-East Timorese Dialogues (AIETD)

IN December 1993, an unprecedented and much publicized meeting took place between two groups of leading East Timorese personalities, one composed of those from Indonesia (East Timor), the other of East Timorese living abroad.

This meeting was not a political meeting; it did not discuss the political status of East Timor. Rather, it was meant to be the first step towards reunion and "reconciliation" between the two groups of East Timorese who had been in conflict with each other since 1975, namely those for and those against integration of East Timor with Indonesia.

An exclusively East Timor affair

This process was the brainchild of Dr. Abilio Araujo, a former Chairman of FRETILIN, who at that time was residing in Portugal where he had settled down as a businessman. In the spring of 1993 he proposed the convening of such a meeting to Mr. Francisco X. Lopes da Cruz, who by then had been appointed Ambassador-at-Large for Special Affairs by the Government of Indonesia. The latter enthusiastically welcomed it.

After several consultations to thresh out details, Dr. Araujo and Ambassador Lopes da Cruz jointly sponsored the meeting, which was held from 14 to 16 December 1993 at the Hanbury Manor Hotel, near the town of Ware, Hertfordshire, approximately 25 miles from London. It was attended by 12 participants from East Timor and 10 from the "diaspora" – East Timorese personalities then living in Portugal, Macau and Australia.

The staff of the Indonesian Embassy in London provided some help in arranging for the meeting, but it was attended only by the East Timorese themselves and the entire proceedings were therefore conducted in the Tetum language.

Although the meeting was strictly non-political and was essentially a reconciliation effort, the organizers had expected that it would also generate ideas on how to assist the development efforts in East Timor.

In the discussions, the East Timorese from abroad asked questions and those from Indonesia gave explanations on such issues as the possibilities of trade and investment, access into East Timor, the military presence in the territory, the possibility of the release of political detainees, compensation for land and other properties that those living abroad had left behind, and the preservation of the culture of East Timor.

The participants from inside East Timor also presented detailed explanations on various aspects of development in East Timor and on the role of the Church. No longer involved in government administration, the Church retained its authority on pastoral and private educational matters.

The meeting did not produce any statement or declaration, but it brought about a new awareness on the part of the East Timorese diaspora of the actual situation in East Timor. Both groups gained a better understanding and appreciation of each other's views, concerns and positions on the question of East Timor. This new atmosphere would later be known as the "London Spirit".

The London meeting drew varied responses from several quarters. Mar'i Alkatiri, joined by Ramos Horta and Joao Carrascalao, condemned the meeting as just a maneuver by Jakarta and as an effort to turn the East Timor issue into a "domestic affair" of Indonesia.

Portuguese Foreign Minister Durao Barosso, however, issued a cautious statement that the Portuguese Government had no competence to comment on the initiatives and positions of various East Timorese groups and on the differences between them. Portugal, he said, continued to adhere to the tripartite dialogue under the auspices of the UN Secretary-General as the agreed way to attain a solution.

Members of the international press, including those from the Portuguese media, who at first were suspicious and skeptical, changed their minds towards the end of the meeting and generally viewed it as an encouraging development that would reflect favourably on Indonesia.

One concrete result of the meeting was the formation of an Indonesian-Portuguese Friendship Association in Indonesia, as a counterpart to the earlier established Portuguese-Indonesian Friendship Association (PIFA) in Portugal.

The "London Spirit" grows

Another concrete manifestation of the "London Spirit" created by this first reconciliation meeting was the visit to East Timor at Easter time in 1994 by a number of East Timorese residing in Portugal for a brief reunion with the relatives they had left behind. In turn, a group of East Timorese from Indonesia made a pilgrimage to the Fatima Shrine in Portugal in May of the same year.

After an interval of almost a year, a second reconciliation meeting was convened as a follow-up to the first. It was again held near the city of London, this time in the town of Chepstow, from 29 September to 1 October 1994.

With the agreement of both the Governments of Portugal and Indonesia, Mr. Tamrat Samuel, a representative of the UN Secretary-General, was invited to the second meeting, but only as an observer attending the formal opening and closing sessions. Outside the meetings, however, he was free to talk and consult with all participants.

At the end of this meeting, a Joint Declaration was issued, signed by Ambassador Lopes da Cruz and Dr. Abilio Araujo as leaders of their respective groups. In the declaration, the leaders of the East Timorese living abroad and those from East Timor "recognized the profound division within the East Timorese society caused by the political confrontation which culminated in the tragic civil war in 1975, the abandonment of the territory by the Portuguese Administration, the unilateral declaration of independence by one party and the proclamation of integration into the Republic of Indonesia by the other four parties as well as the subsequent Indonesian involvement upon the request of those four parties.*"*

Acknowledging their responsibility to East Timorese society, they pledged their *"readiness to participate, either directly of indirectly, in the development of East Timor in all its aspects."*

In response to the express desire of the UN Secretary-General that the meeting be expanded to include other groups, the leaders also indicated their "willingness to hold talks with others in an 'all-inclusive intra-East Timorese Dialogue,' provided that all sides agree to the London Spirit as a basis of these talks and to promote mutual confidence in the interest of peace, stability and harmony within the East Timorese society*"*.

Apart from supporting and encouraging the ongoing tripartite dialogue between Indonesia and Portugal under the auspices of the

UN Secretary-General and the common efforts at promoting Confidence-building Measures, the leaders of the East Timorese society living abroad requested their counterparts from East Timor to convey to the government of Indonesia a number of special requests, including the following:

- Special consideration to be accorded to the administration of East Timor, given its distinct historical background;
- Consideration of the special situation of those East Timorese in custody and to take further appropriate measures aimed at their release;
- The continued implementation of the gradual reduction of troops in East Timor.

The UN takes a keen interest

These developments were closely observed by the UN Secretary-General and his team. Since the first London Meeting, they had shown great interest in the process and pointed out the desirability of convening the meeting on a wider scale, either under the auspices of the United Nations or moderated by a mutually acceptable NGO such as the New York-based International Peace Academy. The Secretary-General argued that, while very encouraging, the London process did not yet include East Timorese belonging to the group of Ramos Horta and that it was therefore desirable to try to include them.

During the fourth round of the ministerial tripartite dialogue, an intensive debate took place on this issue and it was clear that at first the Secretary-General had wanted to bring the intra-East Timorese dialogue under the umbrella of the United Nations as part of his CBM efforts.

I argued that organizing an intra-East Timorese dialogue, especially under United Nations auspices, would detract from the ongoing process of reconciliation, which was initiated and sustained by the East Timorese themselves. The process should therefore be left to them to develop further. I conceded that, so far, those East Timorese identified as the so-called "hard-liners" grouped around Ramos Horta, Mar'i Alkatiri and Joao Carrascalao had not yet joined in the London process, but I pointed out that Dr. Abilio Araujo was already trying to bring this group into the process.

Finally, I emphasized that if this intra-East Timorese dialogue were also to discuss political issues, it would become an unacceptable parallel track to our common efforts to find a solution to the East Timor problem by way of the tripartite dialogue.

The Secretary General took Indonesia's arguments into account but continued to push for a United Nations role in an expanded intra-East Timorese dialogue.

At the fourth round of the ministerial tripartite dialogue, a compromise wording on this question was agreed to be worked into the statement to be released after the end of the round. It simply stated that "the two Ministers took note of the Secretary- General's initiative to explore appropriate efforts to be undertaken towards facilitating an all inclusive intra-East Timorese dialogue."

During the fifth round of the tripartite dialogue, held in Geneva on 9 January 1995, intensive debate on this issue again occurred, which in the end finally yielded the concurrence between the two Foreign Ministers "to note positively the Secretary-General's intention…to facilitate and offer the necessary arrangements for the convening of an all-inclusive intra-East Timorese dialogue."

As could be seen from the language used, Indonesia's view was vindicated, i.e. that the initiative for this dialogue should remain in the hands of the East Timorese themselves and not be taken over by the UN Secretary-General.

The objective of the all-inclusive intra-East Timorese dialogue also became a subject of prolonged debate, but finally it was agreed that it would "provide a forum for continuing the free and informal exchange of views to explore ideas of a practical nature that might have a positive impact on the situation in East Timor and assist in the establishment of an atmosphere conducive to the achievement of a solution to the question of East Timor. The dialogue will not address the political status of East Timor and will in no way constitute a parallel negotiating track or be a substitute for the Ministerial talks under the auspices of the Secretary-General."

An unfortunate complication

Pn the basis of these understandings, preparations began for convening a dialogue. Unfortunately, an unfortunate complication arose soon thereafter.

On 23 February 1995, USG Ismet Kittani, on behalf on the UN

Secretary-General, sent out invitations to prospective participants of the All-inclusive Intra-East Timorese Dialogue (AIETD), to be held from 24 to 26 April 1995 at Schloss Leopoldskron in Austria.

The invitations were extended to 12 East Timorese personalities from Indonesia/East Timor and 14 from outside. The list of invitees was entirely decided upon by the United Nations Secretariat, without prior consultations with either Indonesia or Portugal or indeed with any of the organizers of the earlier London meetings, Ambassador Lopes da Cruz and Dr. Abilio Araujo, as had been agreed upon earlier.

Indonesia protested this way of handling the arrangement for the AIETD by the UN Secretariat, pointing out that this *fait accompli* went beyond the agreed understanding that the UN Secretary-General would only "*f*acilitate and offer the necessary arrangements for the convening of an AIETD." Particularly objectionable to Indonesia was the one-sided and unbalanced determination of the number and choice of participants. In separate letters to the UN Secretary-General, Ambassador Lopes and Dr. Araujo also conveyed their protest and demanded to be consulted first on the composition of the participants and I even had a special meeting with Secretary-General Boutros-Ghali on this issue in Copenhagen on the sidelines of the Social Summit Conference.

As a result, after due consultations by USG Kittani with Lopes da Cruz, Abilio Araujo and Ramos Horta, the list of invited participants was revised and a new date and venue were set for the meeting.

The First AIETD

The first AIETD was convened in Burg Schlaining Schloss, a medieval castle located some 75 miles south of Vienna, Austria, from 3 to 5 June 1995. It was attended by 30 participants, 16 from inside East Timor and 14 from outside. At this meeting, the so-called Ramos Horta group was represented by individuals like Joao Carrascalao, Mar'i Alkatiri, and Jose Luis Guterres, apart from Ramos Horta himself. On the side of those from within East Timor, this time the list included Bishop Carlos Ximenes Belo, Governor Abilio Osorio Soares and several others representing the local government.

After three days of frank and often heated discussions (the meeting ended a day earlier than scheduled, on 5 June, because Bishop Belo had to leave the following day), the AIETD adopted by consensus the

Burg Schlaining Declaration.

Although, as agreed, the discussions did not touch on the political status of East Timor, the Declaration inevitably did contain political nuances. It also contained several references that did not conform to earlier agreed understandings between Indonesia and Portugal and which were apparently brought in deliberately by Ramos Horta and his group during the negotiations over the composition of the text.

For example, in proposing to the United Nations Secretary-General the holding of another Intra-East Timorese Dialogue, it was suggested in the Declaration that such a dialogue "should precede each round of negotiations between the diplomatic heads of Portugal and Indonesia." This proposal was obviously aimed at establishing a linkage between the AIETD and the ministerial tripartite talks.

Where the Declaration noted with appreciation the consultations undertaken by the United Nations with the various shades of Timorese opinion, the idea was slipped in that this was "aimed at their gradual involvement (in the tripartite talks)," something that had been agreed would be ruled out since the start of the tripartite talks.

What provoked the sharpest controversy was paragraph 6 of the Declaration, which cited the importance of the ongoing ministerial tripartite talks aimed at "finding a just, comprehensive and internationally acceptable solution to the question of East Timor." The paragraph was innocuous enough until Ramos Horta c.s. managed to add the phrase "according to the provisions, letter and spirit of United Nations General Assembly resolution 37/30".

When Lopes da Cruz and the East Timorese from Indonesia were reminded that the tripartite talks, at the insistence of Indonesia, were by agreement not to be based on GA Resolution 37/30, but rather on the general authority and competence of the UN Secretary-General, Lopes da Cruz deemed it necessary to write a protest letter to the Secretary-General, setting clear his group's understanding and correction on this and some other parts of the Burg Schlaining Declaration. Dr. Abilio Araujo also sent a similar letter.

This incident unfortunately marred an otherwise encouraging start in the process of dialogue between the contending East Timorese groups. However, as the Declaration itself also acknowledged, in spite of the frank and open spirit in which this Intra-Timorese Dialogue was conducted, the fundamental, adversarial political positions remained unchanged.

The Second AIETD

Another All-Inclusive Intra-East Timorese Dialogue was convened nine months later, again in Burg Schlaining Austria, from 19 to 20 March 1996, involving practically the same participants as the previous AIETD.

Invoking urgent pastoral commitments in Dili, especially on the eve of Easter Week, Bishop Carlos Belo conveyed his regrets for not being able to attend and proposed that Vicar General Mgr. Jose Antonio da Costa represent him at the meeting. This was accepted by all sides. Another absentee was Mr. Guilherme M. Goncalves, a participant from East Timor who, according to the UN Secretariat, claimed he had received the invitation and plane tickets too late and also cited health reasons.

As at the previous meeting, Mr. Tamrat Samuel attended as the representative of the UN Secretary-General without taking part in the discussions.

Despite frequent heated debates and increasing polarization between the East Timorese from Indonesia and the Ramos Horta group and Mar'i Alkatiri, the 1996 AIETD proceeded in a generally constructive atmosphere, with most participants actively participating in the exchange of views.

After four days of intensive discussions, the meeting adopted by consensus the "Burg Schlaining Declaration – 1996". Among the concrete, agreed decisions taken was the expression of interest and readiness on the part of the participants to continue the AIETD, should it be requested by the UN Secretary-General, within the same framework and under the same conditions.

They also conveyed to the Governments of Indonesia and Portugal their "interest in the establishment of an East Timorese Cultural Center in Dili, with the aim of undertaking research on the culture, language, customs and traditions of the East Timorese." They further declared that they would "welcome assistance from Portugal to help East Timor's human resources development by concrete measures, such as technical and financial support for the University of East Timor and practical training for the youth in all areas of relevance to the needs of the East Timorese people."

And "encouraged by the substantial role of the East Timorese in the administration and development of East Timor," they proposed to the Indonesian Government "the provision of further opportunities for East Timorese to have a greater role in the administration of the territory as well as economic policy, trade and investment activities."

Unrealized projects

As earlier recounted, at the eighth round of tripartite talks held in Geneva in June 1996, the two Ministers considered the concrete proposals that had emanated from the 1996 AIETD, notably the proposal to establish an East Timorese Cultural Centre in Dili and the development of human resources in East Timor.

Both sides agreed to endorse these proposals and to conduct further consultations on the details of their implementation. However, Portugal's suggestion to create a "United Nations Trust Fund" for the financing of the Cultural Centre could not be accepted by Indonesia, which preferred to structure it as a bilaterally supported institution.

As to the promotion of human resources development in East Timor, Portugal among other things indicated its preparedness to donate books to the University of East Timor. However, as it turned out, none of these projects could be realized as they were overtaken by events, i.e. the succession of UN Secretary-General Boutros Boutros-Ghali by Kofi Annan towards the end of the year and subsequent change in substance and direction of the tripartite talks.

After the conclusion of the meeting and as previously agreed, the participants of AIETD-1996 met with Portuguese Foreign Minister Jaime Gama on 22 and 23 March in the SAS Hotel in Vienna. These meetings were arranged at the request of the Portuguese Foreign Minister, as he had not had a chance yet to meet with the participants, as did his predecessor.

At the meeting, Foreign Minister Gama expressed his appreciation of the results of the AIETD meeting as he considered them realistic and practical. He reported that he looked forward to cooperating constructively with Indonesia on certain aspects of East Timor's development as laid out in the framework of the AIETD proposals.

The Third AIETD

At the ninth ministerial tripartite talks, held in New York on 19 and 20 June 1997, this time under the auspices of the new UN Secretary-General, Mr. Kofi Annan, the two Foreign Ministers agreed that the AIETD process would be continued under the same terms of reference as the previous meetings, except that the number of participants would be increased from 30 to 35.

The third AIETD was held from 20 to 23 October 1997 in Krumbach Castle, about a hundred kilometers from Vienna. Krumbach Castle was chosen because it was in an even more isolated location than Burg Schlaining, and as such, more conducive to avoiding press exposure. The media, however, quickly came to know of it and were, as usual, very much present during the event.

On this occasion, Bishop Belo again participated, while the UN Secretary-General this time was represented by his newly appointed Personal Representative, Ambassador Jamsheed Marker of Pakistan.

Despite occasional inferences to political issues by the East Timorese participants from the Mar'i Alkatiri/Ramos Horta group, the exchanges during this AIETD meeting generally focused on the main agenda item—the substantive discussion of the relevant aspects of the proposed Cultural Centre, and support for human resources development in East Timor.

Even then, heated debates flared up on such topics as the choice of location for the Cultural Centre, which the Mar'i Alkatiri group proposed to be headquartered in Paris, with a representative office in Dili, while the East Timorese from Indonesia naturally insisted that it be situated in Dili, East Timor. On the composition of the Board of Trustees, a sharp division also emerged between the two groups.

After three days of intensive debates, the two groups finally agreed on the text of the Krumbach Declaration of 1997, which maintained the general outlines of previous AIETD Declarations, but in concrete terms also recorded the consensus reached on the name, objectives, organic structure and sources of financing for the Centre for Culture and Development of East Timor (Centro de Cultura e Desenvolvimento de Timor Lorosae), which was elaborated in an annex to the Declaration.

In the same annex, however, it was acknowledged that as to the Juridical Form, there was no consensus on: "a) the location of the legal headquarters, at Dili or outside of Portugal and Indonesia, bearing in mind the juridical system under which the Cultural Centre is being established; and b) the establishment of a Board of Trustees consisting solely of Timorese or with the participation of Portugal, Indonesia, the United Nations and other potential donors."

The Krumbach Declaration also reflected the agreement that the AIETD participants residing in the diaspora invite their brothers and sisters residing in East Timor to visit the Timorese communities in Australia,

Portugal and Macau on a date to be jointly decided upon. Conversely, the participants residing inside East Timor would invite their brothers and sisters in the diaspora to visit their homeland on a date to be agreed upon.

In the course of the deliberations, Bishop Carlos F.X. Belo proposed that the meeting issue, apart from the agreed declaration, a joint appeal to "the armed forces of both sides and the East Timorese groups who favour integration as well as those favouring independence" to decide among themselves "to establish a permanent truce." This proposed appeal would also request the Government of Indonesia "to issue to elements of the Armed Forces deployed in Timor instructions to ...eliminate for all time the practice of torture in prisons."

This proposal was rejected by the East Timorese participants from inside Indonesia and in the end Bishop Belo decided to issue a written appeal on his own behalf and on behalf of the "Catholic Bishops of the Church of Timor."

Although in the end compromises could be struck on the issues of contention that arose during the discussions, the 1997 AIETD left the distinct impression that instead of reconciliation, the various East Timorese groups participating in the process were becoming increasingly polarized, with the group of Mar'i Alkatiri and Ramos-Horta clearly intent on pursuing their own political objectives.

The AIETD breaks up

A fourth and last AIETD meeting was held from 31 October to 3 November 1998, again in Krumbach, Austria. This meeting took place under fundamentally changed circumstances as it was convened after Indonesia earlier in the year formally proposed the granting of wide-ranging autonomy and a special status to East Timor, as part and parcel of a final, peaceful and comprehensive solution to the East Timor question.

While the Indonesian Government made this offer as a major act of accommodation, the members of the Mar'i Alkatiri/Ramos Horta group in the AIETD apparently interpreted it as a sign of weakness to be relentlessly exploited as they began to demand ever more stridently that the AIETD openly discuss political issues, including the political status of East Timor.

The pro-integration group just as vociferously rejected these demands as being against the agreed terms of reference of the AIETD and contrary to the agenda that was supposed to be limited to such practical issues as the Cultural Centre. From the first day, heated debates marked the discussions, and the pro-integration and the pro-independence groups expressed increasingly polarized views.

Jose Ramos Horta was quoted as saying that he no longer cared what the Portuguese and Indonesian Foreign Ministers and the United Nations had to say about AIETD. He was only interested, he said, in talking politics.

The opening statement made by Ambassador Jamsheed Marker, unfortunately, also gave rise to misinterpretation in this respect, especially in the light of his reference to the agreement reached at the tripartite talks in New York in August of that year, using such phrases as: "the time is fast approaching when East Timor will deservedly run its own affairs, whatever the framework and legal issues may be," and, "to prepare for the imminent prospect of self-determination."

Neither was it helpful that he stressed, "Your input to the discussions of the tripartite process is of crucial importance. We believe that the East Timorese have the primary responsibility for developing and producing ideas and for building consensus amongst themselves. It should not be expected that ideas and initiatives will come from the United Nations or the tripartite process alone."

The Ramos Horta group gave no sign that they took into account Ambassador Marker's reiteration that consultations with and among East Timorese leaders "will also continue on the sidelines of this meeting." For if any of the groups in the dialogue wanted to convey its views on political issues to the tripartite process, they could have done so, as previously agreed upon, by going into consultations with Ambassador Marker on the sidelines of the dialogue. This avenue for the discussion of political issues had been opened up to keep the dialogue itself purely a process of reconciliation.

To the consternation of the pro-integration group and the group of Abilio Araujo, which now styled itself as the "Third Way," Ramos Horta presented on the second day of the dialogue a document issued by the *Concelho Nacional da Resistencia Timorense* (CNRT), the national council of the Timorese resistance, insisting that it be adopted as the final declaration of AIETD 1998. To make matters worse, without giving notice to the other groups, he distributed the CNRT document to the press, calling it the Krumbach Declaration. The document was signed by members of the Ramos Horta group while everybody else were working hard overnight to craft a "Krumbach Declaration" that was moderately worded and reflecting a consensus.

Not all the CNRT members who attended the dialogue signed the CNRT document as the "Krumbach Declaration." Jose Luis Guterres, who heads the CNRT political committee, and another member, Joao Carrascalao, criticized the tactics used by Ramos Horta. The Bishops of East Timor, Carlos Ximenes Belo and Basilio Nascimento did not attend and their representatives did not sign the CNRT document.

When the pro-integration group and Abilio Araujo's group realized that the Ramos Horta group had stolen the show, they were furious. Ambassador Lopes da Cruz spoke for them when he remonstrated that they had "been betrayed and stabbed in the back." And, of course, the consensus draft declaration that they had worked so hard to complete could not be issued. The dialogue broke up with each of the three groups issuing their own separate statements.

Thus ended a serious effort at reconciliation among the contending East Timorese groups, its purposes defeated by the apparent incapacity of the East Timorese personalities to overcome their mutual mistrust and enmity.

Chapter 7
The Idea of Special Autonomy for East Timor

AS EARLIER recounted, during the fifth round of the tripartite ministerial dialogue held in Geneva on 9 January 1995, it was decided that starting with the next round of talks, substantive issues and possible ways of achieving a solution to the East Timor question would begin to be considered.

In anticipation of this "substantive phase" of the talks and in preparing for possible questions by the UN Secretary-General on Indonesia's position on this score, I took the initiative of developing a draft proposal towards a just, comprehensive and internationally acceptable solution to the East Timor question.

Five options

On 7 December 1994, I presented to a limited Cabinet session of the political and security Ministers, chaired by the then Coordinating Minister for Political and Security Affairs, Gen. (ret.) Soesilo Soedarman, a list of possible options towards resolving the deadlock.

By way of introduction, I explained that the tripartite talks were about to move into substantive discussions at a time when the global situation had radically changed: decolonization was no longer high on the agenda of the United Nations. Moreover, in the eyes of the world, the conflict was no longer between Portugal and Indonesia but between Indonesia and East Timor.

The Cold War had been over for some time and new issues such as human rights, democracy and what was called "micro-nationalism" were on the rise. It was therefore imperative for Indonesia to try, as expeditiously as possible, to break the logjam in the East Timor negotiations and come up with a proposal to solve the problem in a comprehensive and final way.

I stressed that considering Indonesia's position at that time as Chairman of the Non-aligned Movement, and its role in solving the

Cambodian problem, the present timing to offer such a compromise proposal would be most favourable and could be viewed as being given from a position of strength instead of weakness.

Thus I presented five options towards a solution: the holding of a referendum; the application of the same scenario as proposed in 1986-1987 (the sending of a UN fact-finding team to East Timor); the grant of wide-ranging autonomy and special status to East Timor; maintaining the status quo while improving the political and socioeconomic conditions in East Timor; and a return to the pattern of voting in the UN General Assembly.

For each of the options, I elaborated the advantages and disadvantages, if chosen as a mode of solution. From the outset and as a matter of principle, however, I conveyed my view and that of the Department of Foreign Affairs that our preference was for the option of granting wide-ranging autonomy and special status to East Timor.

The referendum option was a non-starter, as it would so obviously go against Indonesia's basic policies on East Timor and the very notion of integration on which they were based.

The option of sending a UN fact-finding mission as was contemplated in 1986-87 was also considered as of doubtful value, since conditions both in East Timor and in the United Nations (after the break-up of the Soviet Union) had so substantially changed and had therefore become more unpredictable.

To maintain the status quo, albeit coupled with efforts to improve the political and socioeconomic situation in East Timor, would be tantamount to not preparing ourselves for the expected substantive discussions at the tripartite dialogue.

Latly, a return to the pattern of voting in the UN General Assembly, as happened prior to 1983, would presuppose the termination of the tripartite dialogue and having to gird ourselves for a long battle to win the showdown vote in the General Assembly, on the basis of our own draft resolution.

The recommended option

In arguing for the option of granting special status to East Timor with wide-ranging autonomy, I referred to the fact that Article 18 of the 1945 Constitution contained provisions for granting such a status to regions in Indonesia that possessed certain characteristics and that

Law No.7/1976 on the Establishment of the Province of East Timor specifically provided for this possibility. In fact, in its General Explanation, Law No. 7 *inter alia* states:

"... it should be realized that before its integration into the Unitary Republic of Indonesia, East Timor had a different history and development as compared to the other regions in Indonesia. The condition of its society, its system of law, government, economics, education as well as its defense and security system, was of a different nature and had a different background and development, thus requiring a different arrangement . . . ."

I also pointed out that this option was in conformity with the general policy of Indonesia, in that special autonomy would be given within the framework of the Unitary Republic of Indonesia. In addition, I proposed negotiating a lasting solution to the East Timor question instead of continuing to attempt to arrive at an interim or intermediate solution.

As expected, the proposal gave rise to a lively debate at the coordinating meeting of political and security Ministers, primarily focused on the special autonomy idea. Those who were initially against it brought up the argument that the institution of "special regions" in Indonesia's system of government, such as in Aceh and Yogyakarta, was being phased out, hence proposing it for East Timor would appear as "going against the current."

There was indeed such a shift in policy. What once made Aceh unique and therefore qualified for special status was its adoption of the Islamic courts system. Yogyakarta was in a class by itself because its Governor was by law a hereditary ruler, the Sultan of Yogyakarta. Events, however, were to deprive these provinces of their special place in the political architecture of Indonesia: Islamic courts were being set up in all the other provinces of Indonesia, so that Aceh would no longer be unique, while the hereditary system of choosing the Governor of Yogyakarta was about to be abolished.

In the end, however, the meeting reached consensus on the option to create a Special Province of East Timor with wide-ranging autonomy, based on the 1945 Constitution and relevant laws, especially Law No. 7/1976.

Accordingly, Coordinating Minister Soesilo Soedarman, on 15 December 1994 wrote a letter to the President conveying in general terms the consensus reached at the meeting and requesting that he together with the Foreign Minister and the Minister/Secretary of State be allowed an audience with the President in order to explain the proposal in greater detail.

The kiss of death

Before the meeting with the President could take place, however, a number of events occurred which doomed all our efforts to convince the President.

Firstly, in one of his periodic statements touching on East Timor politics, Bishop Belo expounded his view that perhaps the best solution for East Timor would be to give a form of special autonomy to the territory. This statement, far from being helpful, actually gave the "kiss of death" to my own autonomy proposal, as the President's dislike and suspicion of Bishop Belo's views were well known.

In fact, subsequently the President reportedly told Mr. Moerdiono the Minister/Secretary of State that he suspected that Bishop Belo was voicing the view of Ramos Horta in talking about autonomy. At that time, Ramos Horta on various occasions espoused a solution to the East Timor question by way of a grant of autonomy to the territory for a period of three to five years, followed by a referendum.

A few days after Bishop Belo's statement, the Governor of East Timor, Mr. Abilio Soares, called on the President to report on developments in the province. When he also touched on the idea of granting special autonomy to East Timor, the President reportedly brushed it off rather brusquely.

Subsequently, when Coordinating Minister Soesilo Soedarman met with the President on another matter, the issue of autonomy for East Timor also surfaced. Again, the President was not in favor of autonomy.

In the light of these developments, both the Co-ordinating Minister and the Minister/Secretary of State viewed the circumstances as not conducive to presenting the idea to the President and were seriously thinking of aborting the plan to meet the President to discuss the matter of special autonomy.

But I persisted, arguing that it was important for the President to be apprised of the considerations and objectives of our proposed solution, which were quite different from those aired by Bishop Belo and the Governor. The two Ministers in the end relented and agreed that I alone should request a meeting with the President in order to report on our proposal.

A final effort

When I finally had the opportunity to meet with the President, I went with some trepidation knowing that he had earlier made it clear that he rejected the idea. So I was pleasantly surprised when he patiently listened to my plan without interruption. I provided a detailed background to the problem, considerations that needed to be taken into account and the objective of granting special status with wide-ranging autonomy to East Timor as a proposed end-solution to the East Timor question at the forthcoming tripartite talks.

However, when I was finished, he smiled and shook his head and asked me a problematic question: "Do you believe that the Portuguese will accept this proposal?"

I could only truthfully reply: "I don't know, Sir, but I will certainly try my utmost to convince them."

He quickly responded: "They will not, for sure - and therefore we should not present this proposal at the tripartite talks."

The President added that, in fact, a measure of special autonomy had already been granted to the province of East Timor since its integration with Indonesia and this had been confirmed by law. East Timor's development efforts have also been given priority treatment. So if it were felt that this autonomy should be further expanded, then we could certainly discuss it within the government and implement it when approved.

Finally, he reminded me that over the years many sacrifices had been made and many people, including many Indonesian soldiers, had died in the process of integrating East Timor with Indonesia. He was implying that those sacrifices would be in vain if further autonomy were given to East Timor.

On 20 December 1994, these views were re-iterated in a written deposition by the President in a formal response to the letter of the Coordinating Minister for Political and Security Affairs.

This effectively terminated my efforts to propose a compromise solution for the East Timor question.

In retrospect, had this proposal been accepted, the negotiations on the East Timor question would have taken an entirely different course.

For I believe, that if this proposal had been rejected by Portugal and by the pro-independence group of East Timorese, Indonesia, by showing its willingness to compromise, might have been able to recapture the high ground in the opinion of the member states of the United Nations.

Chapter 8
The Tripartite Talks Intensify

IN November 1996 Mr. Kofi Annan, a Ghanaian national, was elected Secretary-General of the United Nations, succeeding Dr. Boutros Boutros-Ghali, an Egyptian national.

A former UN Under Secretary-General for Peacekeeping Operations, Mr. Kofi Annan is the first Secretary-General elected from the professional ranks of the Organization. And though in UN circles, he enjoyed a reputation of competence and integrity, his election had more to do with the insistence of the African Group in the UN on having a second five-year term for an African Secretary-General and the objection of the United States to a second tenure for the incumbent, Dr. Boutros-Ghali. Mr. Kofi Annan started his tenure on 1 January 1997.

A new impetus

Soon after taking office, the new Secretary-General on several occasions announced his intention to give a new impetus to his good offices on the question of East Timor. One of the first things he did was to appoint, in February 1997, Mr. Jamsheed Marker, a retired Pakistani Ambassador, as his Personal Representative for East Timor, to represent the Secretary-General in all aspects of his good offices function on this issue.

Jamsheed Marker was a very senior and experienced diplomat who had served his country as Ambassador for thirty consecutive years in some eleven different posts, the last of which as Ambassador/Permanent Representative of Pakistan to the United Nations in New York.

I know him personally, for as former Ambassadors/Permanent Representatives to the UN, in Geneva as well as in New York, we had often waged the same diplomatic battles in what was then the so-called "North-South dialogue" and in the various disarmament forums. In the process, we had developed a close personal relationship, which served us in good stead in the ensuing negotiations. When Indonesia was approached on his proposed appointment, therefore, we readily gave our consent.

In January 1997, I had the first opportunity to have an informal meeting with Kofi Annan, the new UN Secretary-General, on the sidelines of the World Economic Forum in Davos, Switzerland, which we both attended. On that occasion, I confided to him my views and suggestions on how best to structure the tripartite talks, which would be resumed under his auspices, in order to get optimum results. I found the new Secretary-General quite receptive to my suggestions, For his part, Ambassador Marker, soon after his appointment, went into intensive consultations with the Governments of Indonesia and Portugal. He visited Portugal from 5 to 8 March 1997, and Indonesia, including East Timor, from 20 to 31 March 1997.

In Lisbon he held discussions with President Sampaio, Prime Minister Guterres and Foreign Minister Jaime Gama. In Indonesia he met and held extensive discussions with President Soeharto and myself, as well as with other Ministers and senior officials. He also went into extensive consultations with East Timorese figures, both those in favour and those against integration, including Bishop Belo and Bishop Basilio do Nascimento, and Mr. Xanana Gusmao in Cipinang prison.

He also met and talked with military officials like General Prabowo Subianto, at that time Commander of the Special Forces (KOPASSUS). General Prabowo was also at that time married to a daughter of President Soeharto and Ambassador Jamsheed Marker had probably hoped that the General's special link to the President could help the cause of the Secretary-General's good offices.

A tortuous history

During Ambassador Marker's stay in Jakarta, I had wide-ranging discussions with him. I briefed him thoroughly on the tortuous history of the East Timor problem and shared with him my views on to how to improve the modalities for our forthcoming, resumed dialogue so as to obtain the best results.

I told him that during the first period of tripartite talks, from 1983 to 1991, negotiations were conducted in secret and were held for too long at an informal level, without directly involving the two Foreign Ministers.

Thus, when the negotiating ambassadors on both sides thought that they had achieved a breakthrough agreement, the Government of Portugal could claim that their negotiator "had gone beyond his instructions" and at the last minute reneged on the arrangements agreed at the ambassadorial level. I had always believed that this was a rather ingenuous and unfair excuse, as I knew my counterpart negotiator, Ambassador Rui de Medina, to be a professional who would not have failed to report every development in the talks to his superiors at home.

I pointed out that during the second period of tripartite talks, 1992 to 1997, under the auspices of UN Secretary-General Boutros Boutros-Ghali, the pendulum swung to the other extreme: the negotiations were all held at the ministerial level (although preparatory work was done at the ambassadorial level). They were all formal affairs and always accompanied by full media publicity. After each session, the two Ministers had to face the press and each of them would tend to "speak to the gallery" at home.

I therefore suggested that at the forthcoming tripartite dialogue, this time under the auspices of UN Secretary-General Kofi Annan with the assistance of Ambassador Marker, serious, substantive negotiations be held at the senior officials level and that the substance of the negotiations be kept confidential. The ministerial level talks would be convened only when needed to check on the progress of the dialogue and to overcome deadlocks that might arise.

During my conversations with Ambassador Marker, I also stressed that even more important than agreeing on the right modalities for the conduct of the upcoming tripartite dialogue was ascertaining whether Portugal was still committed to the originally agreed objective of the dialogue when first launched under the auspices of UN Secretary-General Perez de Cuellar.

That original objective was to find a compromise solution between the two opposing basic positions of Portugal and Indonesia, as expressed in the agreed phrase: "to find a just, comprehensive and internationally acceptable solution."

In this context, I expressed my doubts as to whether the Portuguese Government was sincerely willing, prepared and politically capable of negotiating a compromise settlement. The fact that Portugal had twice reneged on earlier agreed arrangements as worked out during Secretary-General Perez de Cuellar's tenure and the constant reference of successive Portuguese negotiators to the need for a solution based on the "*principle of self-determination and other principles of the UN*" were indeed not very encouraging to Indonesia.

Redefining modalities

Subsequently, I noted with pleasure that Secretary-General Kofi Annan and Ambassador Marker had taken to heart my suggestions with regard to the modalities of the tripartite talks.

In a letter dated 5 May 1997, the Secretary-General invited Foreign Minister Jaime Gama and me to a meeting with him in New York on 19 and 20 June 1997 in order to "clearly define the format and modalities of future talks and set them on firm grounds."

To this letter he attached a draft agenda for the discussions and some proposed modalities and procedural issues very much along the lines that I had suggested earlier. Thus, the first ministerial meeting under his auspices, the ninth meeting since UN Secretary-General Boutros-Ghali launched the talks, was going to be devoted to the format of the negotiations and not as yet to their substance.

As was done at previous tripartite talks, the Indonesian delegation provided the meeting again with a written aide memoire itemizing in detail the important developments that had taken place, both in the context of the negotiations and in East Timor itself, since the immediately previous (eighth) tripartite talks in Geneva on 27 June 1996.

A spate of violence

The run-up to the ninth tripartite ministerial talks was unfortunately marred by an increase in violent incidents in East Timor, which seized international attention and were avidly exploited by Indonesia's detractors abroad to heap opprobrium on Indonesia.

One such incident occurred when the 1996 Nobel Peace Prize laureate, Bishop Belo, arrived back in East Timor on 24 December 1996 and was greeted by large demonstrations that turned violent. In spite of the high degree of self-restraint on the part of the law enforcement authorities, one off-duty soldier was killed and 11 innocent bystanders were injured in the melee.

There was a respite from violence when Pope John Paul II, to serve the spiritual needs of the increasing number of Catholics in East Timor, on 6 January 1997 ordained Bishop Basilio do Nascimento as Bishop of the newly created diocese of Baucau, East Timor, which also covered the regencies of Manututo, Viqueque and Lautem.

Bishop Nascimento, who was a Portuguese national, had requested to become an Indonesian citizen; the Government granted his naturalization on 16 March 1997, a few days before the inauguration of his duties in Baucau on 19 March.

But the incidence of violence would pick up again as the general election of 29 May 1997 drew near. The East Timorese people were participating in an Indonesian general election for the fourth time and the anti-integrationist forces sought a failure of the electoral process in East Timor by campaigning for a boycott.

Still, of the 450,000 eligible voters in East Timor, 368,002 or more than 80 percent exercised their right to vote in the election contested by three contesting parties. This was a significant turnout in spite of repeated attempts by the anti-integration forces to intimidate and terrorize the East Timorese people into boycotting the elections.

On Election Day itself, the armed wing of the anti-integration forces, called FALINTIL, carried out armed attacks against citizens on their way to cast their votes. Again, the law enforcement authorities responded with great restraint. Fourteen innocent civilians were killed and many others were injured in those violent incidents.

These acts of terrorism persisted even after the elections. On 31 May 1997, FALINTIL attacked and killed 17 police officers who were on their way back to their base after performing their security duties at remote polling stations. On 8 June 1997, they burned down the market in Dili, causing heavy losses in property and income to hundreds of small-scale East Timorese merchants.

A Portuguese academic mission

There was one positive development during this period. From 19 July to 5 August 1996, the Indonesian Government played host to a group of Portuguese academics comprising Prof. Dr. Antonio Caetano de Maries-Collaco, professor of international relations of the Universidade Lusofona; Prof. Dr. Marco Antonio Leao de Andrade, professor at the same university and director of the Centre of Studies on Geostrategy and International Relations; and Mr. Manuel Leao Marques Lobato, research assistant on old cartography of the Institute for Scientific and Tropical Research.

The aim of the mission was to contribute to efforts at promoting better understanding and mutually beneficial cooperation, especially among the academics of both countries. As a result of the visit, both sides agreed to enhance cooperation through an exchange of historical data and exchange of students. They also agreed to co-produce a historical documentary film.

A new format is agreed on

On 19 and 20 June 1997, after an informal preparatory meeting at the senior officials' level on 17 June, the ninth Ministerial Tripartite talks were convened in New York. As earlier indicated, this was the first tripartite dialogue for the new Secretary-General, Mr. Kofi Annan, as well as for his Personal Representative, Ambassador Jamsheed Marker.

As agreed, the focus of this meeting was the agenda and organization of work of the subsequent sessions of the tripartite dialogue.

After discussions that proceeded in a generally constructive and frank atmosphere, the following format and framework for the negotiations were agreed upon:

- The Foreign Ministers and the UN Secretary-General would meet only as warranted by progress, or lack of it, at the substantive talks at senior officials level;
- Substantive, working-level negotiations would be held at the senior officials level and would be chaired by the Personal Representative of the Secretary-General;
- The confidentiality of the negotiations would be strictly observed. Any statement to the press would be issued by the Personal Representative in consultation with the two sides;
- The negotiators would be mandated to explore possible political arrangements for East Timor without, at this point, determining whether agreement would lead to an "interim" or a "final" settlement of the issue. In this context, it was further agreed that everything would be negotiated as one package, based on the principle that "nothing is agreed until all is agreed,"
- Meetings of the senior officials would be held for a period of one or two weeks at a time, with a gap of about six weeks between them.

Apart from discussing the format and procedures of forthcoming tripartite talks, the two Foreign Ministers were also given the opportunity to air their views on why progress had been so difficult to achieve in the past and what should be done in future.

Opposing views

Foreign Minister Jaime Gama seized the opportunity to complain about insufficient access to East Timor by UN Special Rapporteurs and to expound on what he called the need for a "multi-faceted" and "multi-staged" approach to the solution of East Timor.

He suggested that as the negotiations proceeded, there would be a first stage, at which the agreed Confidence Building Measures (CBMs) would be implemented, followed by a second stage, at which there would be "real" improvement of the human rights situation in East Timor. During the third stage, a "final" solution could be negotiated, but such a solution could only be achieved and be acceptable if based on the expression of the true will of the East Timorese people.

Responding to the views and suggestions of my counterpart, I reminded the Meeting that when the tripartite dialogue was launched under the auspices of UN Secretary-General Perez de Cuellar, both sides were aware and indeed implicitly agreed that the solution that should be sought would be a "compromise" between the two diametrically opposed basic positions of the two sides.

I wondered aloud if this parameter was still valid at that stage of the dialogue since the Portuguese side seemed to have repudiated it.

I pointed out that the proposed solutions offered in the past all conformed to the "compromise" idea. Indonesia's basic position had been to consider the East Timor problem "finished" as it had been integrated with Indonesia. But from this basic position, it had moved to a "compromise" or "middle position," which was agreeable to a visit to East Timor by a UN and a Portuguese Parliamentary Delegation, followed by a full-fledged debate and voting in the UN General Assembly.

On the other hand, the Portuguese on two occasions appeared to agree to such a compromise only to back out and oppose it at the last minute.

I further stressed that the success of this dialogue depended to a large degree on whether both sides could restrain themselves and focus on the relevant issues. I explained that Indonesia had been ready and remained prepared to face Portugal on the question of East Timor at the relevant forums such as the UN General Assembly, the Committee of the 24 of the General Assembly, and the Conference on Human Rights in Geneva.

Portugal, however, did not limit itself to engaging Indonesia at those relevant forums, but continued to attack Indonesia in such irrelevant forums as the EU, the EU-ACP, the Community of Portuguese Speaking Countries and the Ibero-Latin American Group. Moreover, Portugal had continued to try to block Indonesia's participation in various UN endeavours that had nothing to do with the solution to the East Timor question, such as Indonesian's plan to contribute UN peacekeeping troops to Angola (UNAVEM-II) at the request of the UN Secretary-General.

I also cited a recent statement by the Portuguese Foreign Minister declaring his country's opposition to an eventual Indonesian participation in the UN Multi-national Force in Bosnia-Herzegovina (IFOR), despite the fact that Indonesia did not at all plan to participate in IFOR, as it was a Multi-national Force (MNF) and not an official UN Peacekeeping Force. Such an attitude and actions on the part of the Portuguese, I stressed, were clearly not conducive to the success of the tripartite talks.

I was pleased that the meeting provided me with the opportunity to clarify Indonesia's stand on the negotiations. Unfortunately, as usual, the other participants listened politely but no decisions were taken.

Talks at senior officials' level

As earlier agreed upon, the first tripartite talks at senior officials level was held from 4 to 7 August 1997 in New York, under the chairmanship of the Secretary-General's Personal Representative, Ambassador Jamsheed Marker.

The Indonesian side was led by Mr. Nugroho Wisnumurti, my able Director General for Political Affairs at the Department of Foreign Affairs, while Mr. Fernando Neves, a senior official with the equivalent rank of Director General at the Portuguese Ministry of Foreign Affairs, led the Portuguese side. These talks proceeded in a brisk and businesslike manner and went straight to the substance of the negotiations.

Ambassador Marker submitted to both sides a "non-paper" on "models of possible political arrangements," which were nine case studies on various forms of autonomy agreed upon and applied between: Bhutan and India, Hong Kong and China, Macao and China, Catalonia and Spain, Eritrea and Ethiopia, the Aaland Islands and Finland, Puerto Rico and the United States, the Federation of St. Kitts and Nevis, and the Moro National Liberation Front (MNLF) and the Philippines.

According to Ambassador Marker, the "non-paper" had been prepared by a consultant to serve merely as a point of reference for a non-binding, comparative discussion on autonomy as exemplified by the various models. Attached to the paper was an explanatory memorandum by Ambassador Marker, which pointed out that due to the wide variation in the political, historical and social circumstances of the parties involved in the autonomy models, no single model could be feasibly applied to East Timor.

There were, however, several core aspects that all the successful autonomy/self-government models shared, which could be considered in any political arrangement: the establishment of a local police force, a local independent judiciary, a local legislature, a local administration headed by an executive elected either directly or through a local parliament, the presence of a military force tasked solely with external defense and a mechanism to ensure that the autonomous or self-governing status of the territory would not be unilaterally altered in the future.

In responding to the invitation by Ambassador Marker to discuss the models, even in a non-binding way, Mr. Fernando Neves initially showed reluctance, asserting that Portugal had never agreed to a solution by way of autonomy. He reiterated Portugal's basic position that the most important thing was to ensure that the wishes of the East Timorese people could be expressed and internationally verified. He stated that Portugal therefore was only prepared to discuss the various autonomy models if such discussion were also accompanied by a discussion on mechanisms to ensure Portugal's basic position. But later on, he relented.

The Indonesian delegation responded more positively and assured Ambassador Marker that it was ready to have an exchange of views on the non-paper, while keeping Indonesia's Law No.5/1974 on regional autonomy and law No.7/1976 on East Timor as its comparative reference points.

The Mandela interlude

Although not discussed openly, a rather curious incident that drew considerable international attention occurred while the talks were going on. It was then July 1997 and President Nelson Mandela of South Africa was on a state visit to Indonesia. In the course of his talks with then President Soeharto, he brought up the East Timor issue and requested that he be allowed to talk with the imprisoned the FRETILIN leader, Mr. Jose Alexandre "Xanana" Gusmao.

President Soeharto graciously agreed and subsequently Mr. Xanana Gusmao was brought to the State Guest House to meet with President Mandela. They had a two-hour completely private conversation over dinner.

After the meeting, President Mandela briefed President Soeharto on the gist of his conversation with Xanana Gusmao and on his general impressions of the East Timorese pro-independence leader.

He told President Soeharto that he had tried to persuade Xanana Gusmao to cease his armed struggle and instead endeavor to pursue his aims through dialogue and negotiations with Indonesia. Then he urged President Soeharto to consider releasing Xanana Gusmao from prison and including him in the negotiating process. He promised to write President Soeharto and to convey his ideas in greater detail after he returned home.

Back home in South Africa, President Mandela wrote two letters to President Soeharto, respectively dated 22 July and 5 August 1997. Before the first letter could reach its destination, however, a strange incident happened. The letter of 22 July 1997, which was clearly addressed to the President of the Republic of Indonesia, did not reach, as intended, the office of the Indonesian Ambassador in Pretoria for further dispatch to Jakarta, but somehow landed in the Portuguese Embassy in South Africa.

Had the letter been quickly returned unopened to President Mandela's office, as it had been clearly delivered to the wrong address, nothing untoward would have happened. The staff member in the President's office who was responsible for the inadvertence would have been quietly reprimanded and the world would not have gotten wind of it.

Unfortunately, the Portuguese Ambassador held on to the letter and, worse, opened it and leaked its contents to the Portuguese press, a behaviour that can only be described as highly unethical if not downright malicious. The ensuing furore that erupted and the screaming headlines that were bannered in the national press of the three affected countries as well as in the international media so greatly embarrassed the South African Government that it declared the Portuguese Ambassador *persona non grata.*

The Mandela proposals

As to the contents of President Mandela's letters to President Soeharto, these again raised the suggestion that Xanana Gusmao be released from prison.

In his letter of response dated 28 August 1997, President Soeharto reiterated his usual arguments that Xanana Gusmao had been duly tried for common crimes before a court of law, had been found guilty and sentenced to life imprisonment, a sentence subsequently reduced to 20 years and subject to further reductions in future. Thus, releasing him now would be incompatible with the rule of law and would constitute an injustice to the countless victims of his crimes.

President Soeharto then went further and said that, as he had already indicated to the Portuguese at the meeting with Prime Minister Guterres in Bangkok, if the release of Mr. Xanana Gusmao were proposed to be part of a package of an overall solution entailing acceptance of East Timor's integration with Indonesia, Indonesia would not only agree to his release but would also be ready to grant full amnesty to the remnants of his followers who were still waging armed insurrection. They would be free to come down from the mountains and would be given a choice of staying in Indonesia or leaving for abroad.

In his letters, President Mandela had also proposed that a direct dialogue be established between the Indonesian Government and the "acknowledged Timorese leaders," as a way to achieve a peaceful, negotiated solution to the East Timor question.

To this, President Soeharto replied that this course could not be taken because of a fundamental divergence of views between Indonesia, Portugal and the pro-independence Timorese on who were the acknowledged Timorese leaders.

In Indonesia's view, President Soeharto said, the acknowledged Timorese leaders were those who were living in Indonesia and East Timor, who in the past had actually fought or resisted Portuguese colonialism, overcame theFRETILIN reign of terror during the civil war that broke out in August 1975 and who finally opted for independence through integration with Indonesia. They were decidedly not people like Jose Ramos Horta and Mar'i Alkatiri who at most represented only a small minority among the East Timorese people.

A dialogue with them, he said, would therefore be disproportionate and quite unproductive. Thus, Indonesia still saw no better modality towards finding a just, comprehensive and internationally acceptable solution to the East Timor question than the tripartite dialogue that was being conducted between Portugal and Indonesia under the auspices of the UN Secretary-General.

A misunderstanding resolved

Aside from corresponding with President Soeharto upon his return to South Africa from his visit to Indonesia, President Nelson Mandela also wrote to UN Secretary-General Kofi Annan about the discussions he had in Jakarta. Subsequently, Ambassador Jamsheed Marker was sent to Pretoria where he held a useful meeting with President Mandela on 26 August 1997.

This meeting and the press briefing that Ambassador Marker gave afterwards cleared up a misunderstanding that had arisen earlier. There had been an impression in the United Nations that President Mandela was taking a separate initiative towards a solution of the East Timor question or else he was planning to organize an AIETD kind of meeting in South Africa among East Timorese representatives.

Through Ambassador Marker and in personal assurances to the Mr. Kofi Annan, President Mandela reiterated that his sole intention was to support the efforts of the UN Secretary-General on this issue and not to open a separate negotiating track. President Mandela then offered South Africa as a venue for the next AIETD meeting, but this was politely declined by Ambassador Marker, as it was already agreed that the AIETD this time would be held in Austria.

There was no further follow-up and, to my knowledge, this brought to an end President Mandela's short-lived initiative on the East Timor issue.

More meetings

Since the first round of the senior officials meeting, three more rounds were held in New York: from 1 to 3 October 1997, from 5 to 7 November 1997 and from 6 to 8 May 1998.

During the second round of the meeting in October 1997, a "brainstorming" took place on those common elements or core aspects that successful autonomy models shared, as presented in Ambassador Marker's "non-paper" during the first round. From the preliminary reactions of each side to those elements, it was clear that their respective positions were still far apart.

On this occasion, the Indonesian side suggested that in discussing "possible political arrangements," the focus should not only be on elements for a solution based on autonomy but that other possible compromise solutions should also be considered.

In this context, Indonesia suggested a "package solution" for consideration: that Portugal recognize and accept the reality of East Timor's integration and as a *quid pro quo*, Indonesia would free Xanana Gusmao and other East Timorese detainees, guarantee East Timor's cultural and religious identity and consider other appropriate concessions. This suggestion, however, never elicited a positive response from the Portuguese side.

The Marker proposals

At the third round of talks at senior officials level from 5 to 7 November 1997, Ambassador Marker presented a "non-paper" on ideas of possible political arrangements for East Timor, which was essentially a draft proposal towards an autonomous or self-governing status for the territory. However, because the negotiators needed time to study the paper and report on it to their respective governments, it was decided that discussions on the "non-paper" be postponed to the fourth round of the senior officials meeting, scheduled for 6 to 8 May 1998.

Ambassador Marker also came up with an alternative proposal towards a solution. He proposed a three-month ceasefire, the cessation of all clandestine activities by the anti-integration forces and a halt in anti-Indonesian propaganda activities abroad. According to that same proposal, if such a ceasefire and restraint on the part of anti-Indonesia elements could hold for a period of three months, then a certain number of Indonesian armed personnel would be "withdrawn" from East Timor.

But this idea immediately ran into the objections of the Indonesian delegation, primarily because the proposed ceasefire and restraints were linked to a "withdrawal" of Indonesian security forces from East Timor, which could only be appropriate if East Timor were a foreign country.

In Indonesia's view, there could be no symmetry in any ceasefire arrangement between elements that Indonesia considered as secessionist rebels on the one hand and the Government's legitimate armed forces on the other.

What could be agreed on during the round was that the Secretary-General's Personal Representative again visit Indonesia, including East Timor, and Portugal. The purpose of the visits would be to assess the progress of the talks at senior officials level, the assessment to be based on direct talks with the leadership of both countries and also to observe the situation in East Timor.

A proposal from Xanana

The visit to Indonesia took place from 16 to 23 December 1997. Apart from intensive discussions with myself, Ambassador Marker had talks with the Armed Forces Commander; the Chief of the Udayana Military Command in Bali, which covers East Timor; the Commander of the Special Forces (KOPASSUS); Ambassador Lopes da Cruz and other personalities in East Timor. He also had a meeting with Mr. Xanana Gusmao at Cipinang prison.

On the talks he had with Xanana, Ambassador Marker confided to me and to Director General Nugroho Wisnumurti some interesting details. He said he had impressed upon Xanana the urgent necessity of stopping all armed resistance and accepting the reality of East Timor's integration.

If this could be done, he had told Xanana, then there would be a real possibility for the start of a constructive dialogue toward peace. This would be a process of negotiation toward a package solution that would entail a large measure of autonomy for East Timor, his own freedom from imprisonment and other concessions from Indonesia.

He told Xanana that he was now convinced that Indonesia would never accept independence for East Timor. He therefore urged Xanana to demonstrate his leadership and courage to take the necessary steps towards peace for the sake of his people and in order to end their overlong suffering.

According to Ambassador Marker, unlike in the first talks he had with Xanana in March 1997, this time the latter showed a more accommodating attitude. For example, Xanana admitted that a similar appeal was also conveyed to him earlier by President Mandela of South

Africa and by US Assistant Secretary of State Stanley Roth.

He argued, however, that to halt all armed resistance and to embark on the path of peaceful dialogue, he needed the agreement of his followers in East Timor and he could not possibly convince them from his prison cell in Jakarta.

He therefore wondered whether it would be possible for him to go to East Timor for that purpose. Ambassador Marker replied that on this question, everything depended on President Soeharto and on Xanana himself and he could not get involved in it.

After I reported the gist of this conversation to President Soeharto, I received from the President a cryptic directive addressed to me and to the Coordinating Minister for Political and Security Affairs to "arrange the possibility of Xanana convincing his followers through his appointed representative, such as Bishop Belo, or through Ambassador Lopes de Cruz" and that "any meeting of Xanana with his followers should be held in Jakarta."

Marker's idea for a compromise

At the end of Ambassador Marker's visit to Indonesia, I had a long "de-briefing" session with him, in which he conveyed to me his impressions and views.

He frankly told me that he was not satisfied with the progress achieved after three meetings at the senior officials level. He felt that in order to move forward "a major decision had to be made and a strong political impetus needed to be generated." He said he had come to realize that no solution was possible unless East Timor's integration was accepted by Portugal as an unalterable reality.

In his forthcoming visit to Portugal in January 1998, therefore, he would urge for a solution in which, in essence, Portugal would accept integration and as a *quid pro quo,* Indonesia would commit itself to a number of concessions. He expressed the view that, in the framework of such a solution, Indonesia should agree to engage East Timorese leaders in the process. Hence, if in this way a solution could be agreed with East Timorese leaders, then Portugal would be in an awkward position to oppose it.

Among the East Timorese leaders he had in mind, he mentioned such personalities as Xanana Gusmao, Bishop Belo and Bishop Nascimento.

He further observed that despite the material progress achieved in

East Timor, Indonesia had not succeeded in winning the hearts and minds of the East Timorese people. He therefore urged the Indonesian Government to redouble efforts towards this objective by opening a genuine and constructive dialogue with the East Timorese leaders.

Although up to that stage the senior officials meetings had not produced any concrete results, I was left in no doubt as to the friendly disposition of Ambassador Marker towards Indonesia and the sincerity of his efforts to find a compromise solution based on the concept of large autonomy for East Timor.

Elusive progress

During the fourth round of senior officials talks, held from 6 to 8 May 1998, Ambassador Marker put forward a slightly revised version of his earlier "non-paper" containing ideas on possible political arrangements for East Timor. For the first time, this draft was discussed in a trilateral session of the meeting and not only bilaterally between Ambassador Marker and the Indonesian and Portuguese delegations separately, as in the previous rounds.

Although at least some clarity was achieved regarding the still divergent views of the two sides on the substance of the non-paper, not much progress could be achieved. Ambassador Marker promised to prepare a second draft of his non-paper, which would incorporate the results of the discussions at this fourth meeting at senior officials level.

But as it turned out, this particular phase of the negotiations was soon to be overtaken by the dramatic developments that took place in Indonesia since 21 May 1998 in the wake of the financial and economic crisis that ravaged most of the East and Southeast Asian countries, including and especially Indonesia.

(Footnotes)

1 The ongoing Conference between the developed countries of the global "North" and the developing countries of the global "South" on how to achieve a more just and mutually beneficial world economic order.

▲
Meeting with U.N. Secretary General
Javier Perez de Cuellar.
(UN Photo by J. Isaac)

◀ Meeting with U.N.
Secretary General
Boutros Bhoutros
Ghali
(UN/DPI Photo
by Evan Schneider)

Meeting with U.N. Secretary General Kofi Annan. (UN/DPI Photo by Milton Grant)

Greeting Ambassador Jamsheed Marker, the U. N. Secretary General's Personal representative for East Timor.
(Personal collection)

Meeting with Dr. Abilio Araujo, forner Chairmen of the Fretilin and co-initiator, together with Ambassador Francisco X. Lopes da Cruz, of the London Meetings and the All inclusive Intra- East Timorese Dialogue. (Reuters photo)

With Secretary General
Kofi Annan and Portuguere Foreign Minister
Jaime Gama,
facing the press at U. N. Headquarters in New York.
(Reuters photo)

Addressing the United Nations
General Assembly.
(UN/DPI Photo by Evan Schneider)

Welcoming members of the U. N. Security Council Mission, estalished on 6 September 1999, and led by the Permanent Representative of Namibia, Ambassador Martin Anjabar, which visited Jakarta and East Timor from 8 till 12 September 1999. (Reuters photo)

Meeting with Foreign Minister Gareth Evans of Australia.
(Tempo photo by Bachtiar Abdullah)

Alatas speaks in news conference, Wiranto looks on, Dili. (Reuters photo)

Arriving in Komoro Airport, Dili,on one of the numerous visits to the province.
(Antara Photo)

One of the numerous demonstrations by East Timorese dissidents in the Capital city of Dili. (Reuters photo)

Fretilin fighters froudly showing the flag of Timor Leste. (Reuters photo)

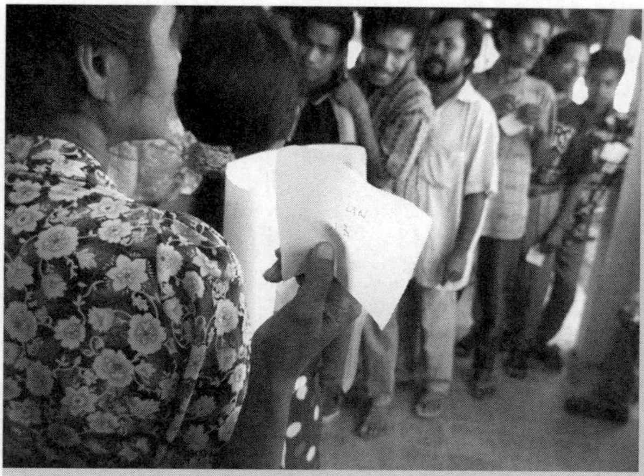

East Timorese register as voters, Dili. (Reuters photo)

Friendly conversation with Mr.Jose Alexandre "Xanana" Gusmao, future President of Timor Leste and Mr. Ramos Horta, future Foreign Minister, on first visit to Jakarta after popular consultation and transfer of authority over East Timor to the United Nations.
(Reuters photo)

Foreign Minister Ali Alatas and M Junisa Alatas with UN Secretary-General and Mrs. Javier Perez de Cuellar
(Personal collection)

Chapter 9
The Offer of Special Status with Wide-Ranging Autonomy for East Timor

A DEVASTATING financial and economic crisis struck the most dynamic Southeast and East Asian economies, including Indonesia, in the middle of 1997. That crisis cut down Indonesia's GDP growth, which had been averaging seven percent during the previous decade, to minus 13.5 percent in 1998.

Indonesia also suffered hyper-inflation, which reached 77.6 percent in 1998, food shortages in several parts of the country, the loss of millions of jobs, the collapse of the banking sector, the sharp depreciation of the Rupiah, a ballooning debt burden and hemorrhagic capital flight.

A full-blown political crisis

Worse still, unlike in the other affected countries, the financial and economic crisis in Indonesia quickly developed into a full-blown political and social crisis, manifested by massive student demonstrations, social tumult, political tension, and ethnic and sectarian strife in some provinces.

Widespread rioting erupted in April and May 1998, culminating in the shooting death of six students of Jakarta's Trisakti University on May 14. This event in turn triggered demonstrations in various parts of the country and the physical occupation of the National Assembly building in Jakarta by students and youth groups.

The upheaval finally led to the abrupt and rather unexpected resignation of President Soeharto, who on 21 May 1998, in a simple public ceremony at the State Palace, handed over the reins of Government to Vice President B.J. Habibie.

The departure of President Soeharto amid country-wide agitation at allegations of rampant corruption, collusion and nepotism committed by his Government over the 32 years that he was in office, brought fundamental changes to the Indonesian political landscape, setting off a far-reaching process of political, economic and constitutional reform which continues until today.

It also thoroughly changed the dynamics of the East Timor question, including Indonesia's approach to its solution.

As the dramatic developments in Indonesia were rising to a climax, I was far away in Cartagena, in Colombia, attending a Ministerial Conference of the Non-aligned Movement, from 18 to 20 May 1998. At the end of the Conference, I returned home, flying by way of Miami, New York, Frankfurt and Singapore.

At every stop on the way home, I was updated on the rapid turn of events in Jakarta by heads of our diplomatic missions.

Thus, while still en route, I had already learnt of President Soeharto's resignation and the consequent dissolution of the VIIth Development Cabinet, which had lasted barely two months. So I was aware that upon arrival home, I would no longer be Foreign Minister.

Joining a new cabinet

When I arrived at Singapore's Changi Airport, our Ambassador handed a message to me: the newly installed President Habibie wished to speak to me urgently. I could not respond from Singapore, but I had just reached the VIP room of the Jakarta Airport, in the early morning of 22 May 1998, when the telephone rang.

On the line was President Habibie, telling me that he was about to announce the composition of his Cabinet to the nation and he wanted me to join as his Foreign Minister and would I please immediately confirm?

It was not a request, but rather an order from the new President. I could, however, fully agree with his observation that the new government had a lot of urgent, unfinished business on its agenda, including in the field of foreign affairs. Thus, he needed to gather some of the experienced people from the earlier government on his team.

So I said, "Yes," without having had the chance of even consulting my wife. The "*Reformasi-Pembangunan*" (Reform-Development) Cabinet was announced at 10:00 a.m. that same morning, 22 May 1998 and sworn in the next day.

A rare opportunity

One of the compelling considerations that moved me to join the new Cabinet was my hope that under the new Government and in the changed political situation of the country, I could find an opportunity to bring the

East Timor question to a final, peaceful solution. That opportunity came rather quickly.

At a private meeting with President Habibie in early June, I seized the occasion to brief him thoroughly on the latest developments in the tripartite negotiations on East Timor and on the need to come up with a compromise solution.

Harking back to the proposal I had submitted in 1994 to former President Soeharto, I suggested the grant of special status to East Timor, with wide-ranging autonomy, within the framework of the Unitary Republic of Indonesia, as part of a comprehensive, just and mutually acceptable end-solution to the East Timor problem. This proposal would be formally presented to the Portuguese and to the UN Secretary-General in the context of the ongoing tripartite talks in New York.

To my great relief and satisfaction, President Habibie agreed to my proposal, directing me to present it to the next plenary Cabinet Meeting for deliberation and official approval. Consequently, I first presented this proposal, with all its considerations and detailed explanations to the limited Cabinet session of the Political and Security Ministers on 5 June 1998. After a spirited debate, the limited Cabinet session approved it on the same day.

Next, I presented it to the plenary Cabinet session on 9 June. Rather surprisingly, the President and the Cabinet approved it without much debate and I received my instructions to convey the proposal as soon as possible to Mr. Kofi Annan, the UN Secretary-General in New York.

Apparently, the enormous problems in the economic and financial field that Indonesia faced at that time weighed so heavily on the minds of Indonesia's President and his Cabinet Ministers that they did not give much thought to the East Timor question.

I seized what I saw as a "window of opportunity" and flew to New York on 16 June 1998. On 18 June, I was received by the UN Secretary-General, who was flanked by Ambassador Jamsheed Marker, Assistant Secretary-General Alvaro de Soto and a number of other Secretariat members.

The Indonesian proposal

To Mr. Kofi Annan I conveyed Indonesia's proposal, verbally at first, which I subsequently followed up with an aide-memoire containing these points:

1. The Indonesian Government is prepared to grant a special status to East Timor, with wide-ranging autonomy, in the context and as part of a comprehensive, just and mutually acceptable end-solution to the question of East Timor. Toward this end, Indonesia is ready to negotiate the substantive elements of such a special, autonomous region of East Timor within the ongoing tripartite talks under the auspices of the UN Secretary-General.
2. Indonesia is of the view that considering the historical, political, socio-cultural, and geographic factors and conditions pertaining to the East Timor question, the creation of a special, autonomous province within the unitary Republic of Indonesia represents the most realistic, viable, and peaceful solution to the problem. On the other hand, the proposal to conduct a referendum would, in view of the long history of bitter strife and bloodshed in the province, only re-open old wounds, re-ignite violent disputes and conflict and may even lead to renewed civil war.
3. Indonesia believes that this proposal reflects, once again, the sincerity and determination with which it has always approached the peaceful solution of this long- standing issue and now expects the same degree of political will and sincerity to imbue and motivate the Portuguese side.
4. A new opportunity is now being provided in order to arrive at a comprehensive settlement of the question and all sides should grasp that opportunity and not allow it to be lost because of an erroneous or speculative assessment of the prevailing situation."

The Portuguese response

Secretary-General Kofi Annan expressed deep appreciation of the proposal, which he described as very important, and stated his preparedness to immediately convey it to the Portuguese Government. Ambassador Jamsheed Marker subsequently traveled to Lisbon for this purpose on 24 June 1998.

The Secretary-General also said that this proposal ought to be acted upon quickly and therefore proposed to convene a tripartite dialogue meeting at the Ministerial level as soon as possible after the return of Ambassador Marker from Portugal.

On 30 June, Ambassador Marker reported the results of his visit to Lisbon to our Permanent Representative in New York, Ambassador Makarim Wibisono.

The Portuguese Government had generally reacted positively to Indonesia's proposal and had expressed its readiness to negotiate seriously on it.

However, they re-iterated their well-known position that they should not be pressured to acknowledge publicly and in advance Indonesia's sovereignty over East Timor or that the integration of East Timor with Indonesia was final, as in that case there would be nothing left to negotiate about.

It was further agreed that Ambassador Jamsheed Marker would visit Indonesia again, including East Timor, towards the end of July and that the ministerial-level tripartite talks would be held in New York on 4 and 5 August 1998, to be followed by a meeting of the senior officials in early September.

A damaging leak

Before the process could reach that stage, however, an unexpected incident occurred, which threw a damper on the atmosphere of goodwill and optimism surrounding the tripartite talks at that time. At the UN, the news broke that a document described as "a proposal of Ambassador Marker for resolving the East Timor problem" was circulating in East Timor.

It was Bishop Belo calling from Dili who alerted Mr. Tamrat Samuel of the UN Secretariat of the existence of this document, which turned out to be the "non-paper" that Ambassador Marker had presented confidentially to the Portuguese and Indonesian negotiators the previous April, containing ideas on possible political arrangements for East Timor in the form of a model for autonomy in East Timor.

According to Bishop Belo, Governor Abilio Soares and the military commander of East Timor had handed him this document, signed by Ambassador Marker, informing him that it was the UN proposal for a final solution to the East Timor problem and hinting that the people of East Timor better accept it.

This development came as an unpleasant surprise to me and to the Foreign Ministry, as the paper had so far been handled correctly as "highly confidential" and for very limited distribution only. It had somehow fallen into the hands of the military command in Dili and of Governor Abilio. Its circulation was clearly a deliberate leak.

Scrambling to contain the damage, I issued a statement

emphasizing that the document was not a proposal made by the UN or by anyone else but a "non-paper" designed to spur a non-binding brainstorming session. The spokesman of the Secretary-General made a similar statement, expressing the serious concern of Ambassador Marker and his protest at this "deplorable breach of diplomatic confidentiality."

These statements seemed to have succeeded in containing the immediate damage caused by the publication of the document, although it did not diminish my sense of unease and foreboding that some quarters in our own ranks were apparently out to sabotage our efforts at compromise.

The Portuguese side, however, depicted the incident in much more serious fashion, accusing Indonesia of deliberately "leaking" the document in a distortive way and stating that it would be very difficult for Portugal to continue the tripartite talks under those circumstances. As it turned out, however, they did not carry out this threat.

The Bishops' Proposal

President Habibie followed up on his decision to grant special status and wide-ranging autonomy to East Timor by arranging to meet with the two Bishops of East Timor, Mgr. Carlos Filipe Ximenes Belo, SDB and Mgr. Basilio do Nascimento, Pr. The meeting took place on 24 June 1998 at the Bina Graha building, the Presidential Office, in Jakarta. However, Bishop Nascimento could not be present because at that time he was abroad.

The meeting, where I was also present, was cordial and animated and it lasted an hour. The two Bishops had obviously prepared themselves well for the meeting: Bishop Belo presented the President with a memorandum containing their views on the situation in East Timor and their proposals and suggestions.

Among other things, they asked for a reduction of combat and territorial troops in East Timor, particularly the Special Forces (KOPASSUS) and the paramilitary forces created by the KOPASSUS, such as the Garda Paksi, the Team Saka, Rajawali, etc.; the freeing and grant of amnesty to all political prisoners; the teaching of the Tetum language at elementary and junior high schools in East Timor and of the Portuguese language in the senior high schools; and the establishment of Dili harbour as a "free trade" port.

In a press conference after the meeting, Bishop Belo spoke glowingly of the new President as being "farsighted" and "sensitive to the concerns" of the East Timorese people. Indeed, President Habibie's reaction to many of these proposals was positive and on 30 June 1998, a special limited Cabinet session was held to discuss and respond to the observations and suggestions contained in the memorandum of the two Bishops.

However, these positive developments would turn sour a few months later when Bishop Belo turned down an invitation by President Habibie to a second meeting in Jakarta. He explained that he could not leave East Timor because of the tense situation in the province as a result of reports, later proven inaccurate, of a massacre in the town of Alas.

After what he considered a flagrant snub, President Habibie would bitterly refer to Bishop Belo in private conversations as "arrogant" and "unreliable."

Marker's visit

Ambassador Jamsheed Marker visited Indonesia from 16 to 22 July 1998. Before that, at the end of June, a troika of European Union Ambassadors stationed in Jakarta, led by the British Ambassador who was then representing the EU Presidency, had visited East Timor. This visit went reasonably well during its earlier part. The EU delegation was able to freely meet and talk with East Timorese of both the pro-and anti-integration groups.

But in the tense political atmosphere prevailing on the island at that time, the situation deteriorated during the later stage of the visit. When the delegation was visiting Bishop Nascimento in the town of Baucau, a clash erupted between pro-integration and pro-independence groups of demonstrators, resulting in a number of casualties. In the end, the troika delegation had to be flown out of the island by special military aircraft.

This incident was widely reported in the press, so that by the time Ambassador Marker arrived in Jakarta, the Government, especially the military authorities, was reluctant to allow any further visits by foreign VIPs to the island. The problem during this visit, therefore, was the trip to East Timor. Ambassador Marker insisted that he had to make the trip despite our appeals that he reconsider.

After a flurry of consultations, a compromise was reached:

Ambassador Marker would not visit Dili but would be flown directly by special military aircraft to Baucau. During this one-day visit to Baucau, he met and talked with various East Timorese leaders and personalities of both camps who were transported there for that purpose.

During the time he spent in Jakarta, Ambassador Marker also met with the leaders of the main Indonesian political parties, notably Abdurrahman "Gus Dur" Wahid, Megawati Soekarnoputri, Amien Rais and high-ranking GOLKAR officials.

When I finally met with him, he pressed for three things: the establishment of "interests sections" in Jakarta and Lisbon; the freeing of Xanana Gusmao or at least his transfer from prison to "house arrest," so that he could be more directly involved in the negotiating process; and the establishment of a UN presence in Dili during the forthcoming rounds of negotiations in New York.

On the first issue, I reiterated Indonesia's longstanding position that, from the outset, we fully agreed to the establishment of interests sections, as long as the Portuguese did not link it to any conditionality.

On the second question, however, I had to disappoint Ambassador Marker, because even in the changed atmosphere in Indonesia at that time the Government, from President Habibie down, could not have possibly agreed to the early release of Xanana Gusmao or even moving him to "house arrest". But I could promise Ambassador Marker greater access to Xanana during the tripartite negotiations.

As to the third question, I had to stick to our earlier position, namely that a UN presence in East Timor could only be considered in the context of implementing an already agreed solution and not before it.

During this visit, Ambassador Marker again met with Xanana Gusmao at Cipinang prison in Jakarta and this time Xanana confided to Ambassador Marker his views on a possible compromise solution to the East Timor problem.

He indicated his agreement to what he called a "phased approach," namely a five-year period of wide-ranging autonomy, at the end of which a referendum would be held to determine whether the East Timorese wished to opt for independence or to remain with Indonesia in a special autonomous status.

He also spoke of a "preliminary phase" that would precede this five-year period in which there would be a cessation of hostilities, a reduction of Indonesian troops and the introduction of a UN presence into East Timor.

Autonomy: final or interim?

As earlier agreed, the Ministerial Tripartite Meeting between the Foreign Ministers of Portugal and Indonesia and the UN Secretary-General was held in New York on 4 and 5 August 1998. On the eve of the meeting, the Secretary-General tendered an informal dinner for the two Ministers.

Throughout the meeting, the discussions proceeded in an open, cordial and constructive atmosphere. I once again formally presented Indonesia's proposal for a special status with wide-ranging autonomy for East Timor.

I stressed that the autonomy being offered was not a unilaterally conceived or a unilaterally granted autonomy but an autonomy that conforms to international norms. And towards this end, Indonesia was ready to negotiate the substantive elements of such autonomy within the ongoing tripartite talks.

The Portuguese side expressed the view that the proposed autonomy should be implemented as an interim arrangement for a certain period of time, to be followed by a referendum. I responded by arguing that such an approach would only be a recipe for continuing conflict.

During the autonomy period, both sides would inevitably prepare themselves for the forthcoming "show-down" referendum by seeking to strengthen their respective political positions. This would result in continuing strife, tensions and conflict in the province and the goals of development and peaceful reconciliation would be set aside.

Furthermore, I said, it was doubtful whether a referendum would solve the problem as the losing side in that contest would surely reject the outcome, thus opening the prospect of renewed fighting and even renewed civil war between the pro-integration and pro-independence forces.

In principle, Foreign Minister Jaime Gama welcomed the Indonesian proposal but he stressed the need for any solution to be subjected to a process of "democratic validation" through a determination of the will of the East Timorese people.

As expected, he would only accept the idea of wide-ranging autonomy as an "interim" arrangement, which should be followed by a process of "self-determination," the form of which could be a referendum or otherwise.

As the talks were in danger of becoming deadlocked, the Secretary-General proposed that the two sides for the time being defered making a decision on whether the autonomy would be a "final" solution or an "interim" one. The idea was to focus first on negotiating the substantive elements of such an autonomy. In other words, both sides would retain their basic positions of principle.

New points of agreement

After some debate, the two Ministers accepted this proposal. Thus, the meeting was saved from a breakdown and proceeded to agree on a number of important aspects. In a Communiqué issued after the meeting, the following agreements were highlight:

- The Ministers agreed to hold in-depth discussions on Indonesia's proposal for a special status, based on wide-ranging autonomy, for East Timor without prejudice to their basic positions of principle. For this purpose, their senior officials would intensify their discussions under the chairmanship of the Secretary-General's Personal Representative, Ambassador Jamsheed Marker.
- The Ministers agreed to involve the East Timorese more closely in the search for a solution. In this connection, the Secretary-General would intensify his consultations with East Timorese representatives in East Timor and outside, in order to take into account their views and to keep them abreast of developments in the tripartite talks.
- The Ministers agreed to establish interests sections in friendly embassies in each other's capital by the end of 1998 and to relax their visa policies towards each other's nationals.
- The next Senior Officials' Meeting of the two sides would take place in New York by the end of September 1998.

Thus, after 15 years of talks, the tripartite dialogue registered what many viewed as a significant breakthrough and embarked on what I hoped would be an accelerated course towards a peaceful solution.

After the August 1998 tripartite Ministerial meeting, two Senior Officials Meetings were held the same year in order, as agreed, to conduct intensified in-depth discussions on the proposed autonomy plan.

An Australian study

Before these meetings, however, I received from the Australian Foreign Minister, Alexander Downer, the results of a study conducted by officials of the Australian Government on "a range of East Timorese views concerning options for progress in light of the Indonesian Government's offer of autonomy for East Timor". The canvassing was done over the period mid-July to mid-August 1998 and views were obtained from East Timorese in Indonesia as well as overseas.

The main conclusion of the study was that almost all those interviewed "maintained that any autonomy package would need to be taken to the people for endorsement at some point, either through a referendum or some other form of consultative process.

There were varying views and degrees of flexibility, even among the FRETILIN and the CNRT, on how such a consultative process might be formulated. Views also varied over the question of a timeframe. Only a negligible number said they would accept international recognition for integration in return for the grant of autonomy.

When apprised of this report, the President and the relevant Ministers did not give it much credence. For one thing, the list of about 30 East Timorese personalities contacted and appended as an annex to the study was regarded as too slanted towards those who were critical of integration and therefore biased in their views.

I thanked my Australian colleague for his Government's efforts, but the report was in effect set aside. However, I remember that at that time it did give me an uneasy sense of foreboding as it foreshadowed the basic change in the Australian Government's stance towards the East Timor issue that would occur a few months later.

First SOM: a backdrop of tension

At the first Senior Officials meeting, convened in New York from 6 to 8 October 1998, Ambassador Marker presented a "non-paper" entitled "Special Autonomy for East Timor: Draft Proposals for a Constitutional Framework for East Timor," containing a more detailed elaboration of the envisaged autonomy, but leaving aside the question of its final status.

As with the earlier draft, this version too was largely drafted by an outside expert, Prof. Hurst Hannum of the Fletcher School of Law and Diplomacy, Tufts University, who this time sat in at the talks. But since both sides needed time to study the draft, the meeting conducted only a "first reading" at which both sides gave their preliminary views and sought clarifications on certain aspects.

The meeting also discussed the technical modalities for the establishment of interests sections and in this context exchanged views on a paper containing "Elements for an Agreement on the Establishment of Interests Sections." It was agreed that this would be carried out in the form of an exchange of notes and that the interests sections would be established at the latest by January 1999, after clearance from the Governments of the Netherlands and of Thailand, the two countries that had agreed to accommodate the interests sections of Portugal and Indonesia respectively.

This first Senior Officials Meeting proceeded in an atmosphere of mutual accommodation and goodwill, in rather sharp contrast to the backdrop of rising tensions and mixed developments in East Timor itself.

On the one hand, at the initiative of the two Bishops of East Timor, a meeting was held in the town of Dare from 7 to 9 September 1998, with representatives of pro-integration and pro-independence factions in attendance. It was the first attempt at peaceful reconciliation between the two conflicting sides in East Timor itself.

On the other hand, apparently emboldened by the political and economic transformation that was taking place in Indonesia, the anti-integration forces were beginning to show an increasingly open defiance of governmental authority, especially that of the military, in East Timor.

Large-scale demonstrations and violent incidents occurred more and more frequently and many instances were reported of elements of pro-independence forces intimidating provincial civil servants, teachers, doctors and other technical expert staff assigned to East Timor by Jakarta.

At the same time, FALINTIL, the military wing of the pro-independence forces also stepped up its operations against Indonesian military units and villages that they considered as having aided the military.

It was in this highly charged and volatile atmosphere that an incident occurred in the town of Alas. Although subsequently presented in a highly exaggerated fashion by the foreign media and certain NGO's, thereby influencing the view of the Portuguese Government, the incident nevertheless almost caused disruption of the ongoing tripartite dialogue.

No massacre

What actually occurred was that an armed attack by pro-independence forces took place on 9 November 1998 against the military post in the town of Alas, Manufahi regency.

The attackers reportedly wore Indonesian military uniforms. In the course of the attack, three military personnel and one civilian were killed. Two other military personnel were abducted and taken hostage. In addition, the attackers seized 35 rifles, a number of hand grenades, rocket-launchers and other military equipment.

A military reaction force quickly gave pursuit and killed one of the attackers and arrested five others. In the days that followed, more arrests were carried out. The tense situation caused panic and confusion among the local people, including those of neighbouring villages, many of whom fled the scene. Rumours flew about that scores of civilians had been massacred.

The local authorities, however, managed within a short time to reestablish peace and order. An ICRC delegation visited Alas from 16 to 19 November 1998 to carry out an on-the-spot investigation. They also visited those who had been arrested. Subsequently, they confirmed that allegations of a "massacre" were unfounded.

News about the Alas incident, sensationalized by the foreign news media, reached New York as the second round of the Senior Officials Meeting had just started on 19 November 1998. It caused a crisis in the talks.

On 20 November, Ambassador Neves told the meeting that in view of what was reported to be happening in Alas, he had been instructed by his Government to suspend the negotiations until "reliable information" could be obtained with regard to the reported "massacre of 50 to 70 civilians" in Alas.

A crisis averted

The Indonesian delegation deplored this unilateral suspension of the dialogue on the basis of still unverified reports and Ambassador Marker also expressed regrets at the interruption of the talks.

Only after the ICRC and the Indonesian Commission on Human Rights confirmed the Indonesian Government's information that the reports were false and after the UN Secretary-General and Ambassador Marker issued statements holding out the prospect of visits by Mr. Tamrat Samuel and Ambassador Marker to East Timor in the near future, did the Portuguese side agree to resume talks on 25 November 1998.

Discussions then continued on the draft text for East Timor's special autonomy and on a draft text of an agreement on the establishment of interests sections, which was agreed and signed by both Ministers on 27 November. It was also agreed that the next Senior Officials Meeting would be held on 28 and 29 January and from 2 to 5 February 1999, to be preceded by a meeting of a working group, which would discuss the economic provisions of the autonomy proposal.

Thus, toward the end of 1998, the negotiations on a draft constitutional framework for a special status and wide-ranging autonomy for East Timor, which were undoubtedly difficult, were nevertheless progressing at an encouraging pace.

At that time, no one among the negotiators could have imagined the bombshell that would be dropped on the tripartite talks a few weeks later.

Chapter 10
The "Second Option"

TOWARDS the end of 1998, the negotiations in New York on a draft constitutional framework for a special autonomous status for East Timor were making encouraging progress, despite inherent difficulties. The situation in East Timor itself, however, as well as reactions against the autonomy proposal by pro-independence East Timorese and their external supporters were far from reassuring.

A worsening situation

Tensions in East Timor continued to escalate. Harassments and attacks on the military, on East Timorese known to be pro-Indonesia as well as on Indonesian technical personnel assigned to the territory were reported with increasing frequency.

The rapidly deteriorating situation was marked by heightened militancy of the pro-independence groups, especially the young among them, and increasing lawlessness, obviously fueled also by the atmosphere of tumultuous reform and newfound freedom that was prevailing in the other parts of Indonesia.

Ambassador Jamsheed Marker and Mr. Francesc Vendrell had again visited Indonesia, making their way to East Timor in mid-December. When they were about to leave Dili, they were surrounded by a hostile throng of demonstrators. With the demonstrators crowding the runway, the regular Merpati Airlines plane could not land. They had to be "rescued" by military helicopter from the tarmac and flown to Kupang in West Timor.

Thus, while I was thinking and talking about a "window of opportunity," the pro-independence faction in East Timor apparently saw it as a door that they needed only to kick wide open so they could rush out into the fresh air of independence.

East Timorese opponents of integration as well as certain foreign governments and NGOs kept up a loud chorus of criticism and deprecation of the proposal for autonomy. They cast doubt on

Indonesia's sincerity in proffering it and argued that a period of autonomy could only be considered if it would be a transition to an act of self-determination.

Such criticisms, coupled with frequent international press reports of human rights violations by the Indonesian military in East Timor were not new to me and I took them in stride. To President Habibie, however, they exacerbated his growing irritation at what he perceived to be a lack of appreciation by certain Western countries of the major concessions his Government had already made.

A fateful letter

It was in this atmosphere and under these circumstances that a letter arrived from Australian Prime Minister John Howard, which in effect reversed Australia's longstanding policy on East Timor and dramatically changed the entire process towards the resolution of the East Timor question.

Although couched in cautious, diplomatic language, the essence of the letter constituted an unmistakable shift in policy as it suggested acceptance of the idea of self-determination for the people of East Timor, albeit after a delay in time.

In his letter, Prime Minister Howard first praised President Habibie's offer of autonomy for East Timor as a "bold and clear-sighted step" that had opened a window of opportunity to achieve a peaceful settlement in East Timor. He also emphasized, "Australia's support for Indonesia's sovereignty is unchanged."

But then he observed, quite unfairly I thought, that the boldness of this offer "has not been matched with the degree of progress in negotiations" and that "the UN process is not producing the desired results quickly enough."

The Prime Minister suggested two ways out of the impasse, one having to do with the approach towards a solution and the other concerning the substance.

On the approach, his advice to President Habibie was "to enter into direct negotiations with representative leaders from East Timor, including the two East Timorese bishops and Xanana Gusmao." His reasoning was that if agreement could be reached directly with the East Timorese, "then the international dimensions would take care of themselves."

On the substance, he suggested that Indonesia consider addressing the East Timorese desire for an act of self-determination in a way that would avoid an early and final decision on the future status of East Timor by "building into the autonomy package a review mechanism along the lines of the Matignon Accords in New Caledonia." (The Matignon Accords between France and the independence movement of New Caledonia provided a compromise solution in which a referendum on the final status of New Caledonia was postponed for at least ten years).

The Prime Minister's reasoning was that such an arrangement would allow time to convince the East Timorese of the benefits of autonomy within the Republic of Indonesia. It was clear from his letter that his original intention was for East Timor to remain within the Republic of Indonesia and that the purpose of his proposal was to minimize the possibility of East Timor separating from Indonesia.

The initial reaction

Prime Minister Howard's letter, dated 19 December 1998, was first sent by fax to Ambassador John McCarthy in Jakarta, with the instruction that it be presented to the President as soon as possible. Ambassador McCarthy was received by the President on 22 December 1998, but one day before that he had called on Dr. Dewi Fortuna Anwar, the President's foreign policy adviser and confidante, to deliver a copy of the faxed cable.

Upon receipt of the advance copy, President Habibie called me to his office to discuss its content. He was visibly agitated with the implications of the letter and at one point he asked me, "What are the Matignon Accords?"

After I explained them to him, he burst out, "But New Caledonia is a French colony and that was a colonial arrangement. Why does he compare us with France and East Timor with New Caledonia?"

He then went on to indicate his preliminary reactions to Howard's proposals. He rejected the idea of transitional autonomy for East Timor and of delaying the determination of its final status for a number of years.

"Why should we continue to carry the political and financial burden of governing and developing East Timor, continue to be responsible and be blamed by the world whenever something goes wrong and then, after five to ten years, only to be told by the East Timorese: 'Thank you, but we now want to be independent'?" he asked rhetorically.

He also declared that accepting a delayed timetable in determining the final status of East Timor would be irresponsible, as it would leave a time bomb for succeeding Indonesian governments.

He would subsequently convey these same reactions to Ambassador McCarthy. Seeing the mood he was in, I suggested that I draft a polite and non-committal letter of acknowledgement to the Australian Prime Minister, but he told me to wait as he would like to further study the implications of the letter. I did not hear anything about it any more for the next few weeks and, frankly, I almost forgot the whole episode.

However, the month of January 1999 witnessed a dramatic turn of events. On 4 January, the original letter of Prime Minister Howard arrived at the Australian Embassy in Jakarta and was relayed to the President's office. It was then submitted to the President on 7 January.

The arrival of the original letter apparently started a process of drastic re-thinking about its contents and ramifications among President Habibie and his circle of close advisers. What actually took place during those discussions and who exactly participated in them is until this writing a matter of conjecture and controversy. But one thing certain was that neither I as Foreign Minister nor the Ministry of Foreign Affairs was consulted.

As a result of his re-thinking, President Habibie on 21 January 1999 scrawled on the margins of the original copy of the letter his views on how best to resolve the impasse on East Timor and sent photocopies to six Cabinet Ministers.

A stunning decision

I only became aware of the existence of this disposition of the President on 25 January 1999, when I attended a regular, limited Cabinet session of Security and Political Ministers. General Wiranto, then Defence Minister and concurrently Armed Forces Commander, alerted me to it.

Before the meeting started, he asked me what I thought of the President's disposition on East Timor. Puzzled, I asked him what he meant. He then showed me a copy of Prime Minister Howard's letter with the scrawled disposition of the President on it.

It was addressed to six Cabinet Ministers: the Coordinating Minister for Political and Security Affairs, the Ministers of Foreign Affairs, Home Affairs, Defence and Justice, and the State Secretary. I checked with the other Ministers to whom the memo was addressed. Like me, they had not yet received it.

When I read the disposition, I was stunned. It was in Indonesian but if translated into English it would read as follows:

"Please analyse contents of this letter from the Prime Minister of Australia.

Please consider also, that if the question of East Timor has become a burden to the struggle and image of the Indonesian Nation and if after 22 years of common history with the Indonesian people, who proclaimed their independence 53 years ago... the people of East Timor cannot become united with us, then it would be appropriate and wise if the People's Consultative Assembly were to decide that this 27th Province of East Timor be allowed to separate honourably from the Unitary Republic of Indonesia, whose people, in fact, had the good intention to accept them in a common struggle to achieve a civil society in the coming millennium."

The text reflected President Habibie's style: impetuous, rambling, imbued with high ideals and yet unpredictable in its ramifications.

General Wiranto asked my view on whether to bring up the matter at the limited Cabinet session although it was not on its agenda and I immediately said yes, noting the extremely important implications of this development.

In the ensuing discussions, I was surprised that almost everyone reacted in such a laid-back manner to this proposed radical change in policy. Questions were asked, some doubts were raised but apart from the pertinent questions I raised, no objections were recorded.

In the end, it was agreed to "welcome the proposal," but also to discuss the issue in greater depth at the forthcoming plenary Cabinet session scheduled for 27 January 1999.

President Habibie's Conviction

Immediately after the limited political and security Cabinet meeting, I went to see President Habibie in his office. I did so without any prior arrangement, as I was eager to hear directly from him the considerations for his extraordinary proposal. I was fortunate: there were no other visitors at that time and we could have an uninterrupted discussion.

Throughout the meeting, in which I put to him a number of questions and arguments, he appeared to have quite made up his mind.

My main argument was that it was, to say the least, premature and unwarranted for Indonesia to come up with the "second option" at that point of the negotiations. I urged him to allow the ongoing tripartite talks, which focused on the proposal of special autonomy for East Timor, to run its course and, then, if and when it really bogged down, that should be the time we cross that bridge.

But he adamantly held on to the view that, given the possibility that the East Timorese pro-independence group would reject the autonomy offer, the need for an "alternative solution" was urgent and should not be postponed until a deadlock occurred. And since he totally rejected the idea of allowing a transitional autonomy for a number of years, followed by some kind of plebiscite, as suggested by Prime Minister Howard, the best way was to let the East Timorese make their choice now.

I warned him that in proposing the second option he would risk the ire and opposition of three groups in society: those East Timorese who had fought so hard for integration with Indonesia; the Armed Forces, especially the veterans among them, and those who had lost husbands, sons and relatives in the armed conflict over East Timor; and the nationalists in Indonesia and by that I meant not only the members of the Indonesian nationalist parties.

I also expressed concern that by offering the second option at this stage, it would completely overshadow the offer of special autonomy, which, I reminded him, was still being negotiated.

President Habibie, however, remained convinced of the urgent need for solving the East Timor problem before the convening of the new People's Consultative Assembly following the June 1999 general elections. He wanted to make sure that any result from the offer of the second option could be immediately reported to and approved by the Assembly.

In response to my question, he assured me that the proposed special autonomy status for East Timor within the Republic of Indonesia remained the preferred solution.

He said, however, that if the East Timorese continued to reject that option, the best and most democratic way was to let them peacefully and honourably separate from the Republic. He urged me to see the merits and positive aspects of this idea, which at any rate would be thoroughly discussed at the forthcoming full Cabinet session.

No cabinet dissent

On 27 January 1999, the Cabinet met in plenary session and, after a debate in which President Habibie allowed all the Ministers to speak, endorsed by consensus the proposed second option. In the course of the meeting, however, it became clear to me that the President had earlier secured the support of key Ministers.

Except for my presentation, in which I reiterated the views that I had already personally conveyed to the President, there were no voices of open dissent—surprisingly not even from the military members of the Cabinet.

Defence Minister Wiranto only stressed the importance of not repudiating Indonesia's policy of integrating East Timor in 1976 and the Armed Forces' military operations there, as this would render their presence and actions in the territory as illegal acts, which would have far reaching consequences on his troops. The President demanded, and received, the Cabinet's reassurance on this aspect, but Minister Wiranto did not object to the proposed second option *per se*.

State Secretary Akbar Tanjung raised some doubts, but he mostly spoke from the viewpoint of GOLKAR, the Government's political party of which he was chairman. GOLKAR had always strongly defended the Government's traditional East Timor policy. Most economic Ministers fully supported the idea of the second option, citing the serious financial and economic straits Indonesia was in.

I emphasized, and got the Cabinet's official affirmation, that the proposed special status with wide-ranging autonomy for East Timor (the first option) was still on the table and in fact remained the preferred option.

Thus, the new proposal was an alternative to the first option and did not supplant it. Accordingly, I was given the task of continuing negotiations on the draft constitutional framework for special autonomy, and at the same time to present the second option to the UN Secretary-General and to the Portuguese.

Towards the end of the session, I made a final pitch and asked for a delay in announcing the Cabinet decision. It turned out to be too late for a postponement, as the decision had already been leaked to the press.

However, the President did yield to my insistence that I would accompany the Minister for Information, General Yunus Yosfiah, at his usual press conference after the Cabinet meeting. I wanted to make sure that this new twist in Indonesia's policy on East Timor, which I was certain would bring out banner headlines in both the national and international press, was conveyed correctly in all its nuances.

The "second option" clarified

At the press conference immediately after the Cabinet session, Information Minister Yunus Yosfiah first explained the gist of the Cabinet decision on East Timor. I then seized the opportunity to clarify and stress the following points:

- The proposed "second option" did not annul Indonesia's earlier proposal to grant special status with wide-ranging autonomy to East Timor, which the Indonesian Government still considered the most realistic, viable and peaceful solution to the problem. It did constitute an alternative proposal, a second option that would be implemented in case the first proposal or first option was rejected by the East Timorese.
- The essence of the proposed "second option" was that if the autonomy proposed were to be rejected, the President would formally propose to the (then) newly elected People's Consultative Assembly (Majelis Permusyawaratan Rakyat – MPR) scheduled to convene in September 1993, for East Timor to part from Indonesia in a peaceful and honourable way. If it agreed, the MPR would rescind its 1976 Decision integrating East Timor with Indonesia and East Timor would then revert back to the UN in its status before integration, namely as a non-self governing territory awaiting decolonization.
- Thus, Indonesia was not "granting independence" to East Timor, which indeed it could not do since it was not a colonial power; however, if in the subsequent decolonization process, the people of East Timor were to opt for independence, they were, of course, welcome to do so.
- In light of this decision, the President and the Cabinet had tasked me to travel to New York and to meet with the UN Secretary-General and the Portuguese Foreign Minister in order to convey and explain Indonesia's position and to continue the tripartite negotiations.

On the same occasion, I also announced the Government's decision to move Xanana Gusmao from Cipinang prison to a house of private detention, which, in compliance with Indonesian penal law was officially designated as an "extension" of Cipinang prison. This was done in response to repeated appeals by the UN Secretary-General and in order to allow Xanana greater access to the process of the East Timor negotiations.

The press conference went reasonably well despite the fact that searching questions were posed and some Indonesian reporters even used words like "abandonment" and "betrayal."

The foreign press, however, and the governments of some Western countries like the United States, Australia, European countries and Japan welcomed the decisions, while still expressing continuing concerns over developments in East Timor itself.

On 5 February 1999, I had to repeat the same explanations before the Foreign Affairs and Security Committee of the Council of People's Representatives (*Dewan Perwakilan Rakyat*) or Parliament. At this forum, I had to answer a number of questions, both on the implications of the new policy option on East Timor as well as on Xanana Gusmao's transfer to private detention.

But again, somewhat to my surprise, the reactions were not as adverse as I had expected. Most probably, this was due to the fact that our legislators, too, at that time were preoccupied with the larger issues of the multi-faceted crisis Indonesia was facing. Or perhaps they needed more time to digest the implications of the newly proposed solution.

Surprised negotiators

The Cabinet's decision on the second option came as a surprise to both the Indonesian and Portuguese senior officials who were on their way to New York for their next round of talks, which were scheduled for 28 January to 5 February 1999. It likewise caught Ambassador Jamsheed Marker and his staff off gaurd.

In answer to the frantic calls of Director General Nugroho Wisnumurti, who received news of the latest developments upon arrival in New York, my office supplied the Indonesian delegation with all the available information by fax and telephone to enable them at least to present a preliminary briefing on Indonesia's latest proposal.

I also received an urgent phone call from Ambassador Marker, who sought confirmation as well as explanation of the fast moving developments. As I furnished him with both, I requested for an early tripartite meeting at the Ministerial level with the UN Secretary-General, which was agreed to be held on 7 and 8 February 1999.

Between 28 January and 5 February 1999, tripartite talks at the senior officials' level were held mainly to further discuss and to try to finalize the text on special autonomy for East Timor. It was also an occasion for the Indonesian delegation to give preliminary explanations regarding the important decision announced by the Indonesian Government on 27 January.

Meanwhile, the two sides exchanged information on their respective diplomatic officers who were going to be posted in the Interests Sections in Jakarta and Lisbon by the end of January, namely Mrs. Ana Martins Gomes for the Portuguese and Mr. Rezlan Jenie for the Indonesian side.

The negotiations on the draft text made good progress except for a number of still controversial issues, such as the questions of control of natural resources, jurisdiction of appeals courts, the opening of a Portuguese office in the territory and the possibility of political parties in East Timor including the goal of independence in their programmes. Both sides put these between brackets and agreed to send them up for the Foreign Ministers to resolve.

The main stumbling block, however, was the basic difference in approach, which continued to persist between the two sides, with the Indonesian delegation viewing special autonomy as being accorded to a province of Indonesia and the Portuguese side regarding it as being conferred to East Timor as a non-self governing territory, albeit with certain links to Indonesia.

UN briefed on a second option

On 7 and 8 February 1999, the tripartite talks at the ministerial level were held in New York. This gave me the opportunity to brief the UN Secretary General and his staff as well as Foreign Minister Jaime Gama and his delegation on the proposed "second option." In the process, I managed to remove whatever confusion and even suspicions that they might have had.

The meeting also discussed the draft text of the special autonomy for East Timor, which the senior officials had been able to prepare so far. This text would be an appendix to the main agreement, which would outline the basic positions of both sides regarding the overall solution of the problem. Consideration of the contents of this main agreement was also started at the meeting.

Good progress was made on the substance of the autonomy text, as the

Ministers were able to agree on most of the major outstanding issues. On the few important issues that remained, it was agreed that further consultations were to be held and for that purpose the senior officials would meet on 9 March and the Ministers would meet on 10 March 1999.

At the end of the two-day meeting, the two Foreign Ministers and the Personal Representative of the Secretary-General held a joint press conference. Mr. Kofi Annan himself could only attend the talks on Sunday, 7 February, as he had to rush to Amman, Jordan to attend the funeral of the late King Hussein.

At the joint press conference, I had to answer a number of still difficult questions. Asked whether Indonesia would allow the United Nations to conduct a referendum to ascertain the views of the East Timorese, I explained that Indonesia's basic position remained as stated before: a referendum was not the way to proceed, because that would only reopen old wounds and re-ignite old tensions and might even lead to civil war again. Indonesia had asked the UN to find a way, short of a referendum, to consult the East Timorese.

I frankly admitted that at that point, neither the UN nor the two sides knew how to achieve it, which was why it was one of the issues still being discussed.

Asked about a United Nations presence during the process, I said that when the stage was reached when the UN was organizing the consultation in implementation of what had been agreed, the UN would have to be in East Timor. At the present stage of the negotiations, however, the UN needed no permanent presence in East Timor, as UN representatives were visiting the territory regularly. Furthermore, a UN presence now would prejudge Indonesia's position on the issue under dispute.

Troubling questions

At that point, President Habibie's decision on offering the second option unfortunately raised more questions than it answered.

All of Indonesian society was abuzz with questions. For example, how would the views of the East Timorese on autonomy be assessed? Would it be by referendum or some other means? The Cabinet decision only spoke of "consulting" the East Timorese on whether they would accept or reject autonomy. How and by whom should such a consultation be conducted?

Considering the limited time frame (with the convening of the MPR session as the apparent deadline), would it be possible to complete the process? What would be the result of the process?

Troubled by these questions, it was not long thereafter that, in having to respond to these hard questions, President Habibie began to backtrack.

Chapter 11
The Negotiations Take a New Turn

IT was inevitable that once the possibility of East Timor separating from Indonesia was put on the table, the tripartite negotiations would take a different turn. Portugal's priority radically shifted from negotiating an acceptable autonomy text to securing the best possible way to carry out what it perceived to be the wishes of the East Timorese people. This could be discerned from the behaviour of the Portuguese negotiators during subsequent discussions on the autonomy model that was to be agreed upon.

What was even more frustrating to me, however, was that at the same time President Habibie and the Cabinet displayed an incomprehensible aversion to an autonomy package that would be more credible and acceptable to the Portuguese and to the world community.

To me, logically, an internationally acceptable autonomy package would be more appealing to the East Timorese and could thus hopefully still sway the majority of them to choose autonomy over separation from Indonesia. But as it turned out, President Habibie and most Ministers in the Cabinet were of an entirely different view.

A draft text for autonomy

On 8 March 1999, a plenary session of the Cabinet was held at the Bina Graha Presidential office with just one item on its agenda: a report by the Minister for Foreign Affairs to the President and the Cabinet on the draft text of the constitutional framework for a special autonomous status for East Timor.

Negotiations on the text of this document had just been completed at the Senior Officials' level and this was the first time that I would be officially presenting it to the Government. Before that, the negotiations had always been coordinated and its progress reported through a working group of the limited Cabinet of Political and Security Ministers.

I first presented a short history of the negotiations, including the development of the first and second options. Then I went into a detailed explanation of the draft text, which consisted of 9 Chapters and 69 Articles. Its main features were the following:

- The autonomous region of East Timor, to be named the "East Timor Authority" (the compromise term agreed at that stage), would be allowed self-government, except in three spheres: foreign affairs, external defense and monetary/fiscal policies, which would remain under the authority of the Central Government;
- In the field of defence, the presence and size of the Indonesian Armed Forces in East Timor would be adjusted to its task of external defence, of East Timor in particular and Indonesia in general;
- Internal security and public order in East Timor would fully be under the authority of the East Timorese police, which would be an independent force responsible to the Executive Council of East Timor;
- East Timor could have its own regional flag and coat of arms, but the national Red-and-White flag must be flown on all occasions and in all places as stipulated by law;
- The East Timorese people could establish their own local political parties and could also join the national parties;
- They could organize elections, especially for representatives to their Legislative Assembly, which would in turn elect the Chief Executive (to be named Governor or otherwise). The Chief Executive thus elected would appoint the Executive Board;
- The East Timor Authority would have its own Courts of the First Instance as well as a Court of Appeal, but the court of highest appeal would be the Indonesian Supreme Court.

A scenario for autonomy

I further explained that once the text on special autonomy for East Timor was agreed on, it would be annexed to the main agreement between Portugal and Indonesia. This main agreement would contain the basic positions of the two Governments on the projected status of special autonomy and on the process by which the views of the East Timorese people on this matter would be assessed.

I also explained that the autonomy text would be finalized and hopefully agreed upon at the next tripartite ministerial talks scheduled for 10 and 11 March 1999, which would be preceded by a meeting at senior officials level on 9 March. Afterwards, the agreed text would be conveyed and "socialized" to the East Timorese, both those residing in Indonesia and those in the diaspora.

Some time before the newly elected People's General Assembly of Indonesia would meet in early September 1999, the UN would organize a popular consultation process to determine the views of the East Timorese people on the proposed autonomy.

A presidential outburst

I then provided a detailed presentation on the articles in the draft text. I was barely at midpoint of the presentation when President Habibie, obviously agitated, interjected. "I am sorry to interrupt," he said, "but you do not have to continue. I can already see that we are headed in the wrong direction! And I think the entire Cabinet agrees with me."

He then went on to argue that the proposed autonomy package went much too far, would amount to "suicide" and lead to the "balkanization" of Indonesia, as it would surely encourage other provinces like Aceh and Irian Jaya to separate from the Unitary Republic of Indonesia.

The "autonomy plus" that he had in mind, he said, should not deviate from the basic laws and fundamental interests of Indonesia. He called the autonomy model negotiated with Portugal under the auspices of the UN Secretary-General an "exaggeration" and wrongly premised.

Neither Portugal nor the UN Secretary-General, he said, "had any right or responsibility" to determine what kind of autonomy would be given to East Timor, as Indonesia was fully entitled to propose the kind of autonomy for East Timor that was in accordance with its own national interests.

He agreed that the UN should conduct the exercise of popular consultation, but in the event the UN was not ready or prepared to do so, Indonesia would invite other countries or a group of countries to supervise the popular consultation.

The case for special autonomy

For an instant, I was completely taken aback by the abruptness and vehemence of his outburst. But I recovered quickly enough and, in as measured a tone as I could muster, I pointed out that:

- From the outset, the mandate entrusted to me as Foreign Minister was to negotiate a model of wide-ranging autonomy for East Timor that was in accordance with international standards. That meant that such an autonomy and a solution in general had to be negotiated through the UN and with Portugal, as had been done since 1983; autonomy unilaterally conceived and extended by Indonesia would not be acceptable to the international community (the UN);
- The nature of the special autonomy proposed for East Timor would by definition be different from the autonomy to be extended to the other provinces for Indonesia. The special autonomy for East Timor was designed to solve an international problem and therefore served quite a different purpose;
- Because of the two options that Indonesia had now placed on the negotiating table, it would be logical to devise a generous and credible autonomy model within the framework of the unitary Republic of Indonesia, so that it would be attractive to the East Timorese and stand a chance of being chosen as the alternative to separation from Indonesia—which would indeed be the real recipe for balkanization;
- If, notwithstanding these considerations, it was the President's and the Cabinet's wish to negotiate a revision or watering down of the text, then I as Foreign Minister and the negotiating team would do our best to carry out their wish. I stressed, however, that the President and the Government needed to be clear whether we still considered the first option as our preference or we would just go straight to the second option.

Revising the draft text

After hearing my remarks, the President calmed down and reassured me that he fully understood that the autonomy proposal needed to be negotiated through the UN and that he did not mean to present a unilateral Indonesian proposal. However, he stressed that Indonesia's basic national interests should be safeguarded and hence the text should be revised accordingly.

For that purpose, the Cabinet session decided to form a special team under the coordination of General Feisal Tanjung, the

Coordinating Minister for Political and Security Affairs and consisting of the Coordinating Ministers for Economic and Social Affairs, the Ministers of Foreign Affairs, Defense, Home Affairs and Justice and the Secretary of State to review and improve the draft text. The team did not have the luxury of time as it had to complete its work by the end of April 1999.

I was further instructed to meet with the UN Secretary-General and explain to him that Indonesia still had difficulties with some parts of the text and that an amended text would be conveyed by the end of April. I would be able to accomplish this at the trilateral ministerial meeting in New York on 10 March 1999.

Contemplating resignation

On returning to my office after the Cabinet session, I was seized by a sense of utter frustration. Indeed, I briefly contemplated tendering my resignation and discussed this possibility with some of my close collaborators.

But in the end, I was persuaded to stay on, mainly on the basis of two considerations: First, my resignation at this stage would have drawn a lot of attention and speculation in various circles in Indonesia and abroad, especially among the foreign media and I would have been portrayed as a "hardliner" opposed to the liberal policies of my President.

This would indeed be quite an unfair depiction of my role and that of the Department of Foreign Affairs after persistently seeking a peaceful compromise solution throughout all the years since 1983.

Second, a new Minister would have a hard time in taking over the negotiations, which had now reached a very sensitive, complex and critical stage.

I therefore decided to stay on if only to ensure that Indonesia would still get the best possible deal in the very difficult negotiations ahead.

A change of mind

It also became apparent that President Habibie had begun to change his mind. In the first days after January 27, he spoke on various occasions of just giving East Timor its independence if it so wanted, "so that we can concentrate our development on the other 26 provinces."

He also stressed that he wanted the East Timor issue resolved as quickly as possible, before 1 January 2000, so that "Indonesia could enter the new millennium free from historical burdens".

On one occasion, the President described East Timor as a place that had neither gold, minerals nor any other valuable natural resources; its integration with Indonesia had only offered "rocks."

But after some time, he appeared to become more aware of the ramifications and consequences of his offer of the "second option," as he also faced a mounting domestic backlash. To me and to the other ministers, he began to speak about "having to win" the popular consultation in East Timor and, indeed, of his confidence that Indonesia would come out the winner.

At least it now became easier to understand why he had rejected the model of wide-ranging autonomy that I had presented. He believed there was no chance that the East Timorese people would choose to separate from Indonesia. Hence, President Habibie and the Cabinet were more worried about a generous autonomy package becoming a precedent for other provinces than the danger of losing East Timor, which they apparently thought was hardly possible.

The UN Secretary-General convened the tripartite meeting at the Ministerial level on 10 and 11 March 1999 in New York. On that occasion, I seized the opportunity to explain the delay in the earlier scheduled wrap-up session on the autonomy text due to the March 8 Cabinet session. I also managed to discuss and clarify some important aspects of the process of popular consultation.

The case against a referendum

With regard to the methodology of assessing the views of the East Timorese people on the autonomy proposal, I stressed that the Indonesian Government would like to develop a mechanism for the popular consultation that was democratic and mutually acceptable, but "short of a referendum."

It could not be said that Indonesia did not agree to a referendum because it was afraid of its possible results, as Indonesia had already put the second option on the table. While acknowledging that theoretically a referendum would indeed be very democratic, Indonesia believed that, considering the situation prevailing in East Timor, it would be a method fraught with great risk of renewed conflict among the East Timorese factions. It would also be so much more complicated in its implementation.

I went on to explain that a full-fledged referendum would require all East Timorese, including those in the diaspora as well as the FALINTIL fighters in the hills of East Timor, to come together first, which would carry a real potential for heightened tension and friction.

Moreover, if a true referendum were to be organized by the UN, Indonesian troops would have to be withdrawn first and replaced by an adequate contingent of UN peacekeeping forces, which would inevitably take time and considerable expense to organize.

In a referendum, the qualifications of those who could take part would have to be decided on. This would be problematic and time-consuming. For example, the pro-integration East Timorese residing in East Timor could oppose the participation of those in the diaspora who have already assumed Portuguese or Australian citizenship.

It was well known that this kind of complication was being experienced in the question of the Western Sahara, where the holding of a referendum had suffered interminable delay.

Alternatives to a referendum

Because of all these considerations, I urged the UN Secretary-General and Ambassador Marker and his team to be "innovative" and to devise a methodology that would be democratic yet "short of a referendum".

In his response, Minister Gama did not go into any explanations but only stressed again that for Portugal, it was important that the method of assessing the views of the East Timorese was done in a democratic way, in accordance with the principles of a free and fair election and that it should be carried out by the United Nations. He said Portugal would then be flexible as to whatever name is given to the mechanism.

The UN Secretary-General then submitted three alternative methods for implementing the popular consultation:

- The conduct of a "sampling assessment" of the views of a number of East Timorese personalities, both those in favour of integration and those against it, in East Timor as well as in the diaspora. The decision to adopt or to reject the proposed special autonomy would be based on the results of the sampling;

- The implementation of a two-stage process: the East Timorese people would first elect a council of representatives of around 35 members; this council would then decide whether to accept or reject the proposed autonomy;
- Directly obtaining the views of the East Timorese people, both in East Timor itself and in the diaspora.

In responding to the alternative methods presented by the UN Secretary-General, I agreed with him that the first alternative would probably not be acceptable to any of the parties; it was apt to be viewed as insufficiently democratic.

As to the second alternative, even if both sides could agree on the composition of the 35 representatives, there would still be many people on both sides who would question the criteria and method of electing them.

In reacting to these first two alternatives, I was also mindful of the difficulties we had in the past in composing the group of East Timorese personalities who would represent both sides in the All-inclusive Inter East Timorese Dialogue (AIETD).

On this question of methodology for conducting the popular consultation, I was fortunate to have had the opportunity of consulting the President before my departure to New York. We both shared the view that at this stage of developments, it would be better for the consultation process to reach and involve the people at the grass-roots or village level than to rely solely on the often unstable views of small elites on both sides.

I therefore told the Secretary-General that Indonesia tended to choose a method that was close to the third alternative, as Indonesia was indeed interested in including as many East Timorese as possible in the process.

For this purpose, I suggested that two UN-led teams be formed, one to conduct the popular consultation in East Timor, the other to conduct it abroad. The details of this exercise would still have to be further discussed and agreed upon, but in this way there would be no possibility of bringing the two opposing groups together at the same place, with the risk of renewed conflict between them.

In his response, Foreign Minister Gama stated that he too tended to prefer the third alternative, although he did not foreclose the second alternative. He again stressed the need for the entire popular consultation exercise to be completed in one day and added that he could not as yet give a detailed response to the Indonesian proposals.

In the end, the third alternative was agreed in principle, but it was decided that further discussions needed to be held on the details.

Toward a UN presence in East Timor

In answering other specific questions subsequently raised by Secretary-General Kofi Annan and Ambassador Jamsheed Marker, I reassured the meeting that the UN presence in East Timor could be established immediately after agreement was reached on the autonomy package and other related documents, so as to facilitate the socialization of the agreement and the preparations for the popular consultation.

I also agreed that the UN Secretary-General and his staff could start making discreet approaches to potential donor countries in order to obtain the necessary funds and technical assistance that would be needed for the implementation of the accords. There was also general agreement that the popular consultation would be conducted after the Indonesian general elections, which were scheduled to take place on 7 June 1999.

It was decided that the next tripartite ministerial meeting would be held on 22 and 23 April 1999, to be preceded as usual by the Senior Officials meeting on 13 and 14 April 1999. It was expected that at these meetings the autonomy package, the text of the main agreements and all aspects of the popular consultation process could be finalized.

A new spate of violence

Throughout most of the month of April 1999 and up to the scheduled meeting on 22 and 23 April 1999, we in the Ministry of Foreign Affairs and the UN Secretary General and his staff were preoccupied with a spate of escalating turmoil and violence in East Timor. There were numerous reports of clashes and incidents between pro-independence groups and the Indonesian military.

The pro-integration East Timorese, who by now had recovered from their earlier shock at the presentation of the second option, had begun to organize themselves politically. They also formed various militia groups, which were now also indulging in acts of intimidation and violence.

On 6 April, some militia members clashed with a pro-independence group and their dependents who had taken refuge in the house of Rev. Rafael dos Santos, the parish priest in Liquica. The killing of a number of the refugees in that incident drew much international disapproval and widespread concern.

The UN Secretary-General issued a strong message of censure, as did several Western Governments, calling upon the Indonesian Government to take stern measures to control the militia, to allow an independent investigation into the incident and to bring those responsible to justice. The Government responded by allowing the ICRC to initiate an objective investigation.

A few days after the Liquica incident, on 17 April, a similar attack by the militia occurred in Dili, in which a number of people were killed. Among the fatalities was the adopted son of Manuel Carrascalao, brother of former Governor Mario Carrascalao.

An unexpected witness was the Foreign Minister of Ireland, Mr. David Andrews, who was visiting Dili at the time as a representative of the European Union. His subsequent report added considerably to the international outrage at the upsurge of violence in East Timor.

Neither was it helpful that in the wake of the Liquica incident, Xanana Gusmao issued from his house of detention a statement of condemnation coupled with a call for FALINTIL and his other followers in East Timor to start a "popular armed insurrection."

Neverthelessm after a few days, he softened his intemperate remarks, which were apparently prompted by the flush of indignation that was his immediate reaction to the killings. He sent a message to the UN Secretary-General reiterating his call for dialogue, reconciliation and peace.

The Liquica and Dili incidents further strengthened the perception of Indonesia's critics of military complicity with the militia and it was diffiult to fend off the resulting criticism from various Western Governments and NGOs.

"Friends of the SG"

Another development worth recounting was the establishment of a group called "Friends of the Secretary-General for East Timor." In late

February 1999, the UN Secretary-General and Ambassador Jamsheed Marker decided to establish this group, which included among its core members the UN representatives of the United States, the United Kingdom, Australia, New Zealand, Japan and Canada. The main purpose of establishing this group, as it was conveyed to me, was:

a) To obtain "material and technical" assistance for the process of consulting the East Timorese on the results of the tripartite dialogue, without having to go to the UN Security Council or the General Assembly; this group would not be involved in the political aspects of the process.
b) To forestall or pre-empt the intention of Australia at that time to propose the establishment of a "contact group" on East Timor; it was feared that such a "contact group" would create complications in the ongoing efforts under the auspices of the Secretary-General to find a solution to the East Timor question, precisely as such a "contact group" might demand to play a political role separate from that of the UN (as in the case of the contact group on Bosnia).

When Indonesia was asked its views on this idea, I gave my green light to it but on the understanding that the involvement and support of such a group of "Friends of the SG" would purely be in the technical and material/financial field.

But later I found out that Ambassador Marker and his team increasingly involved the members of the group in the substantive developments of the ongoing negotiating process. Its members regularly met and acted as informal advisers to the Secretary-General and when tensions escalated in East Timor, they were mobilized as additional channels of pressure on the Indonesian Government.

In effect, therefore, in the process of negotiations, I did not only have to face Portugal and the UN Secretary-General and his staff but also the combined exertions, albeit behind the scenes, of this group of "Friends of the SG".

Some positive developments

Apart from these depressing developments, there were also some events that, however temporarily, provided some rays of hope and basis for optimism. In mid-March, General Wiranto managed to arrange a reconciliation meeting between Joao da Silva Tavares, who was by then chosen to be the leader of the umbrella organization of the pro-integration fighting forces (*Pasukan Pejuang Integrasi, PPI*) and Xanana Gusmao.

The national and international media carried a photograph of Joao Tavares hugging Xanana Gusmao, while quoting both as declaring that fighting between their forces would end.

After the Dili incident of 17 April, through efforts initiated by the Indonesian National Commission on Human Rights with the support of General Wiranto and the Indonesian Government, an Agreement to Cease Hostilities and to Undertake Efforts to Establish Peace in East Timor was reached in Dili on 21 April 1999. The Agreement was signed by representatives of both East Timorese parties to the conflict, i.e. the CNRT (*Concelho Nacional da Resistencia Timorense*) and the pro-integration group, the leaders of the Regional Government, the Regional Military Command and the Regional Police of East Timor.

Defence Minister/Chief of the Armed Forces General Wiranto and Mr. Djoko Sugianto, Head of the National Commission on Human Rights, signed as witnesses, while the two Bishops of East Timor, Mgr. Carlos Felipe Ximenes Belo and Mgr. Basilio do Nacimento, after some vacillation, signed as observers.

The Agreement stipulated that all conflicting parties cease all forms of hostilities, intimidation and acts of terror and violence, and that they assist in efforts to establish peace, to realize reconciliation and to protect human rights. To oversee its implementation, the Agreement provided for the establishment of a Commission on Peace and Stability, with each party to the Agreement having two representatives in the Commission's membership.

When the Agreement was signed and publicized, it was hailed as a breakthrough. It turned out, however, that nothing much could be done to achieve its lofty purposes.

Progress toward acheiving agreement

Despite all these developments, however, work on the draft agreements progressed steadily. By 22 April 1999, the scheduled date of the tripartite ministerial meeting, the following drafts were ready for another round of intensive discussions: the special autonomy text as revised by Indonesia; the draft Agreement between the Republic of Indonesia and the Republic of Portugal, that would be the main agreement to which the autonomy text would be attached; the draft Agreement Regarding the Modalities for the Popular Consultation of the East Timorese through a Direct Ballot; and the draft Agreement Regarding Security Arrangements.

The tripartite ministerial meeting took place on 22 and 23 April, preceded by the preparatory Senior Officials Meeting on 21 April 1999. Although in the end the talks yielded *ad referendum* agreement on all the drafts, there were still some sensitive issues that had to be overcome.

As I expected, Foreign Minister Gama viewed the amendments to the draft autonomy text as of such a substantive nature that it rendered the revised autonomy model as an Indonesian model rather than the earlier, jointly negotiated international model. He therefore demanded that in the text of the Main Agreement, Portugal's non-endorsement of the autonomy model be explicitly stated.

I strongly objected to this demand and after a rather heated debate, agreement was reached on a compromise wording stating that "although the Governments of Indonesia and Portugal each have their positions of principle on the prepared proposal for special autonomy, both agree that it is essential to move the peace process forward . . . ."

I also rejected the original draft formulation in the main Agreement that gave the impression that Indonesia would "give independence to East Timor" in the event the proposed special autonomy was rejected by the East Timorese.

Instead, after some negotiations, agreement was reached on a formulation stating that if the proposed autonomy was not acceptable, "the Government of Indonesia shall take the constitutional steps necessary to terminate the links with East Timor, thus restoring under Indonesian law the status East Timor held prior to 17 July 1976 . . . ."Another issue that occasioned some controversy was the formulation of the questions to be put to the East Timorese to establish whether they would accept or reject the autonomy offer.

At first, the UN Secretariat proposed, in a rather detailed way, that the formulation of the consequences of a "yes" or "no" answer. I rejected this on the grounds that the questions to be put to the East Timorese should be as uncomplicated as possible and after a rather lengthy discussion, the following formulation was agreed upon:

"Do you accept the proposed special autonomy for East Timor

within the Unitary State of the Republic of Indonesia, or, Do you reject the proposed special autonomy for East Timor, leading to East Timor's separation from Indonesia?"

The question of security

The greatest difficulties arose when we discussed the draft text of the Agreement Regarding Security Arrangements. The Secretary-General at first put forward a text containing specific conditions that would have to be met so as to ensure security before balloting could begin.

These consitions included: disarming the pro-integration militia; reduction and restriction of movement of Armed Forces personnel in East Timor; cantonment of all FALINTIL forces one month before the date of the balloting; and assumption of sole responsibility for law and order in East Timor by the Indonesian police, with the assistance of a number of UN-supplied civilian police.

I strongly opposed some of those proposed conditions, as they appeared to be weighted in favour of the pro-independence side. For example, it provided for the disarming of the militia but not of FALINTIL.

Some of the conditions were unrealistic. For example, it was proposed that the Armed Forces would be restricted to specific areas. In the end, a compromise was reached which was to give the Commission on Peace and Stability, established in Dili on 21 April 1999, a greater role to play.

The Commission, in cooperation with the United Nations, would be given the responsibility "to elaborate a code of conduct for the period prior to and following the consultation, by which all parties should abide, ensure the laying down of arms and endeavour to achieve disarmament." The UN Secretary-General agreed not to insist on his list of additional security measures and I agreed to inform President Habibie and the Cabinet informally on this matter.

An unwarranted letter

I was therefore greatly surprised to learn that Secretary-General Annan had directly sent a letter dated 30 April 1999 to President Habibie, again referring to the security conditions which he claimed were "the usual requirements in UN operations of the kind which we are about to initiate, particularly in connection with the Agreement Regarding Security Arrangements."

He further stated, that these security conditions were "*t*he main elements that will need to be in place in order to enable me to decide (as provided for in paragraph 3 of that Agreement) whether or not the necessary security conditions exist for the start of the operational phases of consultation process".

I immediately rang Ambassador Marker in New York and reminded him of the earlier understanding reached on the matter. As usual, he sounded sympathetic to my protest; I thought, however, that he and his collaborators must have had a hand in the drafting of the letter. In the end, we agreed that I would return the letter to the UN Secretariat with the understanding that it would be regarded as not having been sent.

I was aware that the Secretary-General and his team of negotiators at that stage were under strong pressure from Portugal and other Western Governments because of what they viewed as a weak and unsatisfactory text of the Agreement Regarding Security Arrangements. But at this point, I too was under strict instructions not to make any further concessions on issues regarding security as this had become a sensitive issue in the prevailing political situation in Indonesia.

An Australian Effort

Prime Minister Howard of Australia also put in a special effort on this issue. At his request, a meeting was arranged between him and President Habibie in Bali on 27 April 1999.

On that occasion, Prime Minister Howard proposed, both at his private meeting with the President and at a plenary meeting attended by officials on both sides, that Indonesia allow an international peacekeeping force to be stationed in East Timor before the act of popular consultations in order to improve the security situation.

President Habibie rejected this idea with great indignation, saying that if he were to agree to have foreign troops on Indonesian soil even before the result of the balloting, his position would become untenable.

But he softened his stance on other aspects and agreed, among other things, to allow the UN to send up to 300 civilian police advisers. He also agreed to Australia setting up a consulate in Dili.

Agreements reached

At first, the UN Secretary-General proposed 12 September 1999 as the date for carrying out the popular consultation, both in East Timor and certain cities in Indonesia where many East Timorese students and workers were known to reside, as well as certain cities abroad.

However, I had to reject that date because in the national schedule, the newly elected People's Consultative Assembly (*MPR*) would be starting its first session in the first week of September and President Habibie had insisted on being able to report the results of the popular consultation on East Timor to the Assembly.

With great reluctance, the UN Secretariat agreed to 8 August 1999 as the date for the political exercise. But this date also proved to be unfeasible later and twice it had to be postponed.

Finally, after two days of intensive discussions, an *ad referendum* agreement was reached on all the draft Agreements. It was decided that the two Foreign Ministers would seek to obtain the approval of their respective Governments and return to New York on 5 May 1999 for the official signing of the Agreements.

On 3 May 1999, the Cabinet in a plenary session unanimously approved the draft Agreements on East Timor. The stage was thus set for the next milestone in the East Timor saga.

Chapter 12
The 5 May 1999 Agreements and The Establishment of UNAMET

THE FORMAL signing of the Agreements on East Timor, earlier reached *ad referendum* by the two Foreign Ministers, was expected to take place at the Tripartite Ministerial Meetings on 4 and 5 May 1999. However, it turned out that there were still complications which had to be resolved before the Meeting could begin on an agreeable note.

Obstacles

Foreign Minister Gama began by raising the security situation in East Timor, citing reports of threats by militia forces to kill pro-independence personalities, including Aniceto Guterres Lopes, whose house had been assaulted and ransacked. The Foreign Minister demanded greater security assurances and reiterated Portugal's hope that Xanana Gusmao be released.

Meanwhile, Secretary-General Kofi Annan again raised, in a slightly revised version, the security preconditions he had conveyed in his letter to President Habibie, this time in the form of a memorandum addressed to both Ministers.

He listed eight "elements" that should be in place for him to be able to determine that the necessary security conditions existed for the start of the operational phases of the consultation process.

These included the bringing of armed civilian groups under strict control and discipline; an immediate ban on rallies by armed groups; the prompt arrest and prosecution of those who incite or threaten to use violence against others; redeployment of Indonesian military forces; assumption by the Indonesian police of sole responsibility for the maintenance of law and order; the immediate institution of a process of laying down of arms by all armed groups well in advance of the holding of the ballot; and full participation of the UN in the Commission on Peace and Stability, which should be the forum for smoothing friction and resolving disputes on the ground. The Secretary-

General subsequently referred to these points in his report to the Security Council.

I conveyed Indonesia's position to Foreign Minister Gama and provided him with assurances on these issues. As to the Memorandum of the Secretary-General, I again reiterated Indonesia's objections to specific elements while expressing surprise that the Secretary-General had brought them up again in spite of earlier understandings. After some discussion on its contents, the Meeting agreed to treat the Memorandum as a document for "internal reference" only.

During the final discussions on the texts of the draft Agreements, some minor changes and improvements still had to be negotiated and agreed upon. For example, in the Agreement Regarding Security Arrangements, Foreign Minister Gama proposed, and the Meeting eventually agreed, to change the word "endeavour" in the reference towards achieving disarmament and to strengthen it so as to read "take the necessary steps."

In the discussions on the Agreement Regarding the Modalities for the Popular Consultation, specifically with regard to campaigning, the text originally banned all government officials of Indonesia and Portugal from participating in a campaign in support of either option. I pointed out that such a ban should not include the East Timorese officials working in the regional government, as they, like the rest of the East Timorese, had a basic right to do so.

After lengthy arguments, the Meeting agreed that "East Timorese government officials may campaign in their personal capacity. All such campaigning will be carried out strictly according to the Code of Conduct, without use of public funds and government resources or recourse to pressure of office."

Finally, the three Agreements were signed on the afternoon of 5 May 1999, in a ceremony at the UN Press Center in New York, by the Foreign Ministers of Portugal and Indonesia as well as by the UN Secretary-General.

The Main Agreement

The preamble of the "Agreement between the Republic of Indonesia and the Portuguese Republic on the Question of East Timor," the Preamble summarized the positions of each side with regard to the proposed special autonomy for East Timor as follows:

Article 1 of the main Agreement requested the Secretary-General "to put the attached proposed Constitutional Framework providing for a Special Autonomy for East Timor within the Unitary Republic of Indonesia to the East Timorese people, both inside and outside East Timor for their consideration and acceptance or rejection through a popular consultation on the basis of a direct, secret and universal ballot".

Article 2 of the main Agreement requested that the Secretary-General ". . . establish, immediately after the signing of this Agreement, an appropriate United Nations mission in East Timor to enable him to effectively carry out the popular consultation."

Article 5 and 6 of the main Agreement stipulated the actions that the Governments of Portugal and Indonesia had to take, on the basis of the Secretary-General's determination of the results of the popular consultation. In the event of acceptance of the autonomy proposal by the East Timorese people (Article 5), "the Government of Indonesia shall initiate the constitutional measures necessary for the implementation of the constitutional framework, and the Government of Portugal shall initiate within the United Nations the procedures necessary for the removal of East Timor from the list of Non-Self-Governing Territories of the General Assembly and the deletion of the question of East Timor from the agendas of the Security Council and the General Assembly."

In the event of rejection of the autonomy proposal (Article 6), "the Government of Indonesia shall take the constitutional steps necessary to terminate its links with East Timor, thus restoring under Indonesian law the status East Timor held prior to 17 July 1976, and the Governments of Indonesia and Portugal and the Secretary-General shall agree on arrangements for a peaceful and orderly transfer of authority in East Timor to the United Nations. The Secretary-General shall, subject to the appropriate legislative mandate, initiate the procedure enabling East Timor to begin a process of transition towards independence."

Article 7 of the main Agreement requested the Secretary-General "to maintain an adequate United Nations presence during the interim period between the conclusion of the popular consultation and the start of the implementation of either option".

To this main Agreement, a document entitled "A Constitutional Framework for a Special Autonomy for East Timor" was annexed. As earlier mentioned, it was a watered down version based on amendments that had been made as a consequence of the 8 March Cabinet decision.

Inevitably, it became even less attractive to the East Timorese, thus adding to the advantage of the "second option".

The Agreement on Modalities

The second Agreement, entitled "Agreement regarding the Modalities for the Popular Consultation of the East Timorese through a Direct Ballot," set out the arrangements for the implementation of the popular consultation process.

It established 8 August 1999 as the date for the balloting and that the questions to be put to the East Timorese were these:

"Do you accept the proposed special autonomy for East Timor within the Unitary State of the Republic of Indonesia?"or "Do you reject the proposed special autonomy for East Timor, leading to East Timor's separation from Indonesia?"

The United Nations logo would appear on the ballot papers, which would also include symbols for each of the questions to facilitate voting by illiterate persons.

In order to avoid lengthy and complicated debates, the question of vote entitlement was defined in a way that was as simple and as free from controversy as possible. Thus, the minimum age was set at 17 years of age and eligibility was extended to persons born in East Timor, to persons born outside East Timor but with at least one parent born in East Timor and to persons whose spouses fell under either of these two categories.

The Agreement further provided an approximate schedule for the operational stages of the consultation process, starting from 10 May to 8 August 1999, covering the public information programme, registration and the political campaign. As it turned out later, these dates had to be changed and adjusted several times in the following days and weeks.

In the context of the information campaign, the United Nations would make available the texts of the main Agreement and the autonomy document in four languages: Tetum, Bahasa Indonesia, Portuguese and English, and widely disseminate and explain those texts in an impartial and factual manner inside and outside East Timor.

Registration inside and outside East Timor would take place for a continuous period of 20 days. For this purpose, two hundred registration centers would be opened in East Timor. Outside East Timor, special registration centers would be opened in Jakarta, Yogyakarta, Surabaya, Denpasar, Ujung Pandang, Sydney, Darwin, Perth, Melbourne, Lisbon, Maputo, Macau and New York, with adjustments to be made as appropriate.

In the context of the political campaign, it was agreed that the United Nations would devise a Code of Conduct and ensure equal opportunity to both supporters and opponents of the autonomy proposal. As earlier recounted, officials of the Governments of Portugal and Indonesia were forbidden from participating in the campaign, but East Timorese officials could do so in their personal capacity.

Balloting in East Timor would take place in some 700 polling stations located in the 200 polling centers. Balloting outside East Timor would take place in polling stations set up in the same locations as the registration centers.

Portugal and Indonesia would be entitled to send an equal number of observers to all the operational phases of the consultation process, both inside and outside East Timor. International observers would also be allowed to closely monitor the consultation process.

Additionally, the Secretary-General decided to appoint an independent Electoral Commission, consisting of three international jurists: Judge Johann Christiaan Kriegler of South Africa, chairman; Mr. Patrick Bradley (former Chief Electoral Officer for Northern Ireland) and Dr. Bong-Scuk Sohn (Commissioner of the National Electoral Commission of the Republic of Korea), members.

The Commission's functions and tasks included resolving all electoral complaints and disputes and certifying the final results of the popular consultations.

As to funding, the Secretary-General would seek the approval of the Security Council for the operation in order to ensure assessed budgetary funding. Voluntary contributions would be channeled through a trust fund established for the purpose.

The final paragraph of this Agreement stipulated that "The Indonesian authorities will ensure a secure environment for a free and fair popular consultation process and will be responsible for the security of the United Nations personnel. A number of UN security guards will be deployed to ensure the security and safety of United Nations personnel and property."

The Agreement on Security

The third Agreement, entitled "East Timor Popular Consultation—Agreement Regarding Security," dealt exclusively with the security aspect. Though it contained only four paragraphs and thus was the shortest of the three agreements, it had been the focus of the most contentious discussion and was the most strenuously negotiated text.

I was aware that during the negotiations and afterwards, the Secretary-General, Ambassador Marker and their team of collaborators came under heavy pressure and criticism not only by the Portuguese Government and the pro-independence East Timorese and their NGO lobby, but also by various other Western governments that considered the substance of this third Agreement as both toothless and overly pro-Indonesian.

They especially lamented the fact that the responsibility for ensuring "a secure environment devoid of violence or other forms of intimidation" as well as "the general maintenance of law of order" was entrusted to the appropriate Indonesian security authorities. Some of those critics had pushed for the stationing of a UN Peacekeeping Force instead.

But they were not the only ones under pressure. I too went into the negotiations on this issue carrying an extremely rigid and narrow brief. The idea of allowing foreign troops onto Indonesian soil at this stage of the East Timor negotiations was anathema not only to President Habibie and the Government but also to the general Indonesian public. In short, the Indonesian responsibility for security during the popular consultative process was non-negotiable.

However, the compromises agreed upon and stipulated in the Agreement Regarding Security included did give the Commission on Peace and Stability (established in Dili on 21 April 1999) a greater operational role. As stated in paragraph 2 of the Agreement, the Commission, "in cooperation with the United Nations, will elaborate a Code of Conduct, by which all parties should abide, for the period prior to and following the consultation, ensure the laying down of arms and take the necessary steps to achieve disarmament."

Paragraph 4 of the Agreement also emphasized that "The police will be solely responsible for the maintenance of law and order. The Secretary-General…will make available a number of civilian police officers to act as advisers to the Indonesian Police in the discharge of their duties and, at the time of the consultation, to supervise the escort of ballot papers and boxes to and from the polling sites."

Paragraph 3 of the Agreement laid down a stipulation, which later turned out to be a source of controversy between the United Nations Secretariat and Indonesia. At the insistence of the United Nations negotiators, it was stated in that paragraph that "Prior to the start of the registration, the Secretary-General shall ascertain, based on the objective evaluation of the UN Mission, that the necessary security situation exists for the peaceful implementation of the consultation process."

A historic moment

In his remarks at the signing ceremony, Secretary-General Kofi Annan described the occasion as a "historic moment" and expressed the hope that it would start a new and more peaceful chapter in the history of East Timor. In our statements at the ceremony, Foreign Minister Gama and I acknowledged the historic importance of the occasion, while assuring the full support of our respective Governments for the implementation of the Agreements.

As an immediate follow-up, the Secretary-General, in his report to the Security Council and the General Assembly dated 5 May 1999, officially presented the substance of the Agreements and on 6 May 1999, Ambassador Jamsheed Marker, gave a similar oral report to the Security Council.

On both occasions, the Secretary-General and Ambassador Marker, in referring to the "high level of tension and serious incidents of political violence" in East Timor, again mentioned and enumerated the "main elements that would need to be in place in order to enable the Secretary-General to determine that the necessary security conditions exist for the start of the operational phases of the consultation process."

I had the strong impression that, having failed to obtain the official acceptance of these preconditions from the Indonesian Government, they were eager to show to the international public that they had at least tried to establish them and that the message had been conveyed to Indonesia.

The Security Council also swiftly responded to the new developments and on 7 May 1999, adopted Resolution 1236 (1999).

In that Resolution, the Council welcomed the conclusion of the 5 May Agreements on East Timor and the intention of the Secretary-General to establish a United Nations presence in East Timor to assist in the implementation of these Agreements, in particular by conducting a popular consultation of the East Timorese people and making available a number of civilian police officers to act as advisers to the Indonesian Police.

It also welcomed the establishment by the Secretary-General of a trust fund to enable member states to make voluntary contributions.

Further, Resolution 1236 (1999) specifically requested the Secretary-General to keep the Security Council closely informed of the situation in East Timor and to report to the Council by 24 May 1999 on the implementation of this resolution and on the Agreements, specifying the detailed modalities of the consultation process, and after that to report to the Council every fourteen days.

This was generally viewed as an overrly tight reporting schedule imposed on the Secretary-General, but given the tense and fluid situation in East Timor, it could well be that this schedule had been suggested by the UN Secretariat itself in order to keep as informed as possible about ant untoward developments.

After the adoption of this resolution, the Secretary-General and his staff as well as the Security Council immediately commenced work on its implementation, particularly the determination of the size, structure, mandate and budget of the United Nations Mission in East Timor, including the civilian police advisers.

As a first step, the Secretary-General dispatched an assessment team that visited East Timor from 5 to 15 May to gather the necessary information on the political and security situation and the facilities available in Dili and elsewhere for the establishment of the UN Mission, and all other information necessary for the Secretariat to be able to draw up a detailed operational plan for the consultation process.

Then the Secretary-General nominated a British national, Mr. Ian Martin, former Secretary-General of Amnesty International and Deputy High Representative for human rights in Bosnia, as Special Representative of the Secretary-General to head the United Nations Mission in East Timor, which would be better known by its acronym, UNAMET.

I had known Mr. Ian Martin since the days when he was still Secretary-General of Amnesty International and I was Ambassador to the UN in Geneva. In that position, he had been critical of Indonesian human rights policies but I had always found him to be a reasonable person to deal with. I therefore had no difficulty giving clearance for his appointment at the request of Ambassador Marker.

Later on, however, I would be criticized by some of my colleagues for agreeing so readily to someone who had previously been Secretary-General of Amnesty International.

Indonesia does its part

The Indonesian Government, too, was quick in preparing for the implementation of the Agreements, setting up by Presidential Decision No.43/1999, dated 18 May 1999, a *Special Ministerial Team to Ensure the Implementation of the Agreements between Indonesia and Portugal on East Timor.* This team, to be under the direct supervision of the President, was chaired by the Coordinating Minister for Political and Security Affairs, General Feisal Tanjung, and its membership consisted of: the Ministers for Foreign Affairs, Interior, Justice and Defence, the State Secretary, the Chief of Police and the Chairman of the State Intelligence Coordinating Board.

The Secretary of the Coordinating Minister for Political and Security Affairs was designated as Secretary to the Team. Among the tasks of this Special Ministerial Team would be to ensure the "secure and just" implementation of the Agreements between Portugal and Indonesia on East Timor, and to coordinate with relevant agencies in the country as well as with international institutions and bodies abroad.

The team was based in Jakarta, at the office of the Coordinating Minister for Political and Security Affairs, and was supported by a small staff (*Staf Khusus*).

In Dili, at the behest of the Department of Foreign Affairs, the Team set up a Task Force to act as liaison between the UNAMET and the local government and the security apparatus, and generally to be of assistance in the orderly and peaceful implementation of the popular consultation in East Timor.

This Task Force (*Satgas Pelaksanaan Penentuan Pendapat di Timor Timur – SATGAS P3TT)* was headed by Ambassador Agus Tarmidzi, a retired career diplomat backed up by a number of staff officials from various Departments including Foreign Affairs, Defence, Interior, Information and Health. The Armed Forces Command attached Major General Zaki Anwar Makarim, Head of ABRI Intelligence, to the SATGAS P3TT, to act as its own "eyes and ears" on the ground.

The Task Force was deployed in East Timor on 1 June 1999.

The Bali briefings

On 15 and 16 May 1999, I organized a meeting in Bali with leading representatives of pro-integration as well as anti-integration East Timorese groups in order to personally brief them on the 5 May Agreements and their implications.

This was the second meeting of its kind, as from 15 to 17 October 1998, I held a similar "socialization" meeting with East Timorese personalities after the Indonesian compromise proposal to grant special autonomy to East Timor. That first meeting came to be known as the Bali-I Meeting.

This second briefing, or Bali-II Meeting, was attended by 58 East Timorese participants, 33 pro-integration leaders and activists and 25 anti-integration personalities. Also present were the Governor of East Timor, Mr. Abilio Soares; the Speaker of the East Timorese regional Council of Representatives, Mr. Armindo Mariano Soares; Mr. Lopes da Cruz, Ambassador-at-Large for Special Affairs; Major General Adam Damiri, the Udayana Military Region Commander; Colonel Tono Suratman, the Military Commander of East Timor, and Colonel Timbul Silaen, Chief of Police of East Timor.

On both days of the meeting, first separately and then in a joint session with both proponents and opponents of special autonomy, I explained and discussed the detailed aspects of the 5 May Agreements and the requirements for their peaceful and fair implementation. On the surface at least, the sessions proceeded in an encouragingly friendly atmosphere.

In a special meeting with some of the pro-integration political and militia leaders, including Joao Tavares and Eurico Guterres, with military and police commanders also in attendance, I urged them to adopt a peaceful and persuasive approach. I stressed that any attempt to pressure the East Timorese people into opting for autonomy through bullying, intimidation and wanton violence would be totally counterproductive. Furthermore, I said, such crude tactics would reflect negatively on Indonesia and its security apparatus, which would be held responsible for peace, law and order. They all listened attentively, but even then I was not sure that they would heed my exhortations.

Forming UNAMET

UNAMET was formally established by the Security Council only on 11 June 1999 though an advance group had already arrived in East Timor in May, immediately after the signing of the Agreements, looking for space to serve as headquarters and preparing for the influx of the larger UN contingent.

In pursuance of Security Council Resolution 1236 (1999), the Secretary-General submitted his report to the Council on the implementation of that resolution and of the 5 May Agreements on 24 May. This report, which was to become the main input for the subsequent Security Council resolution, also drew heavily on the findings of the UN assessment team to East Timor with regard to the political and security situation on the ground and the facilities available.

In his report, the Secretary-General formally proposed the establishment of the United Nations Mission in East Timor (UNAMET) to organize and conduct a popular consultation in order to ascertain whether the East Timorese people would accept or reject the proposed constitutional framework providing for special autonomy for East Timor within the Unitary Republic of Indonesia.

The Secretary-General also reported on his appointment of Mr. Ian Martin as Special Representative for the East Timor Popular Consultation and as Head of UNAMET. Ambassador Jamsheed Marker would continue to serve as his Personal Representative for East Timor.

UNAMET would include political, electoral, civilian police, information and administrative/financial components. In addition, it would include a small component to monitor human rights and humanitarian developments and to advise the Special Representative on these issues.

At full deployment, the UNAMET would have 241 international staff members, 420 United Nations Volunteers, up to 280 civilian police and around 4,000 local staff. The UNAMET would have its headquarters in Dili and its personnel would be deployed in seven regional centers.

The UNAMET would include a political component, headed by a Chief Political Officer and 15 political officers, who would be deployed in each of the Mission's regional centers. Subsequently, Mr. Beng Yong Chew of Singapore was appointed Chief Political Officer.

In addition, a Senior Political Officer would be posted in Jakarta to serve as liaison with the Indonesian authorities. Mr. Tamrat Samuel, who had already been dealing with the East Timor issue for quite some time, was given this task. The political component would monitor and advise the Special Representative on all matters that had political implications for the effective, free and fair holding of the popular consultation.

The electoral component would be responsible for all activities related to registration and voting. It would be headed by a Chief Electoral Officer and complemented by 16 regional staff. Mr. Jeffrey Fisher was subsequently appointed as Chief Electoral Officer. An additional 400 polling officers would be provided and recruited from the UN Volunteers.

Polling outside East Timor would be conducted and coordinated on behalf of the UN by the International Organization for Migration (IOM) and, for Australia, by the Australian Election Commission. For purposes of the popular consultation, East Timor would be divided into eight regional centres within which there would be 200 registration centres sub-divided into 700 polling stations.

UNAMET would also include an information component to explain to the East Timorese people the terms of the Agreements and the autonomy proposal, the process and procedures of the balloting etc. The information campaign would be conducted in an impartial manner, without prejudice to any position or outcome.

A total of up to 280 civilian police officers would be deployed in Dili, the eight electoral districts and the 200 registration/polling centres. As the head of the civilian police component, a Police Commissioner would be appointed from among Member States contributing police personnel. In due time, Mr. Alan J. Mills of the Australian Federal Police was named to the job.

Military liaison officers

In his report, the Secretary-General also mentioned his intention, "given the important role played by the Indonesian Armed Forces in East Timor," to assign a number of military liaison officers (MLOs). Their primary task would be to liaise with the Indonesian military, both in Dili and in the 13 districts of East Timor and, in cooperation with the UN civilian police, also assist the Special Representative on security matters. This additional issue was not discussed in the talks leading towards the 5 May Agreements and thus became the subject of intensive negotiations.

Reactions by President Habibie and the military against this additional request were not as strong as I had expected. Subject to some conditions, such as that the Liaison Officers would liaise only with the Indonesian Armed Forces and not with FALINTIL, nor bear arms etc., they were willing to accommodate the Secretary-General.

At first, the UN Secretariat asked for 80 MLOs to be posted in the territory. Finally, a compromise of 50 MLOs was agreed upon. In due course, Brigadier Rezaqul Haider of Bangladesh was appointed as Chief Military Liaison Officer.

Further, the Indonesian Government acceded to an additional request by the UN Secretariat to attach a number of military medical personnel to UNAMET to run an emergency medical unit for the Mission's personnel.

On 11 June 1999, a draft resolution was tabled on the Security Council, mainly based on the Secretary-General's report and on the subsequent negotiations on the draft text among its members, in which Indonesia was also consulted. Unanimously adopted on the same day, Resolution 1246/1999 officially established the UNAMET, including all its components, as well as the modalities for the implementation of the consultation process.

In fact, the UNAMET had already been at work well ahead of its official establishment. It began operations in East Timor on 3 June 1999 when its headquarters in Dili were inaugurated.

Chapter 13
The Rocky Road Towards the Ballot

As I had feared, the implementation phase of the historic East Timor Agreements proved to be a period of increasing turmoil and tensions and of seemingly unending dilemmas and difficulties. The complications that arose in the implementation process were brought about not only by the very tight time schedules that the Agreements imposed on UNAMET but also by the progressively deteriorating security situation. For me personally, it turned out to be one of the most trying periods of my diplomatic career.

Militia violence

The deployment of UN personnel and the presence of the UNAMET Headquarters in Dili did result in an improvement in the security situation in the capital and in East Timor's second largest city, Baucau.

It was starkly different, however, in the other parts of the province, where a climate of tension, intimidation and violence continued to prevail. Acts of violence by the pro-integration militias were matched by those by FALINTIL and pro-independence elements.

Briefing the Security Council on 16 June 1999, Ambassador Jamsheed Marker reported that, outside Dili and Baucau, "the security situation remains a serious impediment to a credible and fair popular consultation," as, according to UNAMET reports "pro-autonomy militias have been very active, particularly in the West."

He also reported that "thousands of East Timorese are internally displaced by militia violence and in some cases their humanitarian needs have gone unmet because access to them by humanitarian agencies has been blocked." The number of internally displaced persons (IDPs) was at that time estimated at around 40,000.

Based on this and other reports from East Timor, allegations of Indonesian military involvement, or at least of rogue military elements, in the actions of the armed militia groups were increasingly being voiced, not only by certain NGOs, the foreign press and some Western governments but also by the UN authorities in their official reports as well as in private conversations.

My colleagues and I at the Department of Foreign Affairs had an increasingly hard time trying to refute these allegations.

For example, in a letter to the Indonesian Government on 12 May 1999, Ambassador Marker claimed that "the militias are being allowed to carry out their undesirable activities without restraint" and that "the TNI (the Indonesian military) is fully capable of controlling the violence if it seriously wished to do so."

The Secretary-General, in his report to the Security Council on 22 June 1999, made the same allegation, stating that "*the* pro-integration militias, believed by many observers to be operating with the acquiescence of elements of the army, carry out acts of violence and intimidation."

Towards the end of June and the beginning of July 1999, three violent incidents involving UNAMET occurred in three places in East Timor. They took place successively within a period of one week and drew widespread criticism from several Western governments and urgent protests from the Secretary-General and his staff.

The Maliana Incident

On 29 June 1999, fighting broke out between pro-integration and pro-independence groups in front of the UNAMET office in Maliana, Bobonaro district, which spilled over into the UNAMET premises. Unfortunately, as often happened after incidents of this kind in East Timor, UNAMET and Indonesian sources gave different versions as to what exactly happened.

According to the report from the Indonesian Task Force in Dili, the brawl that erupted between the two groups of East Timorese first started as a heated exchange of political slogans and insults and was followed by a stone-throwing match. While the two groups were hurling stones at each other, the pro-independence group ran for cover into the UNAMET compound, with the result that the stones thrown by the pursuing pro-integration militia landed on the UNAMET building, hitting some of its occupants.

However, the attack on the UNAMET building lasted only for a brief period as the Indonesian police soon arrived on the scene, broke up the crowd and seized control of the situation. Regrettably, one UNAMET staff member, a woman District Electoral Officer from South Africa, suffered a minor injury to her leg, several Timorese suffered head and other injuries and the UNAMET office was damaged.

Thus, from the view of the Indonesian Task Force, UNAMET was clearly the unintended victim in this incident rather than the intended target.

According to the UNAMET version, however, the incident was a deliberate attack on UNAMET property and personnel as well as on those who took refuge in the UNAMET premises, and not a brawl that incidentally spilled over into the compound. Hence, the pro-integration group was regarded as having committed a grave criminal offence.

In its report, UNAMET also blamed the local police for failing to take adequate steps to prevent the incident, in spite of earlier warnings by UNAMET of a planned attack, and failing to take effective measures to stop the attack while it was underway.

The report also claimed that "the passive attitude of the police toward the perpetrators of the attack strongly suggests that the latter are under the control of, and protected by, authorities over whom the police have no effective power" and that "the militia group, Dadurus Merah Putih (DMP), which carried out the attack appears to be supported and controlled by officers of the District Military Command (KODAM)".

The Maliana incident evoked a strong statement from the UN Secretary-General who unsurprisingly based his reaction on the UNAMET version of what took place. Through his spokesman, he deplored "in the strongest possible terms today's attack on the Maliana regional office of UNAMET. The Secretary-General holds the Indonesian Government accountable for allowing such an attack to occur and deems any assault on UNAMET personnel or property completely unacceptable" and as "acts of provocation and vandalism."

The Viqueque Incident

A similar controversy arose about an incident in Viqueque town, which took place on 30 June 1999. A group of pro-integrationists staged a demonstration in front of the UNAMET building, demanding that UNAMET locate the body of one of their group, a certain Duarte Guterres, who reportedly had been killed the day before in the neighbouring village of Waimuri.

The demonstrators sent an ultimatum to the UNAMET that if it failed to locate the body of Guterres by 2:00 p.m. that day, they would expel UNAMET from Viqueque.

This clearly reprehensible attitude was condemned by the Indonesian authorities. But it was apparently provoked by a perception that the UNAMET was partial to the pro-independence group, for when a pro-independence individual was killed a few days earlier, the UNAMET went to great lengths and trouble to retrieve the body, while they did nothing of the sort in the Guterres case.

Fortunately, the demonstrators dispersed peacefully after venting their anger with mere threats. There were no casualties or further disturbances. Nevertheless, UNAMET took the threats seriously and temporarily evacuated their personnel from Viqueque.

The Liquica Incident

The third incident occured in Liquica on 4 July 1999 and again involved UNAMET and its personnel. This incident created a louder outcry and as usual, there were very different versions of what had happened.

On the afternoon of 4 July, a group of militia physically assaulted a convoy consisting of two UNAMET cars carrying UNAMET personnel and six other cars carrying volunteers from a number of NGOs.

The convoy was passing through Liquica on its way back to Dili from a humanitarian relief operation; it had been distributing food and medicine to internally displaced persons in a village south of Maubara.

According to the Indonesian version, the convoy was indeed stopped by the militia. Some of the convoy members were injured and car windows were smashed. The Indonesian police arrived almost immediately on the scene and prevented any further violence. The Indonesian Government soon thereafter issued a formal statement expressing serious concern. It deplored the attack and promised to bring those responsible to justice.

However, in its statement, the Government linked this incident to the shooting on the previous day of a group of pro-integration people who were on their way to harvest coffee in the nearby hills.

A band of anti-integration gunmen ambushed this group, with the result that one man, Paul da Costa, was shot dead. Two others were injured but managed to escape, leaving behind the body of da Costa.

The next day, a police patrol attempted to retrieve the body from the scene of the shooting, but they too were shot at by gunmen. The body of da Costa was never found. The Government likewise condemned the murder and its view was that the the da Costa killing had provoked the pro-integration community in Liquica to attack the convoy.

UNAMET's version of the Liquica incident was substantially different. It focused on how the militia fired their weapons, threatened two UNAMET staff and several NGO workers and beat up one of the drivers. UNAMET also claimed that rocks were thrown and shots fired at a helicopter that was subsequently sent to Liquica to evacuate UNAMET personnel.

Western governments and UN protests came swiftly. They deplored the attack and again accused the police of an "inexcusable lack of action."

Minimal Response

In several letters and reports that I wrote to the President and relevant colleagues in the Cabinet, I repeatedly urged that the competent authorities immediately put a stop to the destructive and wholly counterproductive activities of the militia groups.

I also stressed the necessity of guaranteeing the safety of anti-integration personalities, especially Mr. Leandro Isaac and Mr. David Ximenes, who were members of the Peace and Stability Commission, so as to enable them to participate freely in all activities related to the popular consultation process.

Most unfortunately, however, there was minimal concrete response to my pleas and I was left with a growing feeling of despair at the prospect of losing the forthcoming ballot primarily because of the negative effects of the completely misguided acts of intimidation and violence inflicted upon the East Timorese population in the effort to ensure that they opted for autonomy.

Reacting to the mounting international clamour, President Habibie sent a high-level delegation of several Cabinet Ministers and senior officials to East Timor. It was led by Coordinating Minister Feisal Tanjung and including General Wiranto and myself. The mission's aim was to assess the situation and reassure UNAMET, and the public at large, of Indonesia's strong commitment to ensuring peace and security in East Timor.

Though the Ministerial visit did not put an end to militia activity, it was an encouraging gesture and to some extent it had a calming effect on the situation. On 7 August, a similarly high-powered delegation was sent to East Timor for the second time.

More complications

In this atmosphere of tension and recurrent violence, Ramos Horta issued a decidedly unhelpful statement on 12 June that he intended to visit East Timor and begin campaigning. He planned to fly directly from Darwin, with or without the consent of the Indonesian Government.

This was clearly a breach of the letter and spirit of the May 5 Agreements. Indonesia had clearly objected to a full-fledged referendum and all parties had agreed to first have two separate popular consultations, one in East Timor itself and the other in the Timorese diaspora before campaigning could begin.

To make matters worse, David Wimhurst, spokesman for UNAMET, gave a statement to the press claiming that it would be compatible with the May 5 Agreements for Ramos Horta to visit East Timor to do so.

The next day, 13 June 1999, the Government issued a sharp statement rejecting the views expressed by both parties and warning Ramos Horta not to try to enter East Timor without an Indonesian visa, which even UNAMET personnel were required to obtain. Fortunately, wiser counsel around Ramos Horta prevailed and he did not carry out his plan.

Around this time, another minor complication arose. On 9 June, the Portuguese Government announced that it had established an Assistance Team for the transition period in East Timor, chaired by Father Vitor Melicias. Portugal's intention was to channel various forms of assistance to East Timor within the context of three scenarios: first, as humanitarian aid to be dispatched immediately to improve the humanitarian situation in the province before the popular consultation; second, as special assistance if the majority of the East Timorese people chose to accept special autonomy; and, third, as aid to the people of East Timor in preparing for independence if they were to reject special autonomy. LUSA, the Portuguese news agency, reported that the assistance would initially amount to US$115 million.

The Chairman of the Assistance Team expressed his desire to visit East Timor towards the end of June in order to make the necessary preparations. Through the tripartite talks in New York, I appealed to the Portuguese not to exacerbate an already complicated situation in East Timor and suggested that the Team visit East Timor only after the popular consultation. This appeal apparently persuaded the Portuguese Government not to press the issue.

The UNAMET CONTROVERSY

Another aggravating factor was the fact that relations between UNAMET and the Indonesian authorities were marred by irritants and misunderstandings from the start. In particular, Indonesia considered various UNAMET activities to be highly provocative.

The controversy began with the choice of the building to be used as the UNAMET headquarters. The provincial government assisted in the search and offered UNAMET a number of buildings located at the center of the city. Yet in the end, UNAMET chose a building located in the heart of Becora, a staunchly pro-independence neighbourhood.

According to pro-integration sources, this resulted in the building coming under the "control" of anti-integration elements and this made any visits to the building by pro-integration personalities a potentially dangerous venture. To prove their point, they cited the incident on 28 May 1999, during which Basilio Dias Araujo, a pro-integration leader, was physically assaulted in the UNAMET compound by UNAMET local staff members who were against integration. They also recalled that the cars of Ambassador Lopes de Cruz, Governor Abilio Soares and several others had been vandalized while parked outside the UNAMET building during the official inauguration of the UNAMET Headquarters on 3 June 1999.

Another controversial issue concerned the recruitment of the approximately 4000 East Timorese local UNAMET staff. The pro-integration side charged that the selection of staff was heavily biased and that pro-independence individuals were chosen preferentially. In fact, UNAMET's local staff was practically entirely made up of people who were against integration with Indonesia.

When pressed on this point, both Mr. Martin and Ambassador Marker denied any bias and gave assurances that the recruitment process had been based on objective criteria and qualifications, namely command of the English language. An even more galling and revealing explanation was that since in their view the majority of East Timorese were against integration, this had inevitably been reflected in the composition of UNAMET's local staff.

The intemperate and often biased statements issued by David Wimhurst, UNAMET's chief spokesman provoked considerable irritation and anger. For example, as noted earlier, he had given a press statement defending Ramos Horta's "right" to campaign in East Timor and he had also been quoted as saying that UNAMET was not concerned about disarming FALINTIL, but only about disarming pro-integration groups. He was also responsible for circulating radio and television clips that provided an outlandish explanation of what autonomy would entail. For example, he asserted that choosing autonomy would be like owning a room in a house, while rejecting autonomy and subsequently choosing independence would be like owning the entire house.

On several occasions, I brought the matter of David Wimhurst's behaviour to the attention of Ambassador Marker and Iam Martin, the head of UNAMET. Although they sympathetically listened to my complaints, they never accommodated my request for the replacement of David Wimhurst with a more impartial official. In this regard, it is important to ealize that David Wimhurst is a Canadian national whose wife is Portuguese. I once asked Ambassador Marker, only half in jest, how UNAMET would react if Indonesia were to insist that the spokesman's job be filled with a Malaysian national married to an Indonesian.

Throughout UNAMET's tenure in East Timor, there were also several incidents involving other personnel, such as civilian police (CIVPOLS) and Australian UNAMET members who often caused unnecessary friction and misunderstanding by their insensitive and often provocative behaviour. Unfortunately, this antagonistic relationship between UNAMET officials and staff and Indonesian authorities was a persistant problem.

The Dare Meetings

Apart from these negative developments, however, some encouraging and positive developments could also be noted in the time remaining before the ballot.

From 28 to 30 June 1999, a reconciliation meeting was held in Jakarta at the initiative of the two Bishops of East Timor. This was a follow-up to a similar meeting held at the seminary in the town of Dare, south of Dili, on 10 and 11 September 1998. The earlier meeting had been sponsored and organized by the same Bishops and had brought together representatives of the pro-integration and pro-independence groups. These two events became known as the Dare I and Dare II meetings.

At the end of the Dare I meeting, which was attended by 50 participants representing both warring groups and two persons representing the "minority" (Chinese) group, an eleven-point declaration, calling for peace and reconciliation, was agreed upon and published.

The declaration contained two points, which initially caused sharp controversy. This was solved by a compromise formulation recorded in two key paragraphs. The relevant sentence in Paragraph 7 read: "to consider the establishment of a representative forum of all East Timorese, after a common platform could be achieved" and the relevant sentence in paragraph 9 confirmed that "meetings such as this should in future be attended by representatives of all political and social factions (groups), including leaders of the resistance in the forest, in jail or abroad".

The Dare II meeting, this time held at the Sheraton Hotel near the international airport of Jakarta, brought together leading East Timorese personalities, both from inside and outside the province.

Originally, Bishop Belo wanted to hold the meeting in Australia. In a letter he wrote to me, he also proposed to create a Steering Committee composed of Australian dignitaries, including the Prime Minister and Foreign Minister, as well as bishops from Portugal and the Philippines who would participate as observers. I persuaded him to hold the meeting in Jakarta and not to invite foreign observers or foreign dignitaries to sit on the Steering Committee. Nevertheless, the Government did accede to the Bishops' request to allow the participation of Xanana Gusmao, Ramos Horta and other leading pro-independance personalities to come to participate in the meeting.

Although the Dare II meeting proceeded in a good atmosphere and constituted a significant step towards reconciliation, deep divisions remained. At the end of the meeting a joint statement containing "points of convergence" was agreed upon, but a proposal to form a joint consultative committee to continue the dialogue and to implement the points of convergence in the period before and after the popular consultation failed to obtain consensus.

A suggestion from pro-independence delegates that Xanana Gusmao be released from detention and allowed to campaign was also rejected by the pro-integration group.

The Dare II meeting set back hopes for a reconciliation between the two sides before the popular consultation, although subsequently there were further efforts to bring the warring parties closer together.

Efforts to curb the violence

On 7 August 1999, a high-level delegation of Cabinet Ministers and senior officials again visited East Timor. This was the second mission the Government dispatched to Dili in order to make an on-the-spot assessment of the situation and was again led by Coordinating Minister Faisal Tanjung.

At this visit, the delegation was first briefed by the Chairman of the East Timor Task Force, Ambassador Agus Tarmidzi who, to his credit, painted a relatively realistic picture of the security situation and the prospects of the popular consultation. This was followed by a plenary meeting with the Governor and all senior officials of the provincial government.

At this meeting, I again seized the opportunity to urge all those present to ensure that in the campaign to ascertain the choice of the people for autonomy, persuasion and argumentation should be employed instead of intimidation and violence as these had always proven to be counter-productive.

Afterwards, I had frank and productive meetings with UNAMET Chief Ian Martin and his staff and, later, separately with Bishop Basilio do Nascimento of Baucau and Bishop Belo. At the end of the one-day visit, I held a press conference attended by approximately 100 domestic and foreign journalists.

On 9 August 1999, at UNAMET Headquarters in Dili, a Code of Conduct for Participants in the East Timor Popular Consultation was signed by the Special Representative of the Secretary-General, Mr. Ian Martin, by Mr. Domingos M.D. Soares, on behalf of the United Front for Autonomy for East Timor (*Front Bersama Pro-Otonomi Timor Timur – UNIF*) and by Mr. Leandro Isaac, on behalf of the *Concelho Nacional da Resistancia Timorense* (CNRT).

The Code laid down rules and procedures for the conduct of a peaceful, fair and orderly campaign. It also reiterated that "all participants agree to accept the officially validated outcome of the popular consultation, in accordance with the Main Agreement of 5 May 1999."

Points of agreement

On 11 August 1999, a meeting initiated by UNAMET and supported by the Indonesian Government was held in Jakarta between East Timorese leaders from both sides. After the inconclusive Dare II meeting, this was another effort to try to bring the two sides closer together so that they could agree on important points concerning the conduct of the campaign, security and political issues.

Attending for the pro-autonomy side were Domingos Soares, Lopes da Cruz, Jose Tavaras and Salvador Soares. The pro-independence side was represented by Xanana Gusmao, Manuel Carrascalao, Agio Pereira and Avelino Coelho, while on the United Nations/UNAMET side Ambassador Jamsheed Marker, Ian Martin, Francesc Vendrell and Tamrat Samuel were present.

The most important points of agreement reached at this meeting were as follows:

- The earlier agreed Code of Conduct for the campaign would be promoted and publicized by the UNAMET, with the support of both sides;
- The campaign would be launched jointly, and henceforth both sides would not hold separate public campaign gatherings on the same day;
- Cantonment would be accelerated and both sides agreed on the need for early disarmament;
- The parties reaffirmed their readiness to respect the outcome of the popular consultation;
- If autonomy would be rejected, the right of those who wanted to retain their Indonesian citizenship would be respected;
- The parties agreed that after the popular consultation there would be no winners and no losers, no heroes and no traitors and that this message should be widely disseminated;
- The two sides agreed that an East Timorese Consultative Commission would be established and be launched on 31 August 1999; the Commission would be responsible for fostering East

Timorese reconciliation during the period of political transition until the formation of an elected body under either option;

- The Commission would be made up of 25 members. Each side would nominate ten members and the Secretary-General would appoint five members. After consultation with Indonesia, Portugal and the two sides, the nominations were to be received at UNAMET by 21 August 1999;
- The Commission would issue a statement to promote reconciliation and stability on 31 August (one day after the ballot);
- The Commission should convene a broader meeting of East Timorese leaders after the announcement of the result of the popular consultation to promote a smooth and peaceful transition.

At the conclusion of the meeting, it was proposed that a follow-up meeting would be convened on 21 August with the same participants and under the same conditions. This second meeting of the East Timorese leaders took place on 22 August, again in Jakarta. Agreement was reached on the following:

- A meeting would be convened in Dili on 25 August 1999. The commanders of the four FALINTILregions and the four commanders of the PPI (*Pasukan Pejuang Integrasi* – Force of Pro-Integration Fighters) which was a group composed of all the armed elements of the pro-integration forces. This meeting would be aimed at producing a common position between the commanders of the two sides. It would declare that anyone carrying weapons outside the cantonment areas should be arrested and full investigation should be carried out by the two sides;
- A joint ceremony on the closure of the campaign would be held in Dili on 27 August at 4:00 p.m.
- The proposed composition of the East Timorese Consultative Commission was discussed; there were no significant differences of view on the list.
- The first meeting of the Consultative Commission would be held in Dili on 31 August 1999. It was hoped that Xanana Gusmao would be present at this and subsequent meetings of the Commission.

These two meetings were considered very useful in creating an atmosphere of cooperation and calm during the campaign and in the run-up to the ballot. On 1 September 1999, UNAMET presented their proposal for the final composition of the East Timor Consultative Commission. It consisted of 25 members. 11 members each from the two contending sides and three honourary advisers appointed by the UN Secretary-General, i.e. the two Bishops and Governor Abilio O. Soares.

It would turn out, however, that the lofty plans for the establishment and operation of a Consultative Commission were all for naught because of the post-ballot violence that erupted soon thereafter.

Peaceful voter registration

In the meantime, the tripartite negotiations between Indonesia, Portugal and the UN Secretary-General and his staff were now addressing the various complications and the necessary follow-up measures for the implementation of the May 5 Agreements. But at this stage, most of those negotiations were held in New York at the level of senior officials or of Permanent Representatives.

Much later, during the runoff for the ballot, at the request of and with the agreement of both sides, the tripartite senior officials meetings were scheduled to be held in Jakarta on 12-13 August and reciprocally in Lisbon on 25-26 August 1999. It soon became obvious that the initial date for the start of voter registration, 22 June 1999, was unrealistic. After intensive tripartite discussions, Secretary-General Kofi Annan reported to the Security Council on 22 June that voter registration would start three weeks later, on 13 July 1999.

Anan pointed out that the delay was due to logistic issues. UNAMET was not ready as it was not yet full deployed. However, he also added that he was unable to certify that the necessary conditions existed to begin the operational phases of the consultation process due to the security situation. As it later turned out, the actual date on which registration could have been started was 16 July 1999.

The delay in registration inevitably led to the postponement of the balloting day, originally set for 8 August 1999. The new date became the subject of intense negotiations. Indonesia at first proposed only a two-week delay, to Saturday, 21 August. In the end, however, it was agreed that the date of the popular consultation would be Monday, 30 August 1999 and the Secretary-General accordingly notified the Security Council on 28 July 1999.

In his letter to the UN Security Council dated 14 June 1999, the Secretary-General conveyed his decision "to begin the registration process on July 16, 1999, based on positive assurances by the Indonesian authorities." However, he warned that "*UNAMET will* continue to keep the security situation constantly under review" and that he intended "to make another assessment of conditions... halfway through the registration period."

The process of registration, in spite of the dire warnings of the UNAMET, proceeded peacefully without incident. Yet on 26 July 1999, Secretary-General Kofi Annan still deemed it necessary to issue another warning, that in continuing the registration he did so "on the understanding that the Indonesian authorities will work with UNAMET to achieve the further necessary improvements in the security situation .... The completion of registration and the continuation of the popular consultation process will depend on my being satisfied that these improvements are achieved and sustained."

At the end of the 20-day registration period, the Electoral Commission formally announced the results: total voters registered: 451,792, of whom 438,517 were in East Timor and 13,296 were overseas. The Electoral Commission grudgingly praised "the calm and reassuring atmosphere . . . manifested at the registration centers." Similar words of commendation for the smooth and peaceful proceedings were expressed by the Carter Centre and other NGO observers.

Complaints on the campaign

The next stage of the popular consultation process was the period of campaigning, which was held from 24-27 August 1999. This phase of the process also went reasonably smoothly, with only a few incidents. Nevertheless, it was in this period that the strongest criticisms were leveled by various UNAMET authorities on the security situation in general and on the alleged complicity of certain members of the Indonesian military in the activities of the armed militias.

In a letter to Ambassador Tarmidzi dated 19 August, UNAMET Chief Ian Martin mentioned by name military officers and East Timorese officials who, he claimed, had given open support and direction to the militias in such places as Bobonaro regency, Maliana, Suai, Viqueque and Liquica.

In a letter to Ian Martin dated 20 August, 1999 the Electoral Commission formally complained that "there has still been no proper compliance with the fundamental obligations undertaken by the Indonesian Government under the New York Agreements of 5 May 1999. Unless there is significant and immediate remedial action on the part of the Indonesian Government, we will have to hold that it failed to meet its obligations under the Agreements. Moreover, we may be obliged to conclude that such failure resulted in a perversion of the poll in favour of the pro-autonomy camp."

It then went on to describe what it saw as "a lack of an atmosphere that was free of intimidation, violence and interference that would ensure a secure environment for a free and fair popular consultation process." It also quoted reports of involvement of TNI members in "the training, deployment, payment and arming of the militias."

In similar letters to Colonel A. Muis, East Timor military commander, and Major General Zaki Anwar, the chief of the UNAMET Military Liaison Office (MLO), Brigadier Rezaqul Haider, reported among other things that that "TNI members of KODIM 1638 were wearing pro-autonomy T-shirts, with the message in Indonesian: "Bila otonomi menang darah menetes, bila kemerdekaan menang darah mengalir" which meant: "If autonomy wins, blood will drip, if independence wins, blood will flow".

Post-ballot arrangements

Meanwhile, at the request of the Secretary-General, the Security Council on 3 August 1999 unanimously agreed upon Resolution 1257 to extend the mandate of the UNAMET by one month until 30 September 1999. The resolution came at a time when tripartite discussions had just s begun with a paper prepared by the UN Secretariat titled "East Timor post-ballot planning."

The paper proposed post-ballot arrangements, including the role the UN would have to play, regardless of whether autonomy would be accepted (Scenario A) or rejected (Scenario B). The pre-ballot period was designated as Phase 1; the period between the balloting and implementation of its results as Phase 2 (2A and 2B); and the period of implementation as Phase 3.

On 9 August 1999, in his fortnightly report to the Security Council, the Secretary-General asked the Council's approval for "*UNAMET* to continue through the post-ballot period until the implementation phase of the result." He also indicated that in the post-ballot period, the UNAMET's tasks and structure would be adjusted accordingly. Some of these proposed adjustments were:

- The electoral component would be reduced to a unit that would prepare for the monitoring of the election of the Regional Council, which was foreseen in the autonomy plan, or for general elections that would take place if autonomy were to be rejected;
- The civilian police (**CIVPOL**) component would be increased to 410, to enable it to operate in all 18 regencies/districts. It would be augmented by a small team to prepare for the recruitment and training of a new East Timorese police force. This additional team would eventually number about 50, bringing the overall strength of the CIVPOL component to 460.
- The military liaison component would be increased to 300, to be deployed in all 13 regencies. The military liaison officers would liaise with the TNI and continue to be involved in the work of the East Timorese bodies established to promote peace and reconciliation.
- The political affairs component would be transformed into a civil affairs component, which, apart from continuing to monitor political developments in East Timor, would also assist the Special Representative in the formation and development of a Representative Council, which would be necessary under either outcome.
- Law and order. During the interim period, Indonesia would continue to be fully responsible for the maintenance of law and order, especially by the police.

On 27 August 1999, the Security Council adopted Resolution 1262 (1999) approving the request of the Secretary-General to extend the mandate of UNAMET until 30 November 1999, including the proposed adjustments in the tasks and structure of UNAMET.

Minding partisan passions

One sensitive issue that surfaced in the negotiations during this period was the manner in which the results of the balloting would be announced. The East Timorese pro-integration groups at first insisted that such results be announced on a region-per-region basis.

But after careful consideration, President Habibie and the Government agreed with UNAMET that the results of the popular consultation be announced on a territory-wide basis, with no regional, regency or polling station breakdown in the figures, and the ballots would be collected and counted centrally in Dili. This would be done in order to avoid arousing partisan passions over the results obtained in certain localities or regencies.

Unfortunately, the otherwise peaceful campaigning period was marred by a last-day incident. On 26 August 1999, the last campaign day for the pro-integration side, an armed clash occurred between pro and anti-integration forces in Dili, which resulted in four deaths. The Government expressed its condemnation and regrets over the incident and so did the two opposing groups of East Timorese. The next day, calm was restored.

Chapter 14
The Popular Consultation: The Post-Ballot Upheaval and INTERFET

ON MONDAY, 30 August 1999, the people of East Timor, in their hundreds of thousands went to the 200 polling centers to vote, in generally peaceful and orderly fashion.

The turnout was high, with about 98 percent of registered voters casting their ballot, both within and outside East Timor. The peaceful proceedings again belied the UNAMET's pessimistic and alarmist anticipations of widespread violence on polling day.

The calm before the storm

One day after the ballot, Secretary-General Kofi Annan sent congratulatory letters to President Habibie and me in which he lauded the polling as "a milestone" and a "crucial achievement" in the popular consultation process, which brought "much credit to your Government".

As earlier agreed upon, the counting of the ballots was conducted centrally in Dili, in order to ensure secrecy of the voting in each locality. For that purpose, all ballot boxes were transported to Dili and after all the ballot boxes were accounted for, the actual counting started on 2 September.

However, in sharp contrast to the generally peaceful proceedings on ballot day, on 1 September the security situation in East Timor began to rapidly deteriorate. Droves of armed militias descended on Dili and unleashed a campaign of intimidation and violent attacks on pro-independence supporters and foreign news correspondents.

A surge of violence

The violence escalated after the announcement of the ballot results on September 4. They looted houses and set them on fire. Similar destructive acts were also conducted in other towns and villages where a number of UNAMET local staff members were reportedly killed.

In the process, thousands of East Timorese fled from their homes or were forcibly displaced to the hinterlands and to West Timor. Hundreds of frightened Dili citizens sought shelter at the UNAMET compound. At one point, the UNAMET compound had to accommodate around 2000 internally displaced persons (IDPs).

On 1 September 1999 in New York, the UN Security Council held the first of what was to become an almost daily informal meeting, to hear a report from the Under Secretary-General for Political Affairs, Mr. Kieran Prendergast, on the rapidly worsening security situation in East Timor.

Mr. Prendergast briefed the Council on various security incidents in Dili and other places, such as the torching of houses and buildings in Dili, attacks on several UNAMET houses in the regions and the flocking of East Timorese to the UNAMET headquarters seeking protection.

At the end of the meeting, the Council issued a press statement which, as was to become the pattern, was drafted by the delegation of the United Kingdom. According to the statement, the Council, while "welcoming the smooth conduct of the popular consultation . . . condemned in the strongest terms the violence in Dili that has taken place since." The Secretary-General also made a statement, strongly condemning "The violence that took place outside UNAMET headquarters in Dili, in which it has been reported that at least two people have been killed".

Before the informal meeting, the Portuguese Permanent Representative called on the President of the Security Council to express his Government's deep concern over the developments and to request that a "special mission" of the Council be sent to East Timor to make assess the situation.

Peacekeeping force sought

The Portuguese Permanent Representative also intimated that if the situation continued to worsen, the Security Council should send a "peacekeeping force" to East Timor. At the Council meeting, this Portuguese request was taken up but since no consensus could be reached on the matter at the time, the request was rejected.

On the same day, a tripartite meeting was held in New York at the

Permanent Representatives level to discuss the rapidly evolving events in Dili. The meeting, chaired by Mr. Francesc Vendrell, concluded that tripartite meetings would be held in New York on 19 and 28 September 1999 at the Ministerial level.

On 3 September, the Indonesian Permanent Representative, Ambassador Makarim Wibisono met with the then President of the Security Council, Ambassador Peter van Walsum of The Netherlands. His mission was to clarify Indonesia's position regarding the persistent demand of the Portuguese Government that the Security Council immediately send a UN peacekeeping force to East Timor.

Following my instructions, the Indonesian Permanent Representative conveyed Indonesia's firm position that in the period between the announcement of the results of the balloting and the decision by the Indonesian Consultative Assembly (MPR) formally accepting the result (as earlier agreed to be designated as phase 2), sovereignty over East Timor would still be in the hands of Indonesia. According to the 5 May Agreements, Indonesia would still be responsible for security in East Timor. Hence, Indonesia could not accept UN peacekeeping forces during phase 2, no matter what the results of the balloting would be. However, if at the ballot the autonomy proposal were to be rejected, the Indonesian Government could consider UN peacekeeping operations in the territory, but only during phase 3 (after the MPR decision).

Ambassador van Walsum responded by arguing that according to Portugal, the UN had never acknowledged Indonesian sovereignty over East Timor and therefore the sending of peacekeeping forces or any other UN contingency measure would not require Indonesia's approval.

To this, Ambassador Wibisono replied that if the UN were to insist on sending a peacekeeping force to East Timor during phase 2, it would have to send "peace enforcement forces," as Indonesia would surely resist and, inevitably, there would be casualties on both sides. In the end, the President of the Security Council had to acknowledge Indonesia's determined stand on this matter, and he subsequently conveyed this to the members of the Security Council.

Count completed quickly

Meanwhile, an unforeseen development arose in connection with the counting of the votes. Earlier, UNAMET had estimated that the count would take up to one week to be completed and in everyone's mind it was assumed that the results would be announced around 6 September. The count, however, was completed on the evening of 3 September, much earlier than expected. That night I received a frantic call from Ambassador Agus Tarmidzi in Dili, informing me of this turn of events and of UNAMET's proposal to announce the results as soon as possible lest leaks were to occur that could result in premature press reports.

I immediately reported this development to President Habibie. After discussions with various Ministers and staff as well as with Ambassador Jamsheed Marker, it was agreed that the results would be announced as soon as possible. They were to have been released on the morning of September 4 in Dili by Mr. Ian Martin and simultaneously, (taking into account the time difference) on the evening of September 3 in New York by the Secretary-General.

Before the announcement was actually made, the Electoral Commission had certified the results after first conducting public hearings on 2 and 3 September on a number of protests and accusations of irregularities in the balloting submitted by the pro-integration groups. In refering to these protests, the Electoral Commission, in their report to the Secretary-General, concluded that the allegations of irregularities that could be proven had not had any effect on the outcome of the ballot.

In its overall determination of the results, the Commission stated that "the popular consultation had been procedurally fair and in accordance with the New York Agreements, and consequently provided an accurate reflection of the will of the people of East Timor".

The results are announced

Thus, as agreed, on 3 September at nine o'clock in the evening in New York, the Secretary-General presented the results of the popular consultation to a formal session of the Security Council. At that same moment, which was nine in the morning of 4 September in Dili, Special Representative Ian Martin read out the results at a press conference.

The reported results were: 94.388 votes or 21.5 percent of the ballots cast were in favour of the proposed special autonomy; 344.580 votes or 78.5 percent of the total were against it—a resounding majority for the anti-integrationists.

In conveying the results to the Security Council, the Secretary-

General addressed an appeal to the East Timorese: "Those who voted to accept the proposed special autonomy must not consider this outcome a loss. Nor indeed should the majority consider it a victory; for there are no winners and no losers today. Rather, this moment heralds the opportunity for all East Timorese to begin to forge together a common future in what is to become an independent East Timor."

After the Security Council session, the Secretary-General asked to meet with the Indonesian Permanent Representative to tell him that, unfortunately, he had not succeeded in contacting President Habibie by telephone at 20:30 New York time (07:30 Jakarta Time), as he had wished to convey the results of the ballot to the President before it was made public.

He did, however, write a personal letter to the President, dated September 3, informing him of the results and also praising the President's "wise and historic initiative earlier this year with regard to East Timor. I believe that Your Excellency's decision to allow the East Timorese people to decide their future relationship with Indonesia was fully in keeping with the great processes of democratization which you have presided over throughout the Republic of Indonesia."

Shock and disillusionment

The public had no inkling of how President Habibie, the Cabinet and the TNI must have been shocked at the results of the balloting. For the past two months they had been constantly fed with highly optimistic predictions of a victory for the pro-integration forces in the balloting, although the predicted margin of victory was progressively scaled down as the date of the balloting got closer: from an 80 to 20 winning margin to 60 to 40 and finally to 55 to 45 in the days just before the balloting.

Having access to the more realistic assessments of Ambassador Agus Tarmidzi and his colleagues in the Foreign Affairs Ministry Task Force office in Dili, however, I always had a different view of the probable outcome. In fact, just before the balloting, I already had the uncomfortable premonition that the autonomy proposal would be defeated, although I kept this feeling to myself. But even I was painfully surprised when 87percent of the voters rejected integration. As earlier mentioned, shortly after the announcement of the results of the ballot, there was a sharp escalation of violence and destruction that eventually led to the devastation of Dili and many other towns of East Timor.

Responding to the rapidly worsening situation in the territory and the international outcry, a delegation of Cabinet Ministers including myself, led by the Coordinating Minister for Political and Security Affairs, again paid a one-day visit to Dili to try to assess the situation. Upon arrival in Dili, we were told that security conditions in town were such that it would be advisable for us to remain at the airport.

Instead, Ian Martin, his staff and members of the Electoral Commission, the Head of the Indonesian Task Force office as well as the Governor and his staff were driven to the airport, under heavy military escort, to meet with us. Several leaders of the pro-integration groups were also present.

A city out of control

At the VIP lounge of the airport, the Ministers were briefed, first by the Indonesian officials and then by Mr. Martin and his colleagues, on the upheaval taking place in the city. The fact that the security situation in the city was no longer under control could not have been brought home more starkly than by the fact that we could not even enter it.

In a separate meeting with Mr. Martin and the three Electoral Commissioners, I brought up the complaints of the pro-integration groups that their protests and accusations of deviations and irregularities during the balloting had not been given due consideration. The Electoral Commissioners cited the public hearings they had held on 2 and 3 September as proof that they had done so. They acknowledged, however, that their findings had not been made public but were directly reported to the UN Secretary-General. This, according to them, was normal procedure according to their mandate.

With the help of Mr. Martin, I was able to convince the Commissioners of the importance of making their findings public, for all to see that they were responding to the vociferous protests of the pro-integration groups.

Moreover, I persuaded them to join us on our flight back to Jakarta, where they could hold a press conference to publicize their findings. They could no longer hold such a press conference in Dili since most of the members of the press covering the political exercise had already left for Jakarta because of the deteriorating situation. the Commissioners held this press conference the following day and used ot to make public their conclusions on the complaints. Most unfortunately, the press conference attracted little attention in the media as the press and the public were transfixed over the crisis that was brewing in the territory.

More violence

Meanwhile, in Dili and in other parts of East Timor, the violence and destruction continued unabated. On 6 September, Bishop Belo's residence was attacked and the hundreds of East Timorese who had taken refuge there were driven out and reportedly sent to West Timor. Bishop Belo himself had to be evacuated, first to Baucau by a police helicopter and from there to Darwin the following day.

At the ICRC compound nearby, a similar attack was carried out against a large group of East Timorese who had sought sanctuary there. The police had to rescue the ICRC staff trapped in the compound. These two attacks drew strong condemnation from the UN and from several Western Governments, NGOs and the international press and the UN Security Council was now having virtually daily informal sessions, hearings and discussions and being continuously updated with reports from USG Prendergast and from the Secretary- General.

On 6 September, the Council unanimously decided to send a Security Council Mission to Jakarta to convey its concern to the Government of Indonesia on the intensification of post-ballot violence in the territory and, in particular, violence aimed at UNAMET. The Mission also offered assistance from the international community including UN military force.

The Mission was led by the Permanent Representative of Namibia, Ambassador Martin Anjaba and included the Permanent Representatives of the United Kingdom, Malaysia, Slovenia, the Deputy Permanent Representative of The Netherlands and Mr. Francesc Vendrell of the Secretariat. The Mission arrived in Jakarta on 8 September.

Mounting pressure on Indonesia

The pressure on Indonesia to agree to allow UN troops into East Timor continued to mount. However, a second proposal submitted by

Portugal on 6 September to rapidly dispatch a UN peacekeeping force "to assist Indonesia to restore law and order in East Timor, in cooperation with the Indonesian security forces" failed to garner sufficient support.

The same happened to a subsequent Portuguese request to convene an urgent formal session of the Security Council. The majority of the Council members responded cautiously to this request, preferring to wait for the Security Council Mission to finalize its task, to return from Indonesia and report its findings.

In the meantime, on 7 September and at the behest of General Wiranto and the TNI Command, Indonesia declared martial law in East Timor. Major-General Kiki Syahnakri was appointed martial law commander and fresh troops were dispatched to the territory.

Noting this development, Secretary-General Kofi Annan, in a telephone conversation with President Habibie and through a press statement by his spokesman, let it be known that the Indonesian Government had 48 hours to show that martial law was effective.

I frankly took offense at the way and the tone the statement was delivered by the spokesman and I responded, also by a press statement, with a warning "not to issue ultimatums." I also expressed disbelief that the Security Council could make a decision to send a peacekeeping force to East Timor without Indonesia's concurrence, as it would then have "to shoot its way into East Timor."

Privately, however, I began to have serious doubts whether, even under martial law, the TNI troops could control the situation, not because of technical incapability but because of wavering and indecisiveness to act strongly against the militias.

Martial law proves ineffective

Meanwhile, on the same day, 7 September 2004, the Government decided to release Xanana Gusmao from prison. However, with the upheaval in East Timor, he could not yet return there and, after temporarily taking refuge in the British Embassy in Jakarta, he was flown to Darwin. It was only on 22 October 1999 that Xanana was able to make a triumphant return to his homeland.

After briefing an informal meeting of the Security Council on 8 September, the Secretary-General gave a short press conference in which he revealed UNAMET Chief Ian Martin's recommendation that in view of the conditions in East Timor, the UN staff of UNAMET should be withdrawn. However, since the Secretary-General was also concerned about the East Timorese IDP's in the UNAMET compound, he was thinking of authorizing only a partial withdrawal of UNAMET, with their presence in the premises essentially maintained as long as the military could continue to provide protection.

In this decision, he was subsequently supported by President Habibie who, in a telephone conversation with the Secretary-General, had among other things expressed the hope that UNAMET would not withdraw from East Timor, because that would create a negative image not only of Indonesia but of the UN as well. The Secretary-General also told the press that he had had a series of telephone conversations with President Habibie and that he had conveyed his position and that of the Security Council that, if the Indonesian Government were unable to maintain law and order in East Timor, Indonesia would have to invite and accept international assistance. Asked by the press whether Jakarta's consent would be needed before an international force could be sent in, the Secretary-General said that the governments that had expressed preparedness to make troops available would all wish to have Indonesia's consent first.

The Security Council's informal meeting on 9 September took up a letter by the Brazilian Permanent Representative, Ambassador Gelson Fonseca, requesting the convening of an urgent, formal meeting of the Security Council, based on Rule 2 of the Provisional Rules of Procedure of the Security Council, which requires the President to call a meeting of the Council at the request of any Member of the Council. Brazil was a Member at that time and it was clear that Portugal had succeeded in persuading Brazil to act on its behalf.

This time nobody could reject the request. Still, some Council Members (Malaysia, Bahrain and China) raised questions as to the appropriateness of such a meeting at a time when the Security Council Mission was still in Indonesia. In the end, the Council President was given the discretion to determine when to call the meeting.

In Jakarta, the Security Council Mission had begun meeting with various sides: with me, with Mrs. Megawati Soekarnoputri, who was then the leader of the main opposition party, and with some members of the Diplomatic Corps on 8 September, and with President Habibie, General Wiranto and Xanana Gusmao on 9 September. The Mission also met with a number of NGO leaders critical of the Government's policies on East Timor.

An offer of UN troops

At the meeting with President Habibie, the Mission was told by the President that Indonesia would welcome any form of international assistance to deal with the situation in East Timor, except military assistance. The President rejected the Council's offer of UN troops to help restore law and order in the territory, reiterating assurances that the Indonesian authorities would get the situation under control. He did, however, consent to the Mission's request to visit East Timor and agreed that they could do so on Saturday, 11 September, accompanied by General Wiranto.

According to the Mission's report, the meeting with Mrs. Megawati Soekarnoputri, as leader of the main opposition party, was intended to solicit her cooperation so that she would not criticize the Government's eventual change of heart about an international security presence. She agreed, but when asked to publicly support the idea of such an international intervention, she refused. In addition, in his meeting with the Mission, General Wiranto expressed full confidence that under martial law, his troops would be able to stabilize the situation and he therefore rejected the idea of bringing in UN troops at that stage.

The Mission also met with Xanana Gusmao twice, on 9 and 12 September. At first, Xanana made an emotional appeal for international intervention, with or without Indonesia's consent. However, when it became clear that the Indonesian Government would be announcing its preparedness to request for the assistance of the UN, he was persuaded to issue a more conciliatory statement.

Meanwhile concerted political pressure was also being exerted on Indonesia from another direction. In Auckland, New Zealand, an APEC Summit Meeting was taking place. President Habibie did not attend and he had also asked me not to go in order to focus our attention on the crisis in East Timor.

On 9 September, on the sidelines of the ongoing Summit, a Special Ministerial Meeting was convened to discuss East Timor. The Coordinating Minister for Economic and Financial Affairs, Mr. Ginanjar Kartasasmita, represented Indonesia at that meeting. The Foreign Ministers of Australia, Canada, Chile, Japan, Korea, Mexico, New Zealand, the Philippines, Peru, Singapore, Thailand, the United Kingdom and the United States attended the Summit as did senior officials from Brunei Darussalam, the People's Republic of China, Malaysia, Papua New Guinea, Russia and Vietnam.

After the meeting, the Minister of Foreign Affairs and Trade of New Zealand, Mr. Don McKinnon, gave a chairman's statement to the press. According to Foreign Minister McKinnon, during the meeting, the delegations expressed their grave concern at the deteriorating situation and the growing humanitarian crisis in East Timor. Among other things, he said that "*t*he armed militia continues to carry out violent acts with impunity, while deeply disturbing reports continue to emerge of forcible relocation of large numbers of East Timorese. In the 48 hours since martial law was imposed in East Timor, there has been no improvement in the deplorable security situation. Ministers want to see the results of the ballot implemented in accordance with the Tripartite Agreement and the violence in East Timor brought to an end."

After delivering his chairman's statement, Foreign Minister Don McKinnon called the UN Secretary-General on the phone to brief him on the results of the meeting. He also rang me up for the same purpose. It was obvious that the screws against Indonesia were being tightened.

On 10 September, the Security Council again met in informal session, both in the morning and in the afternoon. During the morning session, USG Kieran Prendergast gave his usual briefing, in which he noted that after 72 hours, martial law in East Timor had failed to restore law and order.

In the afternoon session, the Council addressed the question of convening a formal session in response to the request of Brazil and Portugal. After a spirited debate, the Council decided to convene the formal session in two phases, i.e. the first on 11 September 1999, to be followed by a resumed session after the Council Mission's return from Indonesia.

Harsh words for Indonesia

Separately, the Secretary-General issued a statement to the press on the latest developments in East Timor. This time he used particularly harsh language, calling Indonesia for the first time the "*currently occupying power*" of East Timor. He went on to state:

"Before the eyes of the world, the people of East Timor are being terrorized and massacred because they exercised their right of self-determination... Regrettably, Indonesia has failed to fulfill that responsibility (of maintaining security in East Timor), even with the introduction of martial law in the last 72 hours. East Timor is descending into anarchy. The anti-independence militias, who were overwhelmingly defeated at the ballot box, have engaged in an orgy of looting, burning and killing. I have been in frequent contact with the President of Indonesia, urging him to bring the situation under control, but it continues to deteriorate... The Indonesian forces...have so far been either unable or unwilling to take effective steps to restore security."

"The time has clearly come for Indonesia to seek the help of the international community in fulfilling its responsibility . . . . A number of governments in the region...have assured me of their willingness to participate in an international force for this purpose.

I urge the Indonesian Government to accept their offer of help without further delay. If it refuses to do so, it cannot escape responsibility for what could amount, according to reports reaching us, to crimes against humanity."

I could not imagine what had moved Secretary-General Kofi Annan to use such harsh language at that particular point, although the terrible situation in East Timor could have been enough reason for it. But it was also apparent that he was coming under increasing pressure from the leaders of the United States, West Europe, Canada and Australia to act with greater urgency on the crisis in the territory and to take a tougher stand against Indonesia.

Accompanied by General Wiranto and some of his staff officers as well as a large media contingent, the Security Council Mission visited Dili on 11 September. They toured the city and saw that much of it had been reduced to smouldering rubble. They visited the UNAMET compound, met with local military and police commanders and had talks with Bishop Nascimento.

In the Mission's hard-hitting report, presented to the Security Council after their return, it was stated that "the Mission left with a strong sense of shock at the destruction which had taken place." In its analysis, the Mission's report further observed that ". . . . this activity (of the armed militias) could not have occurred without the involvement of large elements of the Indonesian military and police. There was clearly a disconnect between the situation on the ground and the assessment of the situation in East Timor as presented by President Habibie and his senior advisers."The Mission's report also noted that "During the course of the visit it became clear that General Wiranto's views had also undergone a change."

Indonesia accepts the UN offer

Meanwhile, in a formal session of the Security Council on 11 September in New York, 52 Member States participated in a public debate on the situation in East Timor. The Secretary-General opened the session with a renewed call for Indonesia to accept UN peacekeeping forces. Most of the delegations that took the floor also urged Indonesia to agree to an international peacekeeping presence while condemning the breakdown of security in East Timor.

However, even as the debate was proceeding and taking into account the 12-hour time difference with Indonesia, reports were trickling in from Jakarta that the Government was about to change its policy on not accepting peacekeeping forces. Back in Jakarta, in the almost daily limited Cabinet meetings that took place in those days, it was primarily General Wiranto and the military leadership who had opposed the offer of assistance by the UN in the form of a peacekeeping force and President Habibie, perhaps against his own better judgement, had concurred with this view.

But especially since it became clear that martial law was not effective, I myself had concluded that, under the circumstances, it would be better to accept the UN offer. In this, some other colleagues in the Cabinet and in the Presidential staff supported me. As it turned out, upon returning from his visit to Dili, together with the Security Council Mission, in the early evening of September 11, General Wiranto had changed his view. He reported to the President, and to the assembled Cabinet members, including myself, that he now saw the need to call in the UN troops. Apparently, upon seeing for himself the extent of the destruction, the General had had a change of mind and he now spoke about the "very difficult psychological constraints" under which his troops were operating in facing the militias in East Timor. In effect, he was actually implying that his troops could not take effective action against the militias.

Now that General Wiranto and the TNI Command themselves had changed their stance, President Habibie took action with laudable speed. On 12 September, he made a phone call to the Secretary-General in New York asking him "as a friend of Indonesia and as a personal friend" to assist in arranging for "effective security cooperation between Indonesia and the UN." He duly informed the Secretary-General of Indonesia's "readiness to accept international peacekeeping forces through the UN from friendly nations to restore peace and security in East Timor, to protect the people and to implement the results of the ballot of 30 August 1999." He also told the Secretary-General that he would send me immediately (that same evening) to New York to explain to him and to the Security Council our position and to prepare the details of its implementation.

The President then gave a special statement to the press, which was broadcast nationwide, explaining to the people his decision and Indonesia's preparedness to accept UN peacekeeping forces. In his statement, the President declared that while the Indonesian defence forces "had done their utmost in a very complex and complicated situation, under very difficult psychological constraints," they had to recognize that there were limits to what more they could achieve.

When he received the Security Council Mission for the second time on 12 September, he informed the Mission about the Indonesian Government's decision, and his conversation with the Secretary-General. He also conveyed to them the contents of his press statement.

Preparations for UN deployment

In New York, I immediately started discussions and intensive lobbying to ensure the smooth and appropriate implementation of Indonesia's decision to accept a UN troops presence in East Timor.

From September 13 to 15, 1999 I held a series of talks with the Secretary-General, the President of the Security Council, the Ambassadors of the five Permanent Members of the Council, both singly and as a group, the NAM Caucus on the Council, Foreign Minister Alexander Downer of Australia and Foreign Minister Jaime Gama of Portugal. I also held a tripartite dialogue meeting with my Portuguese counterpart, under the auspices of the Secretary-General. At these meetings, I conveyed Indonesia's new position on the sending of UN troops to East Timor. I also explained that while Indonesia's invitation to the UN was extended without any preconditions, we did have certain "preferences," considering the political sensitivities in Indonesia.

For example, on the composition of the multinational force, I asked them to consider structuring it in such a way as to be composed mostly of ASEAN and Asian troops. With the President and Members of the Security Council I also discussed and negotiated improvements on the text of the Council Resolution, which was being drafted by the United

Kingdom's Permanent Representative.

On this trip to the United Nations, General Wiranto had assigned two high-ranking staff officers, Lt. General Susilo Bambang Yudhoyono (who would later become Indonesia's President) and Rear Admiral Yoost Menko, to join my delegation in order to prepare for and coordinate the technical aspects of the deployment of UN forces in East Timor. Following our intensive lobbying efforts, the UN Security Council was able to adopt unanimously a reasonably balanced resolution (Resolution 1264/1999) on 15 September 1999 establishing a Multinational Force that would be known as the Interim Force for East Timor (INTERFET).

Considering that security in East Timor was not yet entirely restored, it was agreed that the INTERFET would be a "peace enforcement" rather than a "peacekeeping" force, and hence it was designated to operate under Chapter VII of the UN Charter. The Resolution also "authorizes the States participating in the Multinational Force to take all necessary measures" to fulfill its mandate, which meant that they could, if necessary, use force.

Due to the nature of the MNF and the fact that Australia was indeed its largest contributor in terms of troops and other material support, it was inevitable that the MNF command was given to Australia and Major General Peter Cosgrove was duly appointed to the post. However, at Indonesia's insistence, the job of Deputy Commander of MNF was given to an ASEAN country and the Secretary-General was able to persuade Thailand to assume the post and to contribute 700 troops to the Force.

On the other hand, Portugal was persuaded not to immediately participate and contribute troops to the INTERFET, but rather to do so only in phase 3 after the INTERFET had subsequently been transformed to a UN Peacekeeping Force, as agreed. However, in my separate talks with Foreign Minister Gama, as well as in the tripartite talks, it was agreed that Portugal would open a diplomatic mission in Dili in preparation for the implementation of its tasks during phase 3. Additionally, Portugal would establish a "liaison mission" in Darwin and station one frigate in Australia to support the expected Portuguese troop contingent in the UN peacekeeping force in East Timor during phase 3.

INTERFET-TNI coordination

In the meantime, in separate but coordinated discussions between Lt. Gen. Bambang Yudhoyono and Rear Admiral Yoost Menko with their

Australian counterparts, as well as with the UN Department for Peacekeeping Operations, a framework of cooperation was devised to govern the relations between the TNI and INTERFET in East Timor. The following details were agreed upon:

- Australian troops would not be the only contingent arriving when the INTERFET would be initially deployed. A maximum effort would be made to arrange for the deployment of some ASEAN and other Asian countries with the first batch or shortly thereafter;
- There would be no wholesale withdrawal of the TNI upon the arrival of INTERFET. A coordinated downsizing of TNI's presence would be undertaken.
- Coordination and cooperation between INTERFET and the TNI would be executed through "The Joint Security Consultative Group," which would comprise the two Commanders, with the participation of the Indonesian Police, UNAMET Chief MLO/MILOB and UNAMET Chief Commissioner of the CIVPOL.
- The TNI would assist and cooperate with INTERFET in the latter's implementation of the tasks assigned to it by Security Council Resolution 1264 (1999).
- INTERFET would have the authority to take all necessary measures to deal with armed groups, including the disarming of these groups. The TNI would cooperate with INTERFET in carrying out this task.
- The TNI would assist INTERFET in protecting UNAMET, its personnel and its properties.

The first troop contingents of INTERFET, totaling about 1,500 and led by Major General Peter Cosgrove of Australia, landed at the Comoro Airport in Dili and began their deployment on 20 September 1999. They were welcomed by the TNI Command under Major General Kiki Syahnakri, and UNAMET Chief Ian Martin.

In the coming weeks and months, INTERFET would increase to a total of 8000 troops, comprising forces from 22 UN Member States, including Indonesia's fellow ASEAN countries, Thailand, the Philippines, Malaysia and Singapore. Meanwhile, UNAMET officially re-established itself in East Timor on 28 September and started to cooperate closely with INTERFET.

The final act

Cooperation between INTERFET and the remaining TNI troops proceeded smoothly. There were only a few clashes between INTERFET and armed militia groups which at that time were making their way across the border to West Timor. Nevertheless, during this period, there were two notable incidents that drew worldwide media attention and public censure, because the victims were journalists.

On the afternoon of 21 September, a young Dutch journalist working for the *Financial Times*, Sander Thoenes, was shot and killed in the Becora district of Dili while riding pillion on a motorcycle driven by an East Timorese, Florindo Conceicao. He had gone to Becora to gather breaking news. The killer or killers have never been identified, but a National Human Rights Commission investigation has put the blame on personnel in Battalion 745 which had a large East Timorese component and which was in the area at that time as they were in the process of withdrawing to West Timor. The Battalion commander, however, denied the accusation.

Sander Thoenes was the first foreign journalist to die in East Timor since the death of five Australia-based reporters in Balibo in 1975. Four days later, an Indonesian reporter working for a Japanese news agency, Agus Muliawan, became the next journalist victim. He was in a group of nine people who were killed on 26 September as they traveled by car from Los Palos to Baucau. This incident, too, drew wide publicity and condemnation.

On 23 September, the Indonesian Government formally lifted martial law in East Timor and on 27 September Major General Kiki Syahnakri handed over operational command to Major General Peter Cosgrove, Commander of the INTERFET.

Thus, from that date onwards, responsibility over security in East Timor reverted to the INTERFET on a *de facto* basis, although the *de jure* transfer of sovereignty and overall authority still had to wait until the People's Consultative Assembly (MPR) had formally accepted the results of the popular consultation. That formality was to take place at the forthcoming general session of the Assembly scheduled from October 1 to early November 1999.

Meanwhile, the TNI left a residual presence of around 1000 troops and Special Police force personnel in East Timor to cooperate with the INTERFET, especially in guarding some vital public utility installations, and coordinating their efforts with the INTERFET through the Joint Security Consultative Group (JSCG).

Additionally, the Ministry of Foreign Affairs again assigned a special Task Force, under the leadership of former Ambassador Taufik Sudarbo, to be temporarily stationed in Dili for the purpose of maintaining liaison and cooperation with the INTERFET and the UNAMET at this particular stage of developments in East Timor. This was the *Satgas Pasca Pelaksananaan Penentuan Pendapat di Timor-Timur* or SATGAS P4TT.

By then, it was only a matter of time and a few formalities before, for all intents and purposes, East Timor would cease to be part of Indonesia.

Chapter 15
UNTAET and the UN Take-over

ALTHOUGH there was a gradual restoration of security in East Timor because of the presence of INTERFET, the situation remained critical and the condition of the refugees became the focus of global attention and concern. There was a clearly vacuum of authority: the civil administration was no longer functioning. Most civil servants, including the police, had either left the territory or fled to the hinterland. The judiciary and the legal system, too, had ceased to operate as judges, prosecutors and other members of the legal system had also fled. No medical services were available and public utilities such as water and electricity supply systems were in danger of collapse.

Attending to the refugees

Meanwhile, the plight of the refugees in West Timor became an issue of particular concern to the UN and the international community. Apart from the urgent humanitarian assistance that they required, there persisted allegations of intimidation and violence perpetrated against them by pro-integration militia groups who had mingled with them. According to unofficial estimates, about 250,000 East Timorese had either fled or had been forced to move to West Timor.

The subsequent tripartite dialogues in New York, both at the Ministerial level and at the Senior Officials level, focused on these problems. Ad-hoc measures were quickly agreed to address the vacuum created by the early departure of the Indonesian civil administration, including especially the restoration of public utilities such as electricity, water supply and telecommunication services. Plans were also made for the launching of humanitarian relief efforts as well as for the repatriation of the refugees teeming in West Timor.

At the tripartite meeting on 28 September, the Secretary-General specifically requested Indonesia to provide security protection for the refugees and to allow them to return to East Timor as conditions permitted.In response, I informed him that with regard to refugees, the Indonesian Government had formed a special task force led by the Coordinating Minister for Social Welfare, with instructions to cooperate closely with international humanitarian organizations such as the UNHCR, the World Food Programme, UNICEF as well as the UNDP and the ICRC. I also told him of the three options offered by the Indonesian Government to the refugees in West Timor, namely:

- To return to East Timor;
- To remain temporarily in West Timor pending resettlement in other parts of Indonesia; or
- To immediately resettle in any of the other provinces of Indonesia.

The human rights question

In contrast to the generally constructive discussions that were held in New York, an entirely different atmosphere prevailed in Geneva. There, at the initiative of Ms. Mary Robinson, UN Human Rights Commissioner, the Commission on Human Rights convened a Special Session on East Timor. On 27 September 1999 it adopted a Resolution calling for the establishment of an International Commission of Inquiry to investigate the human rights violations in East Timor.

The Indonesian Government protested against both the Resolution and the highly unusual procedure by which the decision to convene the Special Session was taken. It was particularly irregular that the Session had been convened at the request of a non-member, Portugal. Indonesia's objections were brushed aside. Nevertheless, on 15 October the UN Human Rights Commissioner named a five-member International Inquiry Commission, headed by Ms. Sonia Picado of Costa Rica. Simultaneously, the Indonesian Government appointed its own special investigation commission, organized and led by the Indonesian National Human Rights Commission (KOMNAS HAM), which would work in parallel with the international panel.

Meeting with Xanana

During my busy schedule at the UN General Assembly session, I had the opportunity to have a memorable meeting with the future President of independent East Timor, Mr. Jose Alexandre Xanana

Gusmao. On 28 September, at his request, I had a friendly meeting with Xanana Gusmao at the Indonesian Permanent Mission office in New York. He was accompanied by Mr. Ramos Horta and the conversation was conducted partly in English and partly in Indonesian, in which Xanana was much more fluent than in English at that time. This was my first formal meeting with him and it made a deep impression on me.

Xanana assured me of his sincere wish to build close and harmonious relations between East Timor and Indonesia. He expressed his determination not to look backwards, but to conduct a forward-looking policy. He further expressed the hope that national unity and reconciliation would be nurtured among the people of East Timor, between those who were for integration and those for independence. We also discussed some of the urgent problems that East Timor faced, such as the need to rebuild the civil administration, to restore the functioning of public utilities and to establish a new police and security force in the new state. For all these efforts, Xanana expressed the hope that Indonesia would continue to provide its support.

I wholeheartedly reciprocated Xanana's friendly sentiments and assured him of Indonesia's full support for his conciliatory approach and Indonesia's cooperation in his efforts at nation-building. Throughout the meeting I was struck by his candour and sincerity and by his visionary approach to the future of East Timor-Indonesian relations. It would be confirmed in my subsequent meetings and conversations with him that despite years of hardship, struggle and imprisonment by Indonesia, Xanana remarkably showed no trace of rancour or bitterness toward his former adversaries.

The UNTAET concept

On October 4, 1999, in a detailed report required by Security Council Resolution 1264 (1999), the Secretary-General presented a framework and concept of operations for a UN Transitional Administration in East Timor (UNTAET). This Administration was to be deployed in the implementation phase (phase 3) of the popular consultation process, that is, after the results had been approved and certified by the Indonesian People's Consultative Assembly.

In the Report it was envisaged that UNTAET would be endowed with the overall responsibility for the administration of East Timor and empowered to exercise all legislative and executive authority, including the administration of justice. An important part of it would be a UN Peacekeeping Operation.

UNTAET would thus be an integrated, multidimensional operation of exceptionally broad scope, responsible for the governing of East Timor during its transition to independence. UNTAET would operate under mandate of the Security Council and its work would be supervised by a Special Representative of the Secretary General who would be the Transitional Administrator.

The wide-ranging mandate of UNTAET would include:

- To establish and operate an effective administration;
- To provide security and maintain law and order;
- To support capacity building for self-government;
- To ensure the coordination and delivery of humanitarian and development assistance;
- To establish advisory bodies at all levels that would ensure the participation of the East Timorese in the governance of the territory.

Organizationally, UNTAET would comprise three main components: a governance and public administration component; a humanitarian assistance and emergency rehabilitation component; and a military component, which would be the UN Peacekeeping Force that, in turn, would absorb most of INTERFET troops.

The Special Representative and Transitional Administrator would be assisted by two deputy Special Representatives, a Chief of Staff and the Military Force Commander.

A nationalist backlash

Meanwhile, in Indonesia the voting debacle had finally sunk in and had began to produce a nationalist backlash and outbursts of often irrational emotions. In private circles as well as in public forums, President Habibie and the Government were scathingly criticized for bringing about what many thought was "a national humiliation and a loss of national pride" and "the beginning of the fragmentation of Indonesia."

In this atmosphere, the public at large could not see what in reality had happened on the question of East Timor. All people could see was the denigration of national dignity.

On 21 September, the President appeared before a plenary session of the People's Representative Council (DPR or Parliament) to give a full account of his policies on East Timor. In his two-hour speech to Parliament, Habibie attempted to give detailed answers to a number of written questions put to him beforehand by the legislators, mostly on the considerations, background and consequences of his so-called "second option". He also provided the House with a historical flashback of the East Timor issue and ended by expressing the hope that the MPR, when it would meet in October, would ratify the results of the popular consultation. For the first time, he publicly gave vent to the Indonesian Government's irritation at Australia's attitude and role in the East Timor crisis.

After observing that the Government of Indonesia had always highly valued relations with Australia in the shared endeavour to promote peace, stability and prosperity in the region, he pointedly cited "Australia's excessive behaviour and actions on the issue of East Timor, which were not at all conducive to the maintenance of bilateral relations with Indonesia based on mutual respect for national sovereignty, territorial integrity and equality and on the principle of non-intervention in each other's internal affairs".

He went on to say, that "the Indonesian Government deeply regrets this Australian attitude which has harmed relations between the two countries. In this context, therefore, the Indonesian Government has decided to annul the Agreement between the Government of Indonesia and the Government of Australia on Security Cooperation signed on 18 December 1995. The main reason for this abrogation is that Australia's behaviour and actions are no longer in consonance with the letter and spirit of the Agreement."The speech before Parliament was a tightly argued and frank expose, but it failed to elicit a sympathetic hearing.

Even without that speech, there was already a great deal of public bitterness directed at Australia, because it was seen as an erstwhile supporter of Indonesia on East Timor that had suddenly changed sides and had become Indonesia's most strident critic and proponent of "foreign military intervention" in East Timor.

The perception of Australian "triumphalism" among Indonesian nationalist circles was reinforced by an unfortunate and controversial interview given by Prime Minister Howard, which was published in the weekly magazine, *The Bulletin*, on 22 September. In that interview, Howard was quoted as saying that he saw Australia's emerging role as that of America's "deputy sheriff" in the region.

Although the quote was subsequently denied by the Prime Minister, the damage had been done and not only the Indonesian public but those of other Southeast Asia nations saw in it a confirmation of Australia's radical change of stance towards engagement with Asia.

A presidency lost

It was in this kind of mood that Indonesia moved into the crucial month of October 1999, the month in which the People's Consultative Assembly (MPR) would convene to hear and debate the President's accountability report, including his report on the results of the East Timor popular consultation, and to choose a President and Vice President for the period 1999-2004.

The Assembly started its sessions on 1 October 1999 and, after the formal inaugural session, went as usual into ad-hoc committee meetings. On 12 October I received a letter from the Chairman of Ad-hoc Committee II of the Assembly asking clarification about the following question: "Suppose the result of the popular consultation in East Timor is rejected by the People's Consultative Assembly, what would be the consequences (of such a rejection) for Indonesia's position in international relations?"

I replied, also in writing, that such a rejection would be seen as repudiation by Indonesia of its commitments as enshrined in an international agreement and as non-compliance with binding UN Security Council Resolutions. Such an act, therefore, would have far-reaching consequences, ranging from condemnation by the Security Council to the application of economic and/or political and military sanctions by the international community.

The next day the Indonesian press reported a proposal by some MPR members to delay the decision on East Timor until Portugal removed from the text of its Constitution any claim to the territory. It was alleged that in one of the Articles of the Portuguese Constitution East Timor was still referred to as an "ultramarine province" of the country.

Again I had to write to the MPR, while additionally issuing a press release, pointing out that the Portuguese Constitution, dated 1976 and as last amended in 1997, states about East Timor in Article 293:

1. Portugal remains bound by her responsibilities under international law to promote and guarantee the right to self-determination and the independence of East Timor.
2. The President of the Republic and the Government have the power to take all necessary action for achieving the objectives set out in paragraph 1.

Any claim that Portugal might have had to East Timor, and any reference in its Constitution to that territory as a Portuguese "ultramarine province," had thus been negated by this last amendment and by the reestablishment of Portugal as a democracy.

As a follow-up to answering these questions, I started to conduct a discreet lobbying effort with some key members of the Assembly in order to impress upon them the vital necessity of endorsing the results of the popular consultation in East Timor.

Subsequently, on 14 October 1999 and again on 17 October, in response to specific questions from the MPR members, President Habibie delivered his accountability report to the People's Consultative Assembly (MPR). In his accountability speech before the MPR, the President gave an overall review of his record of achievements in the political and economic spheres and in starting the process of national reform and democratization. On East Timor, he reiterated most of the points he made earlier before Parliament. His explanation and arguments, however, were not accepted by the majority of the Assembly members.

After several days of debate and intensive lobbying for and against President Habibie's accountability report, the Assembly rejected it by a vote of 355 to 322. This was tantamount to turning down his presidential candidacy and on 20 October, just before the Presidential election process was to start, Habibie withdrew from the race.

Ratifying the result of the popular consultation

Despite this dramatic development, the question of the Assembly's ratification of the result of the East Timor popular consultation fared much better. Following discussions in the Ad-hoc Committee and in the Plenary, which the Department of Foreign Affairs and I monitored closely, the People's Consultative Assembly on 19 October 1999 formally adopted Decision no. V/MPR/1999 on the Popular Consultation in East Timor.

In Article 1, the final negotiated Decision states: "The People's Consultative Assembly of the Republic of Indonesia recognizes the result of the popular consultation held in East Timor on 30 August 1999 by the United Nations, in accordance with the Agreement between the Republic of Indonesia and the Portuguese Republic on the question of East Timor."

In Article 2, the Decision declares: "Decision Number VI/MPR/1978 concerning the Affirmation of the Integration of the territory of East Timor within the Unitary State of the Republic of Indonesia is no longer in effect."

In subsequent Articles, the Decision affirmed the following:

- "The abrogation of Decision VI/MPR/1978 does not nullify the legality of the actions of the fighters and government officials or all forms of awards accorded to them during the time when East Timor constituted a part of the Unitary State of the Republic of Indonesia…"
- "Recognition of the result of the popular consultation does not diminish the rights of the people of East Timor who are still loyal to the Unitary State of the Republic of Indonesia, which are guaranteed by international law."

The Decision was signed by the Chairman of the People's Consultative Assembly, Prof. Dr. Amien Rais M.A. and co-signed by the seven Vice-chairs.

The ratification of the results of the popular consultation by the TheMPR was not without misgivings and even opposition on the part of some members. But in the end, the Assembly dropped earlier proposals to include in the text of the Decision a directive to the President to hold talks with the United Nations to investigate the alleged partiality of UNAMET in conducting the balloting.

Also dropped, after clarifications and lobbying by the Department of Foreign Affairs, was a reference to the need for Portugal to delete mention of East Timor from its Constitution. In addition, they also agreed to temporarily drop the issue of the transfer of authority over East Timor.

The next day, after a lengthy session full of political maneuverings and switching of political alliances, the People's Consultative Assembly elected K.H. Abdurrahman Wahid, popularly known as "Gus Dur," as President of Indonesia, defeating the leader of the largest political party in Parliament, Megawati Sukarnoputri. Bitterly disappointed at the loss, Megawati recovered sufficiently to run for and win the Vice Presidency at the request of Abdurrahman Wahid.

UNTAET is born

The road was now clear for the UN Security Council to act on the Secretary-General's proposal to put a transitional government in place in East Timor. After three weeks of debate and discussion on the Council, with the Indonesian Delegation contributing its views as usual through its friends among the members, the Security Council unanimously adopted Resolution 1272 (1999) on 25 October 1999. It established the UN Transitional Administration in East Timor (UNTAET) and invested it with wide-ranging authority and responsibility for the administration of East Timor.

It was a sweeping mandate indeed and much broader than the similar body established in Cambodia a few years before, the UNTAC, on which I had personally worked so hard for many years. Therein, in the process of drafting this and all previous Security Council Resolutions on East Timor during that period, the Indonesian Delegation always received the sympathetic support and cooperation of the delegations of China, Russia, Malaysia and Bahrain. Occasionally, Argentina also gave support to Indonesia.

This was not the case with Namibia, a member of the so-called Non-aligned Caucus on the Council and a country that Indonesia had helped so much in its struggle for independence.

The contents of the Resolution, especially in referring to the mandate, objectives and structure of UNTAET, practically adopted all the proposals in the 4 October Report of the Secretary-General. The Resolution also gave UNTAET an initial tenure that extended to 31 January 2001.

Soon after Resolution 1272 (1999) was passed, Mr. Sergio Vieira de Mello was appointed by the Secretary-General as his Special Representative and Transitional Administrator for East Timor. Before his appointment, de Mello, a Brazilian diplomat, was Undersecretary-General for Humanitarian Affairs whom I first came to know when he was with the UNHCR. He assumed the post on 16 November 1999 and served with distinction until East Timor formally assumed independence on 20 May 2002 and UNTAET was replaced by the United Nations Mission of Support in East Timor (UNMISET).

The final parting

On 25 October, Indonesia's newly elected President, Abdurrahman Wahid, in a letter addressed to UN Secretary-General Kofi Annan, officially conveyed the Indonesian Government's acceptance of the results of the popular consultation in East Timor and the adoption of Decision No. V/MPR/1999.

After quoting Articles 1 and 2, he referred to Article 5 (1) of the Decision, which directed the President of Indonesia "together with international organizations to take concrete steps to provide protection for the East Timor people as a consequence arising from the holding of the popular consultation . . . ."

In that letter, President Wahid specifically mentioned that the Indonesian Government was ready to negotiate with the United Nations to find a mutually satisfactory settlementwith regard to matters relating to the consequences of the transfer of authority, including those related to public (state-owned), commercial as well as private assets. He further proposed that his letter and the Secretary-General's reply to it would constitute "an arrangement for the transfer of authority over East Timor to the UN as stipulated in Article 6 of the Agreement between the Republic of Indonesia and the Portuguese Republic on the question of East Timor." and that "accordingly the transfer of authority would take effect on the date of the Secretary-General's reply."

This proposed arrangement was indeed in accordance with the procedure earlier agreed upon at the ministerial level dialogue to signify the transfer of authority, as the United Nations appeared reluctant to agree on a more explicit arrangement for the transfer of authority because it would imply UN recognition of Indonesian sovereignty over East Timor.

On 29 October 1999 came the letter of reply of the Secretary-General acknowledging the President's letter and welcoming Decision No. V/MPR/1999 of the People's Consultative Assembly. The Secretary-General also informed the President of the appointment of Mr. Sergio Vieira de Mello as his Special Representative and Transitional Administrator for East Timor.

With the exchange of these letters, authority over East Timor was transfered from Indonesia to the United Nations. Consequently East Timor formally reverted back to its status prior to 1976, namely as a non-self-governing territory under the United Nations.

Shortly thereafter, on 31 October 1999, Indonesia's remaining troops in East Timor left without ceremony or fanfare. In New York, Portugal and Indonesia agreed that the United Nations put to a close the consideration of the long-standing item, "Question of East Timor," and further concurred that henceforth any discussions on East Timor would be done under the newly titled item: "The situation in East Timor during its transition to Independence".

Finally, on 2 November 1999, I formally handed over my function and responsibilities as Minister for Foreign Affairs to my successor in the new Cabinet of President Wahid, Dr. Alwi Shihab, a long-time friend whom I had known since his student days in Egypt and the United States.

I had served as Foreign Minister since March 1988, a period of slightly less than 12 consecutive years. With the transfer of authority in East Timor and my own transfer of duties to Dr. Alwi Shihab, my official dealings with the question of East Timor, which had lasted for some 23 years, came to an end.

Epilogue

THE ULTIMATE departure of Indonesia from East Timor, preceded by a burst of uncontrolled violence and bloodshed, marked the end of a political saga that was replete with missed opportunities, mutual misperceptions and ill-conceived policies.

This was not the first time that the Indonesian people and Government had to face the opprobrium of certain Western powers in the pursuit of what Indonesia perceived to be an issue of fundamental national interest. But unlike in the case of, for example, the West Irian question in the late fifties and early sixties, the factors that contributed to the emergence and outcome of the East Timor question were far more complex and interconnected.

Historical context

A full understanding of the East Timor issue, therefore, requires a correct knowledge of the historical context in which it arose and evolved, starting from 1975. It should be recalled that the emergence of a new era in Portugal, ushered in by the so-called "Carnation Revolution," and the rise of the question of East Timor's decolonization as an international issue in 1975 coincided with the fall of South Vietnam and the withdrawal of American troops from the former Indo-China.

The unification of Vietnam under communist rule as a result of the military victory of North Vietnam over American-backed South Vietnam stoked fears in the United States and West Europe that the rest of the countries of Southeast Asia would inexorably succumb like "falling dominoes" to the encroachment of communism in that part of the world.

Most Indonesians at that time still had fresh memories of the turmoil the nation went through in the aftermath of a failed communist-led coup in 1965. Hence, Indonesian circles, especially those in the military establishment, were receptive to the "domino theory" that was almost a doctrine in the West. According to this view, an independent East Timor, right in the middle of the Indonesian archipelago, would pose a grave security threat as it would be poor, weak, unstable and easy prey to the influence of communist countries close by.

The reputation, behaviour and pronouncements of the leaders of the dominant political party in East Timor at that time, FRETILIN, only strengthened this perception. For example, FRETILIN was quoted by the international press as saying that they would welcome any assistance from the Soviet Union and China. And yet the Western powers took no visible interest in the turmoil taking place in East Timor as political parties engaged in a struggle for power leading to civil war.

Hence, as the situation in the territory progressively worsened, an initially reluctant President Suharto finally agreed with his military advisers that Indonesia had to be directly involved in East Timor.

Policy shift

More than two decades later, in 1998-1999, Indonesia would make a startling policy shift on East Timor. In this policy shift, a confluence of domestic and international factors and events, both economic and political, also played a significant role.

There was, in the first place, a fundamental transformation of the global environment that attended the end of the Cold War, the impact of globalization in all its manifestations, increased interdependence among states and interconnection among problems, and the high premium being given all over the world to notions of good governance, democracy and democratization, human rights and humanitarian ideals in the foreign policies of Western countries. With the end of the Cold War, security perceptions of the West changed and Indonesia was no longer regarded as a country that could serve as a bulwark against communist expansion in the region. The threat was simply no longer there. Consequently, perceptions of the East Timor question also became increasingly influenced by human rights and humanitarian considerations.

Globalization had a profound impact on Indonesia's policies and way of handling the East Timor question: comprehensive and rapid media coverage on events in the territory and the availability of various means of communication with the outside world had a way of diminishing Indonesia's influence on East Timorese society.

In the economic and financial sphere, globalization contributed to the so-called Asian financial crisis, which undoubtedly precipitated the fall of the Suharto Government. This in turn, led to economic collapse and socio-political crisis in Indonesia. Total catastrophe could only be prevented through the institution of wide-ranging reform in all fields. Within this overall context of rapid and pervasive change, the need for a new approach towards a solution of the East Timor issue became increasingly apparent.

However, the way and the speed with which the East Timor problem was resolved by President Habibie in 1999 was entirely unexpected - even by Indonesia's opponents.

The role of ASEAN

Another issue that needs to be clarified is the widespread accusation leveled against ASEAN —that it failed to play a commensurate role in resolving the East Timor question. According to this view, ASEAN remained passive throughout the crisis and only joined the international community in addressing the problem, somewhat hesitantly at first, when the multinational force was formed. I believe this is a patently erroneous and unfair judgment.

From the outset ASEAN, like Indonesia, regarded the question of East Timor as an unfinished decolonization issue. Hence, it correctly considered the United Nations to be the right context for resolving the conflict. Over the years, as Indonesia patiently pursued a peaceful solution through the tripartite dialogue under the auspices of the UN Secretary-General, ASEAN gave its full support and cooperation, all the while loyally backing Indonesia's stand.

However, when the East Timor question, in the wake of the popular consultation process, threatened to become a regional security threat rather than simply a decolonization issue, ASEAN did join in the international effort to restore peace and stability by contributing its forces, first to INTERFET and subsequently to UNTAET. Thus in my view, the substance and timing of ASEAN's role in the resolution of the East Timor issue was perfectly correct.

The PR angle

The East Timor conflict was, apart from anything else, also a public relations war which was waged successfully against Indonesia by the pro-independence East Timorese. It was supported by the Portuguese Government and a vociferous and well-financed NGO lobby. Throughout the conflict, Indonesia was first depicted as an aggressor and expansionist state, intent on swallowing a small neighbour and later on as a systematic and gross violator of human rights.

The Department of Foreign Affairs, and I personally, had to spend a great deal of time and energy in rebutting these accusations and debunking the many myths that were spun around the East Timor conflict by our opponents. For example, we pointed out that throughout its short history as an independent state, Indonesia had never showed any interest in territorial expansion. For example, had Indonesia been inherently expansionist, it could have taken over East Timor when India marched into the small Portuguese colony of Goa, in 1961. At that time, Portugal, under the Salazar/Caetano dictatorial regime, was shunned by the West and recieved neither support nor sympathy for this expansionist policy.

If Indonesia had coveted East Timor that would have been the perfect time for it to make its move to grab another neglected Portuguese colony, and not when Portugal was being hailed by the world for restoring its democracy. Moreover, the fact of the matter is that it was only in 1975, when East Timor was abandoned by the Portuguese and descended into a raging civil war, that Indonesia felt compelled to intervene.

In the end, however, I had to admit that Indonesia was losing the propaganda contest. This was partly due also to our underestimation of the power of the NGOs and the international press in influencing the policies of Western governments and in swaying world public opinion.

From pebble to boulder

In its campaign, the Portuguese Government also tried, especially after the Santa Cruz incident, to paint Indonesia as a "pariah" state, shunned by most of the international community because of its human rights record, and as a country heavily burdened by the East Timor issue.

It was in this context that when a foreign journalist asked me to comment on this image being promoted by Portugal, I gave an answer that was to be quoted widely for quite some time. The East Timor issue, I said, contrary to what Portugal would like the world to believe, was far from being a problem of such overwhelming proportion to Indonesia as to make it a "pariah" state.

In fact, Indonesia's election to the chairmanship of the Non-aligned Movement (1992-1995), its prominent role within ASEAN, APEC and the East Asian region and its acknowledged contributions in the UN and outside it to regional and international peace and security, completely belie such a characterization. Thus East Timor, in my mind, was a problem for Indonesia, but it was only as bothersome as the proverbial "pebble in the shoe." This was the original context and meaning of that remark.

In retrospect, however, I have to admit that in its final years, the East Timor problem was no longer a mere pebble in the shoe but had become a veritable boulder, dragging down Indonesia's international reputation to one of its lowest points.

Reconciliation and the way forward

As far as my personal role in the East Timor saga was concerned, the hatchet was finally buried when I visited Timor Leste in September 2003, at the invitation of President Xanana Gusmao, followed by my visit to Portugal in June 2004, at the invitation of the Foreign Minister, Dra. Teresa Patricio Gouveia.

From 8 to 10 September 2003, my wife and I paid a visit to Dili at the personal invitation of President Gusmao and the First Lady, Mrs. Kirsty Sword-Gusmao. This was not the first time for me to visit independent Timor Leste, as I had accompanied President Megawati Sukarnoputri to Dili when, on 20 May 2002, she attended the official, midnight inauguration ceremony of Timor Leste's independence. But that was a short visit of only a few hours. This time it was quite a memorable stay of three days, not the least because of the warmth of the welcome and hospitality extended to us by our Timorese hosts.

One item on the programme of the visit was a public seminar on the topic: *Timor Leste, Indonesia and the World*, specially organized for the occasion, in which I was the featured speaker. Other speakers included Foreign Minister Jose Ramos Horta; Ambassador Kamalesh Sharma, Special Representative of the UN Secretary General and Head of the UNMISET (UN Mission of Support in East Timor); and Ambassador Paul Foley of Australia. President Xanana Gusmao, apart from giving the introductory speech, took on the role of moderator of the proceedings, an extraordinary thing for a Head of State to do.

Among those present were the Speaker of Parliament, Francisco Gutteres; members of the Cabinet; the Commander of the UN Peacekeeping Forces, Lt. Gen. Khaeruddin bin Mat Yusof; the Timor Leste Armed Forces Commander, Brig. Gen. Taur Matan Ruak; Bishop Carlos Felipe Belo; as well as members of Parliament, academics, representatives of national and international NGOs, heads of diplomatic missions and members of the press. I also had the opportunity to meet again with old acquaintances or erstwhile protagonists in the East Timor saga such as Mar'i Alkatiri, now Prime Minister of Timor Leste; the brothers Joao and Mario Carrascalao; Xavier do Amaral; Clementino Dos Reis Amaral and others.

In my remarks, I first touched on the substantive progress that had already been made in consolidating the ties of friendship and cooperation between the two countries, starting even before Timor Leste assumed independence on May 20, 2002. I then described the fundamental changes that had occurred and continued to take place on the global scene, to which all states and international institutions had to adapt themselves and which inevitably posed challenges to our respective national interests and the state of our bilateral relations.

After the presentations, a lively question-and-answer session followed, during which President Xanana as moderator occasionally deflected some of the more sensitive questions directed to me, although I was quite ready to respond to them.

But apart from the official and unofficial meetings and receptions organized in our honour, including a pleasant informal dinner offered by Foreign Minister Ramos Horta at his home, the highlight of the visit was the private dinner the President and Mrs. Gusmao gave for us at their residence, in the village of Balibar high up in the hills south of Dili.

There, in the intimacy of his home, surrounded by his wife, his two children and his mother-in-law who was visiting them, I really came to fully appreciate the admirable qualities of this remarkable leader. The same cordial welcome was accorded to me and my wife when we visited Portugal from 2 to 5 June 2004, at the invitation of Foreign Minister Teresa Gouveia.

Actually, the invitation was originally extended to me by one of her predecessors, former Foreign Minister and negotiating counterpart Jose Durao Barosso who had unofficially visited Jakarta in July 2001. But by the time I went to Portugal, Mr. Barosso had become Prime Minister and so the invitation was issued by his successor. As in the case of the visit to Timor Leste, the ostensible reason for the journey to Lisbon was a speaking engagement. This time I was invited to a conference on *Changes in South East Asia and its Relations with the European Union*, which was organized by the *Instituto Diplomatico*. But obviously, the real resaon for the event was "reconciliation."

After officially paying a call on Minister Gouveia, I had the opportunity to meet over dinner with members of the newly established Association of Portuguese-Indonesian Friendship and Cooperation, *the Associaçao Luso-Indonesia para Amizade e Cooperaçao (*ALIAC*)*. Chaired by an old friend of Indonesia, Ambassador Antonio Pinto da França, the Association comprised a number of eminent Portuguese academics, representatives of the cultural establishment and the industrial/business community, all with great interest in promoting Portuguese-Indonesian relations.

The conference was opened by the Foreign Minister and I spoke there about the ASEAN Security Community, a new concept that had just been launched on Indonesia's initiative. Other speakers included Prof. Tim Huxley, Senior Fellow at the London Institute of International and Strategic Studies (IISS); Jose Ramos Horta, Foreign Minister of Timor Leste; Prof. Antonio Barbedo Magelháes and Mr. Aldo Dell 'Ariccia of the European Commission.

During the luncheon offered by the Secretary of State for Foreign Affairs, Dra. Manuela Franco, I had the opportunity to meet with old friends such as former Foreign Minister Jaime Gama, Ambassador Rui de Medina and Ambassador Ana Gomes. We were also fortunate to be able to squeeze in a short trip by car to the city of Porto for some sightseeing, hosted and accompanied by another good friend of Indonesia, Mr. Luciano da Silva and his Indonesian wife. On our return journey to Lisbon we dropped by at the ranch-home residence of Ambassador Pinto da França and his wife in the village of Tomar, where we spent a delightful evening reminiscing about old times.

Our visit to Portugal was most enjoyable in all respects. But as earlier noted, throughout my two visits to Timor Leste and Portugal and notwithstanding the larger agenda in which they were framed, the future of Indonesian-Timor Leste ties was a major topic of discussion.

It was also a subject that long occupied my mind. I thought then as I think today that as the Timor Leste and Indonesia step into a new era in their relationship, given the historical and geopolitical framework within which this bilateral relationship is cast, there is no option but for the two countries to draw closer to each other.

In an increasingly globalized and interdependent world, we must nurture and continuously strengthen good-neighbourly and forward looking policies of friendship and cooperation in the interest of our respective national development goals as well as of the peace, progress and stability of our region.

(Footnotes)

[1] Indonesia went on the brink of war with the Netherlands on the issue of the much-delayed return of West Irian to Indonesian administration and control in the early 1960s. Diplomatic efforts by the United States and the United Nations persuaded both sides to settle the dispute through negotiations. West Irian is today the Indonesian province of Papua.

Appendix 1

MEMORANDUM OF UNDERSTANDING

1. The Portuguese Government reiterated that the fundamental responsibility for the decolonization of Portuguese Timor lies with Portugal and that Portugal should rightly assume to undertake all efforts towards the speedy and orderly implementation of the act of self-determination by the people of Portuguese Timor. The Indonesian Government reiterated its position that it recognizes the Republic of Portugal as the sole authority in Portuguese Timor until such time when the people of Portuguese Timor shall exercise their lawful rights of self-determination.

2. Both sides expressed their continued adherence to the principles of decolonization as enunciated in the pertinent resolution of the U.N. and to the scrupulous safeguarding of the principle of respect of the will of the people of Portuguese Timor.

3. In accordance with those principles, the two sides agreed that it is urgently necessary that conditions of stability and order in Portuguese Timor are created which will enable its people freely to decide their own future.

   To this end, the two sides agreed to exert concerted and coordinated efforts in order to convince the political parties of Portuguese Timor of the necessity to resume talks with the Portuguese Government aimed at finding a solution in accordance with the wishes of the people of Portuguese Timor.

4. The two sides further agreed that such talks must be convened at the earliest possible time between Portugal and all political parties simultaneously and be based on a precise agenda including at least the following subjects for discussion ;

   - the establishment and maintenance of an effective cease-fire in Portuguese Timor ;
   - the problem of the return of Portuguese Timor refugees now residing in Indonesian territory;
   - the problem of 23 Portuguese nationals detained by the UDT ;

- 2 -

- the establishment of a transitional governing mechanism in Portuguese Timor, in which all the political parties are equitably represented, to prepare for the implementation of the act of self-determination.

5. With regard to the achievement of a cease-fire, the two sides agreed to exert all efforts to persuade all the parties concerned in Portuguese Timor to agree on a cease-fire.

6. With regard to the effective maintenance of such a cease-fire, the Indonesian side proposed the contribution of an Indonesian military contingent to a joint Portuguese-Indonesian Peace-keeping force. The Portuguese side expressed its position that it would regard it as inconvenient to accept the proposition of a joint peace-keeping force as it would run contrary to Portuguese authority over Portuguese Timor. Instead, the Portuguese side requested Indonesia's cooperation in providing logistic facilities to tthe Portuguese Government in Timor, especially facilities to Portuguese air and sea transport. The Indonesian side expressed its readine to study this request in the light of overall efforts to restore peace and stability in Portuguese Timor.

7. The Portuguese side acknowledged that the refugees constitute an acute and pressing problem to the Indonesian Government and people. With regard to the return of the refugees to their places of origin under adequate security protection, as demanded by the refugees of the Indonesian Government, the Indonesian side proposed that these refugees be escorted by Indonesian police units into Portuguese Timor. The Portuguese side expressed the view that such a proposition would be equally unacceptable to the concept of Portuguese authority and sovereignty over Portuguese Timor. The Portuguese side expressed its understanding of Indonesia's urgent need to resolve this problem, inter alia by endeavouring to secure the concurrence of the political parties now in control of the various areas of Portuguese Timor to provide such security protection to the refugees. However, in the view of the Portuguese side the refugee problem must be solved by both sides endeavouring to obtain the security protection of the political parties and by involving the collaboration of the International

Red ....

Red Cross.

8. The Indonesian side acknowledged that the question of the 23 Portuguese nationals detained by the UDT is of utmost importance to the Portuguese Government. The Indonesian side reitarated its readiness to convey the concern of the Portuguese Government on this matter to the UDT and to exert all efforts in order to effect their speedy release. The Portuguese side expressed its conviction that this release would represent a gesture of the political goodwill of the UDT with which Portugal has never considered itself to be at war. In Portugal's view, continued unjustified detention would create an unfavourable climate to the success of the talks.

9. Both sides agreed on the need to avoid external interference in the process of decolonization in Portuguese Timor, especially those which may lead to further fratricide and armed fighting in the territory.

10. Both sides agreed that under the present circumstances premature involvement by the U.N. and other forms of "internationalization" of the problem of Portuguese Timor would be inopportune. It is acknowledged however, that at a certain stage U.N. involvement and endorsement would be considered appropriate and necessary.

11. The Portuguese Government reiterated that in the implementation of the decolonization in Portuguese Timor it will be necessary to safegard the legitimate interests of the countries of the region, particularly the interests of the Republic of Indonesia as the closest neighbouring country.

12. The two sides agreed on the necessity to continue to maintain close cooperation and consultation between them on all aspects

and phases of the orderly and peaceful process of the decolonization in Portuguese Timor. They also agreed to maintain close cooperation and consultation in facing the issue of the decolonization of Portugues Timor in the U.N.

Done in Rome, November 3, 1975 .

the Government of the Repul lic of Portugal,	For the Government of the Repu. of Indonesia,
(E. MELO ANTUNES) Minister for Foreign Affairs	(ADAM MALIK) Minister for Foreign Affairs

Appendix 2

Appendix

Act Number 1/A.D. 1976 of "Provisional Government of East Timor" in the English version delivered to the special representative by representatives of the "Provisional Government"

Article 1:

The fate and future of the people of East Timor are in the hands of the people of East Timor. The right of self-determination according to the principles of democracy is recognized as inalienable and undisputable.

Article 2:

This basic democratic right is to be implemented in accordance with the traditions and identity of the people of East Timor, meaning a representative system by means of consensus and consent.

Article 3:

To constitute a representative body for the whole of East Timor the existing representation of the region of East Timor, designated the Deliberative Council of East Timor, established at the same time with the Provisional Government of East Timor, needs to be complemented with representatives from all conselhos.

Article 4:

Conselho Popular Assemblies comprising 13 conselhos, complementing the regional East Timor representation, are to be formed in conformity with the principles of consensus and consent.

Article 5:

Solely for the capital city of Dili the representatives for the Conselho Popular Assemblies and the Regional Popular Assembly will be elected in accordance with the one-man/one-vote.

Article 6:

These Popular Assemblies on their respective levels and in their respective areas of jurisdiction have popular sovereign powers.

Article 7:

Every Popular Assembly in administrative conselhos/regions comprise 15 to 20 members in accordance with the number of residents of the area.

S/12106
English
Annex
Page 6

Article 8:

At the latest, one month after the promulgation of this act the formation of the Conselho Popular Assemblies and the perfection of the Regional Popular Assembly of East Timor should be implemented.

Article 9:

(a) The members of the Popular Assembly are elected from the people residing in the administrative postos/conselhos/region concerned in accordance with the principles of consensus and consent and with consideration of the traditional and cultural values prevailing and developing in the area. (b) The Regional Popular Assembly, besides being represented by prominent citizens of East Timor, is complemented by representatives from the conselhos, comprising two or three members, and should also include representatives of the tribal chiefs/kings and representatives of the religious groups.

Article 10:

This act is drafted legally on the second day of April 1976 and is sanctioned by the Deliberative Council of the Region of East Timor.

Appendix 3

STRICTLY CONFIDENTIAL

Memorandum of Understanding

I. The Representatives of Indonesia and Portugal held preliminary consultations in New York between 19 February and 12 March 1986, under the auspices of the United Nations. Recalling the Secretary-General's progress report to the fortieth session of the General Assembly, they agreed to continue their substantive talks, building upon the measure of understanding already achieved during the first phase of talks, so as to prepare the ground for a just, comprehensive and internationally-acceptable settlement of the question of East Timor. Accordingly, it was agreed that the first round of the second phase of the process would be held from 1-4 April 1986. Further rounds of talks will be held as required, on the understanding that all aspects of a definitive solution will have been considered before the opening of the forty-first session of the General Assembly.

II. The agenda of the substantive talks will be the following :

(a) Consideration of the framework and modalities of a comprehensive and internationally-acceptable settlement.

(b) Consideration of guarantees for religious freedom and for the preservation and promotion of the linguistic and cultural heritage, as well as for the humanitarian, economic and social conditions of the people of East Timor.

(c) Consideration of topics of current relevance, including certain aspects concerning resumption of diplomatic relations.

III. It was agreed that the Secretary-General would be invited by Indonesia to dispatch a team to observe the Indonesian general elections, including in East Timor, in April 1987. However, the terms of reference of the observer team and its composition remained to be determined. It was understood that the report of the team of observers would be factual in nature.

IV. The report of the Secretary-General to the forty-first session of the General Assembly will, in principle, be issued by mid-September 1986 (prior to the opening of the session but following the conclusion of the Non-Aligned Summit in Harare). It was understood that the report would cover the following topics, as appropriate :

(a) Summary of contacts made and issues discussed during 1985-1986.

(b) Invitation to send a team to observe the Indonesian general elections, including in East Timor (as agreed under III).

- 2 -

(c) Guarantees for the people of East Timor (as agreed under II (b)).
(d) Implementation of repatriation programmes.
(e) Humanitarian activities of the UN and other organizations.

V. It was agreed that, following the issuance of the report of the Secretary-General, deferral of the item on the question of East Timor until the forty-second session would be sought, referring specifically to the invitation extended to the Secretary-General to send an observer team at the time of the Indonesian general elections. Should conditions permit and if it is deemed desirable by both sides, the item could be re-introduced at the resumed forty-first session of the General Assembly. A procedural mechanism to accomplish this would have to be found.

VI. The deferral will be construed as giving the Secretary-General the clearance to accept the invitation extended to him by Indonesia.

VII. It was further agreed that, in the light of the report of the observer team and upon consideration of the item by the General Assembly, one or more Member States may propose a draft resolution determining that a comprehensive settlement of the problem has been achieved and that East Timor no longer falls within the purview of Chapter XI of the Charter.

VIII. If such a resolution were to be adopted by the General Assembly, Portugal would request that the item, "The Situation in Timor", be deleted from the list of matters of which the Security Council is seized, and the two countries would subsequently take appropriate steps to normalize their relations.

New York, 12 March 1986

Appendix 4

New York, 17 July 1986

Assurances

During the substantive talks, Indonesia assured that the guarantees embodied in its Constitution, including Article 18, which recognizes the traditional rights and special character of particular territories as further prescribed by statute, are applicable to East Timor. It provided re-assurances on religious freedom, the preservation and promotion of the cultural heritage of East Timor, and humanitarian, economic and social conditions. It further provided assurances on political and civil rights, as well as other aspects of the question of East Timor. In this context, reference was made to the relevant provisions of the Indonesian Constitution, i.e. Articles 27-34. Indonesia also re-affirmed its commitment to the Universal Declaration of Human Rights.

Religious Freedom

Indonesia reiterated its assurances on complete freedom to profess and practice all religions, including the Catholic faith. The Catholic Church is allowed to participate, with other humanitarian organizations, in the provision of humanitarian assistance to the population. Members of the clergy have complete freedom of movement to carry out their apostolic duties and foreign-born missionaries have free access to the Territory, in accordance with immigration regulations. The Catholic Church also has full authority over the parochial school system in East Timor.

Preservation and Promotion of the Cultural Heritage of East Timor

Assurances were given concerning the protection and preservation of the cultural heritage of the people of East Timor, and the specific influence of the Portuguese heritage was noted. Accordingly, all aspects of the culture of the people of East Timor, encompassing their ethnic and linguistic heritage, their cultural and religious ceremonies and practices, and the specific expression of their artistic forms and customs, including music, dance, art, folklore, handicrafts and traditions, are fully respected and exercised freely. Historical monuments are also being identified, restored and preserved.

- 2 -

Detailed information was provided by Indonesia regarding activities which have been undertaken in the territory to promote policies consistent with these assurances. In particular, the Government has undertaken programmes to develop the education infrastructures in East Timor and to ensure access to all levels of education, especially primary education, on a widespread and non-discriminatory basis. Measures have been taken for East Timorese to receive teacher-training, so that schools in the territory may eventually be fully staffed by East Timorese. Assistance is also provided to the Catholic teachers-training school in East Timor, and programmes are being developed to promote religious teachings in the schools. In addition, Tetum, the most-widely spoken of the several dialects in East Timor, is being used as the language of instruction in schools through the third grade, and courses are being developed to teach Tetum as a separate linguistic subject in the higher grades. The Portuguese language is also the language of instruction in some parochial schools.

Indonesia also provided information regarding the development of the communications infrastructures, including the production of radio and television programmes in the local dialects of the East Timorese, in order to promote the availability of information on socio-cultural, economic, educational and agricultural matters. Assurances were given that the ethnic and cultural identity of the East Timorese was being respected in the formulation of development projects for the territory.

Humanitarian, Economic and Social Conditions

The concerns of the international community regarding the improvement of the humanitarian situation of the people of East Timor were discussed. In this connection, Indonesia assured that it was committed to continued co-operation with the international humanitarian organizations engaged in providing assistance and protection to the people of East Timor. The need to encourage access to the territory for the purposes of, inter alia, assessment and verification of conditions prevailing in East Timor was also recognized. Indonesia assured that it would continue to facilitate general access to the territory, including regular visits by foreign journalists, diplomatic personnel and others.

Information was provided concerning the protection and relief-assistance activities of the International Committee of the Red Cross. The situation of the displaced persons on the island of Ataúro and their resettlement on the main island was discussed, in particular. The progress made in the implementation of the repatriation programme for former Portuguese civil servants was also reviewed. In addition, agreement was reached on the formulation and implementation of a programme for the repatriation of certain East Timorese expatriates now residing in Portugal.

As is consistent with Article 25 of the Universal Declaration of Human Rights, Article 27 of the Indonesian Constitution protects the right to work and to expect a reasonable standard of living. Information was provided regarding the policies which have been adopted to promote the improvement in living conditions of the people of East Timor. In particular, Indonesia reiterated its determination to make every effort to ensure increased production and adequate distribution of food in the Territory and indicated the measures which have been taken to stimulate economic activity and local industrial development. Priority consideration is also given to the improvement of the availability of health and medical facilities for the population, by establishing hospitals, clinics, rural public health centres, and preventive health care programmes, and by increasing the number of doctors and medical personnel. Indonesia also reaffirmed its policy of promoting the balanced and harmonious administration of government in East Timor, inter alia, by staffing all levels of the civil service in the territory by East Timorese, as far as possible.

Political and Civil Rights and Other Aspects

Assurances were given that the people of East Timor enjoyed the rights and privileges guaranteed by the Indonesian Constitution and laws in the same way as all citizens of Indonesia. In particular, Indonesia stressed that the East Timorese are assured of equal status and rights of citizenship and equal guarantees of fundamental rights and freedoms without any distinction or discrimination. They also had equal rights and opportunities for representation and effective participation at all levels of government, including access to and participation in the conduct of public affairs through freely-elected representatives, to vote and to be elected at elections, which are by universal and equal suffrage and held by secret ballot.

Assurances were given by Indonesia on freedom of movement of the population of East Timor throughout the territory in the same way as for the citizens of Indonesia in other provinces. Information was provided concerning the current trial proceedings against East Timorese detainees. Indonesia assured the right of the East Timorese to an effective remedy by the competent tribunals for acts violating the fundamental rights granted by the Constitution or by law and to due process and equal protection of law, including the right to be tried at public proceedings, conducted in full conformity with Articles 10 and 11 of the Universal Declaration of Human Rights, and the right of appeal to a higher court. In addition, assurances were given on complete amnesty for those who renounce insurgency. Assurances were also given regarding respect for the rights provided in Articles 5, 9, 12 and 13 of the Universal Declaration.

Appendix 5

UNITED NATIONS

A

General Assembly

Distr.
GENERAL

A/46/456
13 September 1991

ORIGINAL: ENGLISH

Forty-sixth session
Item 105 of the provisional agenda*

QUESTION OF EAST TIMOR

Progress report of the Secretary-General

1. In my last report (A/45/507), dated 17 September 1990, I indicated that, in the framework of the substantive talks that Indonesia and Portugal have been holding under my auspices, the two sides were considering the terms of reference of and modalities for a visit to East Timor by a delegation from the Portuguese Parliament. I further reported that considerable progress had been achieved in that regard.

2. During the course of the past year, I and Under-Secretary-General Rafeeuddin Ahmed, who has been assisting me in these endeavours, have continued our consultations with the two Governments. Discussions have been held with the President, Prime Minister and Foreign Minister of Portugal and with the Foreign Minister of Indonesia, as well as with other officials from both Governments concerned with the issue. In the course of those consultations, both sides have reiterated their determination to seek a comprehensive and internationally acceptable solution through continuing dialogue and negotiation.

3. At a meeting held under my chairmanship on 27 June 1991, Indonesia and Portugal reached agreement, ad referendum, on a number of pending issues related to the terms of reference of the proposed visit. That agreement, a copy of which is annexed to the present report, was subsequently approved by the competent authorities of the two sides.

---

* A/46/150.

91-29613 2712d (E)

/...

A/46/456
English
Page 2

4. Since then, three rounds of the substantive talks have been held to consider the practical arrangements for the visit of the Portuguese parliamentary delegation to East Timor. In the course of those talks, the Indonesian side confirmed its readiness to receive a small advance team in order to prepare the logistical and technical aspects of the visit of the Portuguese parliamentary delegation. It is foreseen that the visit of the advance team would take place a few weeks prior to that of the delegation of the Portuguese Parliament, subject to agreement being achieved on the itinerary and other practical details. I will continue, within the context of my good offices, to make every effort to assist in the realization of that visit, in the hope that it can help to create an atmosphere conducive to a comprehensive and internationally acceptable solution to the question of East Timor.

Appendix 6

ANNEX

Terms of reference of the visit to East Timor by a delegation from the Portuguese Parliament

1. With a view to facilitating the achievement of a comprehensive and internationally acceptable settlement of the question of East Timor, Indonesia and Portugal have agreed to a visit by a Portuguese parliamentary delegation to East Timor. The terms of reference, modalities and timing of such a visit were decided in the course of the talks held under the auspices of the Secretary-General. The realization of the Portuguese parliamentary delegation visit, in all its aspects, shall in no way be construed as prejudicing the respective positions of principle of the parties with regard to the substance of the question.

I. OBJECTIVE

2. The objective of the Portuguese parliamentary delegation visit is to obtain first-hand information on the situation in the territory, on the understanding that the visit will not be investigative in nature.

II. COMPOSITION

3. The delegation will be composed of 13 Portuguese Parliamentarians, accompanied by 13 Portuguese officials and 10 Portuguese journalists. The list of the delegation and those accompanying it will be submitted by Portugal to Indonesia at least three weeks prior to the commencement of the visit.

III. INDONESIAN JOURNALISTS

4. Indonesia may designate 10 Indonesian journalists to accompany the delegation.

IV. INTERNATIONAL JOURNALISTS

5. The Portuguese parliamentary delegation will be joined by 12 international journalists, 6 selected by each side. Each side will communicate its list of international journalists to the other at least three weeks prior to the commencement of the visit.

V. REPRESENTATIVES OF THE SECRETARY-GENERAL

6. The Portuguese parliamentary delegation will also be joined by representatives of the Secretary-General, dispatched in the exercise of his good offices.

/...

VI. ACCESS

7. The question of visa formalities for the Portuguese parliamentary delegation and those accompanying it is treated in the unilateral declaration submitted by Indonesia and attached to the present document as appendix I.

8. On its way to Dili, the Portuguese parliamentary delegation will make a stop-over at Jakarta airport and the leader of the delegation will accompany the representatives of the Secretary-General to pay a courtesy call on the Speaker of the Indonesian House of Representatives. A unilateral declaration submitted by Portugal in that regard is attached to the present document as appendix II.

VII. FREEDOM OF MOVEMENT AND OF CONTACTS

9. The Portuguese parliamentary delegation shall have unhindered access to all parts of the territory, within the context of the agreed objective of the visit, in conditions of peace and security.

10. The Portuguese parliamentary delegation shall be free to meet whomever it wishes and anyone who wishes to meet the Portuguese parliamentary delegation will be allowed to do so. No action, including of a security nature, may be taken by the Indonesian authorities that could prejudice any potential or actual contacts. Individuals who meet the Portuguese parliamentary delegation shall not be made to suffer any adverse consequences as a result of those contacts.

11. The visit of the Portuguese parliamentary delegation shall be undertaken on the basis of a predetermined but flexible itinerary and list of contacts. During the visit, the delegation may request that changes may be made to the itinerary and the list of contacts, provided they are of a reasonable nature, taking logistical constraints into account.

12. The Portuguese parliamentary delegation will provide its own interpreters and the contacts may be undertaken in private and on the basis of confidentiality.

13. Indonesia will extend full cooperation to the Portuguese parliamentary delegation and those accompanying it for the realization of the visit, in accordance with the principles defined above.

VIII. TIMING AND DURATION

14. The visit will take place during the dry season and will last for approximately 10 to 12 days.

/...

IX. PREPARATORY STEPS

15. An advance team will travel to East Timor to prepare the practical arrangements for the visit of the Portuguese parliamentary delegation. The advance team will be lead by a representative of the Secretary-General and will include two representatives from the Indonesian side and two representatives from the Portuguese side.

Appendix 7

A/46/456
English
Page 6

APPENDIX I

Unilateral declaration by Indonesia concerning visa formalities

The Government of Indonesia believes that the visit by the Portuguese parliamentary delegation to East Timor upon the invitation of the Speaker of the Indonesian House of Representatives will constitute an important step towards the achievement of a comprehensive settlement of the question of East Timor acceptable to all parties concerned. In order to facilitate the visit, therefore, and out of respect for the noble efforts by the Secretary-General - made under his general mandate accorded by the Charter of the United Nations - to promote the reaching of an agreement between Indonesia and Portugal on the modalities and timing of the visit, the Government of Indonesia - in the exercise of its sovereignty - has decided to waive visa requirements for the members of the Portuguese parliamentary delegation and those accompanying it.

APPENDIX II

Unilateral declaration by Portugal concerning the stop-over in Jakarta

The stop-over in Jakarta and the visit of the leader of the Portuguese parliamentary delegation to the Indonesian House of Representatives, accompanying the representatives of the Secretary-General of the United Nations to pay a courtesy call on the Speaker, constitute only a gesture of good will testifying to the continuing availability of Portugal to achieve, through dialogue and negotiation with all parties directly concerned and under the auspices of the Secretary-General of the United Nations a just, comprehensive and internationally acceptable settlement to the question of East Timor.

UNITED
NATIONS

A S

General Assembly
Security Council

Distr.
GENERAL

A/53/951
S/1999/513
5 May 1999

ORIGINAL: ENGLISH

GENERAL ASSEMBLY
Fifty-third session

SECURITY COUNCIL
Fifty-fourth year

Question of East Timor

Report of the Secretary-General

1. The Security Council will be aware of the efforts which, since 1983, the Governments of Indonesia and Portugal have undertaken through my good offices to find a just, comprehensive and internationally acceptable solution to the question of East Timor. These efforts have culminated with the signature, on 5 May 1999, of an overall Agreement, attached herewith (annex I), between the two Governments entrusting me with the organization and conduct of a popular consultation for the purpose of ascertaining whether the East Timorese people, both inside and outside the Territory, accept or reject a proposed constitutional framework providing for a special autonomy for East Timor within the unitary Republic of Indonesia, which is appended to the Agreement. The Agreement requests me to establish immediately a United Nations mission in East Timor for the purpose of conducting the popular consultation.

2. The Council will note that, under article 5 of the Agreement, in the event of the popular consultation resulting in the approval of the proposed special autonomy by a majority of the East Timorese people, the Government of Indonesia would initiate the constitutional measures required for the implementation of the autonomy framework, and the Government of Portugal would initiate within the United Nations the procedures necessary for the removal of East Timor from the list of Non-Self-Governing Territories of the General Assembly and the deletion of the question of East Timor from the agendas of the Security Council and the General Assembly. Article 6 of the Agreement provides in parallel that, should the popular consultation result in a majority of the East Timorese people rejecting the proposed special autonomy, the Government of Indonesia would take the constitutional steps necessary to terminate Indonesia's links with East Timor, thus restoring under Indonesian law the status that East Timor held prior to 17 July 1976, and that the Governments of Indonesia and Portugal would agree with the Secretary-General on arrangements for a peaceful and orderly transfer of authority in East Timor to the United Nations, which would then initiate a process enabling East Timor to begin a transition towards independence.

99-12629 (E) 050599

/...

A/53/951
S/1999/513
English
Page 2

3. I should further point out that, under article 7 of the Agreement, it is foreseen that the United Nations will maintain an adequate presence in East Timor during the interim period between the conclusion of the popular consultation and the start of the implementation of either the special autonomy or the assumption of authority by the United Nations. Also, in the event that the East Timorese people approve the special autonomy framework, I am authorized under article 56 of the framework to establish in East Timor such offices as I may deem necessary in order to carry out my responsibility to monitor and verify compliance with its provisions.

4. The Governments of Indonesia and Portugal have also signed, on 5 May 1999, the two attached supplementary agreements, on the modalities for the popular consultation of the East Timorese through a direct ballot (annex II) and on security arrangements (annex III), which, inter alia, stipulate that 8 August 1999 will be the date for the ballot to take place, both inside and outside East Timor, that a secure environment devoid of violence or other forms of intimidation is a prerequisite for the holding of a free and fair popular consultation, that the appropriate Indonesian authorities have the responsibility to ensure such an environment as well as for the maintenance of law and order, and that the United Nations will ascertain whether the necessary security exists for the peaceful implementation of the consultation process.

5. Under the terms of the supplementary agreements, I have been requested by the two parties to deploy, immediately upon signature, United Nations personnel adequate for the execution of the various phases of the consultation process. I have also been requested, in paragraph 4 of the Agreement regarding security, to make available a number of civilian police officers to act as advisers to the Indonesian police in the discharge of their duties and, at the time of the consultation, to supervise the escort of ballot papers and boxes to and from the polling sites.

6. I do not wish to minimize the logistical and other problems that the United Nations will face in carrying out the consultation in such a short time-frame. The Security Council will be aware of the high level of tension and serious incidents of political violence that have recently occurred coupled with the reported opposition to the proposed consultation by some political elements in East Timor. I have emphasized to the parties the main elements that will need to be in place in order to enable me to determine that the necessary security conditions exist for the start of the operational phases of the consultation process. These include the bringing of armed civilian groups under strict control and the prompt arrest and prosecution of those who incite or threaten to use violence, a ban on rallies by armed groups while ensuring the freedom of association and expression of all political forces and tendencies, the redeployment of Indonesian military forces and the immediate institution of a process of laying down of arms by all armed groups to be completed well in advance of the holding of the ballot. I intend to report to the Security Council periodically on the evolution of the situation, the status of the United Nations presence and other matters regarding the implementation of the Agreements.

7. Given the limited period of time between the signature of these Agreements and the date of the ballot, I have opened a trust fund to which Member States

/...

may channel voluntary contributions, which would enable me, without waiting for the assessed budgetary process, to proceed as soon as possible with the establishment of a United Nations presence in East Timor.

8. Once the logistical and personnel requirements of the mission have been identified, I shall report them to the Security Council and to the General Assembly. I shall also be presenting to the Council, for its approval, my recommendations regarding the deployment of civilian police personnel.

/...

Appendix 9

Annex I

Agreement between the Republic of Indonesia and the Portuguese Republic on the question of East Timor

The Governments of Indonesia and Portugal,

Recalling General Assembly resolutions 1514 (XV), 1541(XV), 2625(XXV) and the relevant resolutions and decisions adopted by the Security Council and the General Assembly on the question of East Timor;

Bearing in mind the sustained efforts of the Governments of Indonesia and Portugal since July 1983, through the good offices of the Secretary-General, to find a just, comprehensive and internationally acceptable solution to the question of East Timor;

Recalling the agreement of 5 August 1998 to undertake, under the auspices of the Secretary-General, negotiations on a special status based on a wide-ranging autonomy for East Timor without prejudice to the positions of principle of the respective Governments on the final status of East Timor;

Having discussed a constitutional framework for an autonomy for East Timor on the basis of a draft presented by the United Nations, as amended by the Indonesian Government;

/...

Noting the position of the Government of Indonesia that the proposed special autonomy should be implemented only as an end solution to the question of East Timor with full recognition of Indonesian sovereignty over East Timor;

Noting the position of the Government of Portugal that an autonomy regime should be transitional, not requiring recognition of Indonesian sovereignty over East Timor or the removal of East Timor from the list of Non-Self-Governing Territories of the General Assembly, pending a final decision on the status of East Timor by the East Timorese people through an act of self-determination under United Nations auspices;

Taking into account that, although the Governments of Indonesia and Portugal each have their positions of principle on the prepared proposal for special autonomy, both agree that it is essential to move the peace process forward, and that therefore, the Governments of Indonesia and Portugal agree that the Secretary-General should consult the East Timorese people on the constitutional framework for autonomy attached hereto as an annex;

Bearing in mind that the Governments of Indonesia and Portugal requested the Secretary-General to devise the method and procedures for the popular consultation through a direct, secret and universal ballot;

/...

Agree as follows:

Article 1

Request the Secretary-General to put the attached proposed constitutional framework providing for a special autonomy for East Timor within the unitary Republic of Indonesia to the East Timorese people, both inside and outside East Timor, for their consideration and acceptance or rejection through a popular consultation on the basis of a direct, secret and universal ballot.

Article 2

Request the Secretary-General to establish, immediately after the signing of this Agreement, an appropriate United Nations mission in East Timor to enable him to effectively carry out the popular consultation.

Article 3

The Government of Indonesia will be responsible for maintaining peace and security in East Timor in order to ensure that the popular consultation is carried out in a fair and peaceful way in an atmosphere free of intimidation, violence or interference from any side.

Article 4

Request the Secretary-General to report the result of the popular consultation to the Security Council and the General Assembly, as well as to inform the Governments of Indonesia and Portugal and the East Timorese people.

/...

Article 5

If the Secretary-General determines, on the basis of the result of the popular consultation and in accordance with this Agreement, that, the proposed constitutional framework for special autonomy is acceptable to the East Timorese people, the Government of Indonesia shall initiate the constitutional measures necessary for the implementation of the constitutional framework, and the Government of Portugal shall initiate within the United Nations the procedures necessary for the removal of East Timor from the list of Non-Self-Governing Territories of the General Assembly and the deletion of the question of East Timor from the agendas of the Security Council and the General Assembly.

Article 6

If the Secretary-General determines, on the basis of the result of the popular consultation and in accordance with this Agreement, that the proposed constitutional framework for special autonomy is not acceptable to the East Timorese people, the Government of Indonesia shall take the constitutional steps necessary to terminate its links with East Timor thus restoring under Indonesian law the status East Timor held prior to 17 July 1976, and the Governments of Indonesia and Portugal and the Secretary-General shall agree on arrangements for a peaceful and orderly transfer of authority in East Timor to the United Nations. The Secretary-General shall, subject to the appropriate legislative mandate, initiate the procedure enabling East Timor to begin a process of transition towards independence.

/...

Article 7

During the interim period between the conclusion of the popular consultation and the start of the implementation of either option, the parties request the Secretary-General to maintain an adequate United Nations presence in East Timor.

DONE in New York, on this 5th day of May, 1999.

For the Government of Indonesia

Ali Alatas
Minister for Foreign Affairs

For the Government of Portugal

Jaime Gama
Minister for Foreign Affairs

Witnessed:

Kofi A. Annan
Secretary-General
United Nations

/.

Appendix **10**

A/53/951
S/1999/513
English
Page 29

Annex III

East Timor popular consultation

The Governments of Indonesia and Portugal and the Secretary-General of the United Nations,

Agree as follows:

1. A secure environment devoid of violence or other forms of intimidation is a prerequisite for the holding of a free and fair ballot in East Timor. Responsibility to ensure such an environment as well as for the general maintenance of law and order rests with the appropriate Indonesian security authorities. The absolute neutrality of the TNI (Indonesian Armed Forces) and the Indonesian Police is essential in this regard.

2. The Commission on Peace and Stability established in Dili on 21 April 1999 should become operational without delay. The Commission, in cooperation with the United Nations, will elaborate a code of conduct, by which all parties should abide, for the period prior to and following the consultation, ensure the laying down of arms and take the necessary steps to achieve disarmament.

3. Prior to the start of the registration, the Secretary-General shall ascertain, based on the objective evaluation of the UN mission, that the necessary security situation exists for the peaceful implementation of the consultation process.

4. The police will be solely responsible for the maintenance of law and order. The Secretary-General, after obtaining the necessary mandate, will make available a number of civilian police officers to act as advisers to the Indonesian Police in the discharge of their duties and, at the time of the consultation, to supervise the escort of ballot papers and boxes to and from the polling sites.

DONE in New York on this 5th day of May 1999

For the Government of Portugal	For the United Nations	For the Government of Indonesia
Jaime Gama Minister for Foreign Affairs Portugal	Kofi A. Annan Secretary-General United Nations	Ali Alatas Minister for Foreign Affairs Indonesia

Appendix 10

Appendix 11

04-05-99:ect

ANNEX

A CONSTITUTIONAL FRAMEWORK FOR A SPECIAL AUTONOMY FOR EAST TIMOR

PART ONE

RESPECTIVE AREAS OF COMPETENCE

Chapter I

The Indonesian (Central) Government

Section A: Foreign Relations

Article 1

The Indonesian Government, hereinafter referred to as the Central Government, shall have responsibility for and competence over the foreign affairs of the Special Autonomous Region of East Timor (SARET). It shall consult the Government of the SARET for the purpose of taking into account the views of the Government of the SARET on issues of particular relevance to the SARET.

Section B : Defence

Article 2

The Central Government shall have responsibility for and competence over the external defence of the SARET, as part of the territory of the unitary state of the Republic of Indonesia.

Article 3

For such purpose, the Indonesian armed forces (Tentara Nasional Indonesia - TNI) shall maintain a military presence in the SARET in the context of defending and safeguarding the external security of the SARET.

PR 56

Article 4

In the event of an external armed attack, or an imminent threat of such an attack, the Indonesian armed forces (TNI) may be deployed outside their bases or normal areas of operation in the exercise of its duty to defend the sovereignty and territorial integrity of the unitary state of the Republic of Indonesia.

Section C: Economic and Fiscal Policies

Article 5

The SARET shall be a part of the Indonesian monetary and customs unit subject to those national monetary and fiscal policies, and laws and regulations of Indonesia which are consistent with this Agreement.

Article 6

The Central Government will continue its assistance to the development of the SARET.

Article 7

The Central Government shall have exclusive competence over national taxation and the Government of the SARET shall have exclusive competence over local taxation, in conformity with the existing laws and regulations.

Article 8

Natural resources in the SARET, except those considered to be strategic or vital under national laws, shall be under the control of the Government of the SARET. In the exploitation of all natural resources, the Central Government and the Government of the SARET may establish cooperative or joint undertakings.

Article 9.

For the purposes of its overall development, the Government of the SARET may receive foreign assistance which is to be channelled through the Central Government.

Article 10

The Government of the SARET can enter into domestic loans to finance part of its budget, with the consent of the Regional Council of People's Representatives of the SARET.

2

Section D : Continuity of Indonesian Laws

Article 11

Indonesian laws in force upon the date of the entry into force of this Agreement that fall within the competence of the Central Government, as defined in this Chapter, shall remain in force for the SARET.

Chapter II

The Government of the Special Autonomous Region of East Timor

Article 12

All matters, other than those listed within Chapter I of Part One, and as provided in other relevant provisions of this Agreement, shall be within the responsibility and competence of the Government of the SARET.

Article 13

The powers of the Government of the SARET shall be exercised in accordance with the provisions of this Agreement, and also in accordance with the Constitution of the Republic of Indonesia.

Article 14

The Government of the SARET shall not:

a. restrict the rights of workers as recognized by law; and

b. reserve any occupation or public office solely to persons with East Timorese identity.

Chapter III

Jurisdictions of the Central Government and the Government of the SARET

Article 15

The Government of the SARET shall have jurisdiction over crimes committed in the SARET with the exception of those related to treason and terrorism, narcotics and other international crimes, over which Indonesian laws and jurisdiction shall prevail.

PART TWO

EAST TIMORESE IDENTITY AND IMMIGRATION

Chapter I

Definition

Article 16

Any person,

a. who was a lawful resident of East Timor prior to or in December 1975,

b. whose father, mother, grandfather, or grandmother was a lawful resident of East Timor prior to or in December 1975, or

c. who has permanently resided in East Timor for a period of at least five years at the time of the entry into force of this Agreement,

shall be considered to have East Timorese identity, irrespective of nationality, and have the right to permanent domicile in East Timor.

Chapter II

Acquisition of Identity and Immigration

Article 17

The Government of the SARET shall have the exclusive right to establish the rules and procedures under which persons who do not have East Timorese identity may acquire such identity.

Article 18

The Central Government shall have the power to apply immigration controls on entry into and departure from the SARET of persons who are neither citizens of Indonesia nor have East Timorese identity, pursuant to its authority under Article 1 of this Agreement.

Article 19

The SARET shall have the authority to issue documents to individuals in order to identify those who have East Timorese identity.

Chapter III

Symbols of Identity

Article 20

The SARET may adopt its own coat of arms. The Indonesian national flag and Indonesian national anthem "Indonesia Raya" shall be flown and performed at such places and occasions as required by the existing laws and practices.

Article 21

The SARET may participate under its own name, with the concurrence of the Central Government, in international cultural and sports events in which other non-state entities participate.

PART THREE

POWERS AND INSTITUTIONS OF THE SARET

Chapter I

Legislative Powers and Institutions of the SARET

Article 22

The legislative power of the SARET shall extend to all matters not within the jurisdiction of the Central Government, as defined in Chapter I of Part One. This power shall include, the establishment of political, economic, and social policies in the SARET; cultural and educational matters; designation of a second language or languages in addition to the official language, Bahasa Indonesia; the establishment of courts of first instance pursuant to Article 40; rules of family law and succession; and public order, including the creation of an East Timor police force that shall be responsible for enforcement of all laws and regulations in the SARET, in accordance with the laws and regulations of the Republic of Indonesia.

Article 23

The SARET may adopt legislations regulating or restricting the ownership of property by persons who do not have East Timorese identity without contravening legitimately acquired rights.

Article 24

The SARET shall have the authority to establish a Land Claims Commission, whose members shall be selected in accordance with the manner prescribed for the selection of judges in Article 42, which shall make recommendations in order to decide on all disputed claims to title over real property through the court.

Article 25

The Regional Council of People's Representatives of the SARET

1. The legislative power of the SARET shall be vested in and exercised by the Regional Council of People's Representatives of the SARET, elected by persons of East Timorese identity as defined in Part Two, on the basis of universal adult suffrage. The implementation of elections for the Regional Council of People's Representatives of the SARET shall be further determined by the SARET and need not coincide with national elections.

2. Members of the Regional Council of People's Representatives of the SARET shall be persons who fulfill the eligibility requirements for membership. No racial, ethnic, religious, nationality, or other requirement unrelated to the exercise of the functions of a member of the Council shall be imposed.

3. Members of the Regional Council of People's Representatives of the SARET shall be immune from legal action in respect of their oral or written statements or actions relating to the business of the Council, or made or taken in their capacity as members of the Council.

Chapter II

Executive Powers and Institutions of the Government of the SARET

Article 26

The executive power of the Government of the SARET shall be exercised by a Governor who will be assisted by an Advisory Board whose members shall be appointed by the Governor upon the recommendation of the Regional Council of People's Representatives of the SARET.

Article 27

The Government of the SARET shall have the competence to design, guide and implement policies and programmes and issue executive decrees and regulations within the scope of the laws of the SARET. It shall also be responsible for ensuring that all laws and regulations applicable in the SARET are faithfully administered and enforced

Article 28

The Governor of the SARET shall be elected by a majority of the members of the Regional Council of People's Representatives of the SARET and responsible to it. The list of candidates for the post of Governor of the SARET shall first be consulted with and approved by the President of the Republic of Indonesia.

Article 29

The Governor-elect shall be formally confirmed to the post by the President of the Republic of Indonesia and shall be formally invested before the Regional Council of People's Representatives of the SARET.

Article 30

The Governor shall designate officials who shall be in charge of the executive services and other bodies of the SARET.

Article 31

The Government of the SARET shall have responsibility for the maintenance of public order in the SARET and for the administration and enforcement of all laws and regulations within the SARET.

Article 32

There shall be a Police Force of the SARET which shall be organized in accordance with regional laws.

Article 33

The Police Force of the SARET shall be subject to the authority and control of the Government of the SARET.

Article 34

Members of the Police Force of the SARET shall be recruited, without discrimination on racial, ethnic, or religious grounds.

Article 35

The primary functions of the Police Force of the SARET shall be :

a. to preserve internal peace and good order in East Timor; and
b. to maintain and, as necessary, enforce the law in an impartial and objective manner.

Chapter III

Judicial Powers and Institutions of the SARET

Article 36

The judicial power of the SARET shall be vested in and exercised by an independent judiciary.

Article 37

The judiciary of the SARET shall have jurisdiction over all civil, criminal, administrative, and other matters that fall within the competence of the SARET.

Article 38

In any civil suit, with the consent of all of the parties to such suit, the judiciary can apply any customary law applicable between such parties and recognized as such by the judiciary of the SARET.

Article 39

The judiciary of the SARET shall consist of such Courts of First Instance as may be established by regulations of the SARET, a Court of Appeal, a Court of Final Appeal and a Public Prosecutor.

Article 40

Courts of First Instance

1. There shall be Courts of First Instance in the SARET for the administration of justice. Such courts shall have such original civil, criminal and administrative jurisdiction as may be necessary to administer the laws in force in the SARET.

2. The Courts of First Instance shall consist of such judges as may be required for the proper administration of justice.

Article 41

The Court of Appeal

1. There shall be a Court of Appeal, consisting of a President and as many other judges as may be required, which shall have appellate jurisdiction from judgments of the Courts of First Instance.

2. The Court of Appeal also shall have original and appellate jurisdiction over all cases that concern the interpretation of Indonesian laws applicable to the SARET or the interpretation of Parts One, Five and Six of this Agreement.

3. The President of the Court of Appeal shall be appointed by the Chief Justice of the Supreme Court of the Republic of Indonesia, upon the recommendation of an independent Judicial Commission, which will be established in accordance with procedures adopted by the Regional Council of People's Representatives of the SARET.

Article 42

Judges of the Courts of First Instance and the Court of Appeal shall be selected by the Judicial Commission.

Article 43

The Judicial Commission also shall be responsible for disciplinary and other issues related to judicial performance, as specified by the Regional Council of People's Representatives of the SARET.

Article 44

Court of Final Appeal

1. The court of final appeal of the SARET shall be the Supreme Court of Indonesia.

2. An appeal shall lie from decisions of the Court of Appeal to the Supreme Court of Indonesia which is the right of the disputing parties:

   a. in all cases concerning laws and regulations of Indonesia applicable in the SARET;

   b. in all cases concerning the interpretation of this Agreement, provided that the Supreme Court shall establish a special chamber to hear such cases composed of an odd number of judges drawn from the Supreme Court of Indonesia and ad hoc judges drawn from the East Timor Court of Appeal of the SARET.

3. An appeal shall lie from decisions of the Court of Appeal to the Supreme Court of Indonesia with the leave of the Court of Appeal :

   a. in all cases concerning the interpretation of the regional laws and regulations of the SARET;

   b. on questions of law arising in criminal and civil cases.

Article 45

The Public Prosecutor shall be appointed, discharged and shall have such duties, as provided for by the regional laws and regulations of the SARET.

PART FOUR
PROMOTION AND PROTECTION OF HUMAN RIGHTS AND FUNDAMENTAL FREEDOMS

Article 46

The Central Government and the Government of the SARET shall promote, protect and respect human rights and fundamental freedoms without discrimination of any kind, as set forth, inter alia, in the Universal Declaration of Human Rights, the 1993 Vienna Declaration on Human Rights and the Decree of The People's Consultative Assembly No. XVII/MPR/1998 Concerning Human Rights. These rights and fundamental freedoms include : :

a. freedom of thought, conscience, and religion;

b. the right to life, liberty, and security of person;

c. freedom from torture, violence, arbitrary arrest, detention, or exile;

d. the right to a full and fair hearing by an independent and impartial tribunal in the determination of any civil rights or obligations or any criminal charge;

e. freedom of expression in all its forms, association, and peaceful assembly;

f. the right to form political parties specific to East Timor without restrictions of any kind and subject to the provision of Article 57;

g. the right to participate in government without discrimination, through free periodic elections and non-discriminatory access to public service, subject to the provisions of Article 25;

h. the right to participate in Indonesian national political life, including the right to vote in general elections and to be elected as a member of the Indonesian national Parliament or be appointed as a member of the People's Consultative Assembly;

i. the right to participate in Indonesian public and administrative services without discrimination on any grounds;

j. freedom of movement throughout the territory of the Republic of Indonesia;

k. the right of everyone to enjoy and participate in his or her culture;

l. the right to own property and not to be arbitrarily deprived of it;

m. the right to protection for family life, privacy, home and correspondence;

n. the right to education, including, as a minimum, the right to a free primary education for all;

o. the right to an adequate standard of living, subject to available resources and capabilities;

p. the right of women to full and equal participation in political, civil, economic, social, and cultural life;

q. the rights of the child, without discrimination of any kind, as set forth in the UN Convention on the Rights of the Child.

PART FIVE
RELATIONSHIP BETWEEN THE CENTRAL GOVERNMENT AND THE GOVERNMENT OF THE SARET

Article 47

The Central Government shall take into account the views of the Government of the SARET in the adoption of laws, regulations and policies within the competence of the Central Government that may have a direct effect in the SARET.

Article 48

In the implementation of those laws, regulations or policies of the Central Government that are applicable in the SARET, as set forth in Chapter I of Part One, the Government of the SARET shall coordinate, with the relevant offices of the Central Government.

Article 49

The Central Government shall appoint a senior official, who shall reside in Dili, to exercise the competences of the Central Government in the SARET, and to coordinate and supervise such Central Government officials in the SARET as may be necessary to assist the Government of the SARET in the implementation of laws, regulations and policies within the competence of the Central Government, as set forth in Chapter I of Part One, and to perform the functions provided for in Article 50 below.

Article 50

The Central Government and the Government of the SARET may create bodies or other arrangements to facilitate consultation, cooperation and coordination on such matters as police matters, tourism, transportation, telecommunications, education, health and the environment.

Article 51

In the performance of its duties, the Police Force of the SARET shall consult and cooperate with the Central Government authorities with respect to the enforcement of Indonesian national laws in the SARET.

Article 52

The Police Force of the SARET shall take the necessary action, at the request of the Indonesian National Police to apprehend persons in the SARET accused of having committed crimes outside the SARET.

Article 53

The Indonesian National Police shall take the necessary action, in cooperation with the Police Force of the SARET, to apprehend persons outside the SARET accused of having committed crimes in the SARET.

Article 54

In exceptional cases the Indonesian National Police will assist the Police Force of the SARET in the performance of its functions.

PART SIX
RELATIONSHIPS BETWEEN THE SPECIAL AUTONOMOUS REGION OF EAST TIMOR AND OTHER ENTITIES

Article 55

Without prejudice to the responsibility and competence of the Central Government, as set forth in Article 1,

a. the Government of the SARET may, with the consent of the Central Government enter into agreements and engage in social, cultural, trade, environmental, transportation, scientific, technical, tourism, and sports activities with regional governments / cities of foreign countries and international organizations;

b. the Government of the SARET may seek and obtain international development assistance with the consent of the Central Government; and

c. foreign governments may open, with the consent of the Central Government, non-diplomatic representative offices in the SARET.

PART SEVEN
THE UNITED NATIONS

Article 56

The United Nations Secretary-General shall have the responsibility and authority to monitor and verify compliance with this Agreement. This authority includes monitoring the election of members of the Regional Council of People's Representatives of the SARET and verifying that such elections are free and fair. For this purpose, the United Nations Secretary-General may establish in the SARET such offices as he deems necessary which would operate within a specific time-frame to be further agreed upon between the United Nations and the Indonesian Government.

PART EIGHT
GENERAL PROVISION

Article 57

The special autonomy for East Timor as provided in this Agreement is granted within the framework of the Constitution of the Republic of Indonesia.

PART NINE
BASIC LAW OF THE SARET

Article 58

The SARET shall be governed by a basic law, enacted by the first elected Regional Council of People's Representatives of the SARET and which shall be in accordance with the provisions of this Agreement.

PART TEN

TRANSITIONAL PROVISIONS

Article 59

The following provisions shall be in effect during the time between the entry into force of this agreement and the election and assumption of office by the the Regional Council of People's Representatives of the SARET and the Government of the SARET:

a. There shall be a broadly representative Transitional Council, composed of no more than 25 persons of East Timorese identity, whose members shall be appointed by the United Nations Secretary-General in consultation with relevant individuals and groups within the SARET and with the Government of Indonesia.

b. The Transitional Council can enact the regional laws and regulations for the election of the first Regional Council of People's Representatives of the SARET and for such subjects as may be agreed upon by the parties to this Agreement, in accordance with existing laws, while maintaining the smooth functioning of the general administration, public services and public order.

c. The Secretary-General of the United Nations, the Government of Indonesia and the Transitional Council shall engage in consultations to ensure the effective implementation of this Agreement, and the smooth and peaceful process of transition in the SARET.

d. The Secretary-General of the United Nations, the Government of Indonesia and the Transitional Council shall establish a working group that will address transitional security arrangements.

----

a:english.fin\270499

Appendix 12

AGREEMENT REGARDING THE MODALITIES FOR THE POPULAR CONSULTATION OF THE EAST TIMORESE THROUGH A DIRECT BALLOT

The Governments of Indonesia and Portugal and the Secretary-General of the United Nations,

Agree as follows:

Immediately following the conclusion of the agreement between the two Governments requesting the Secretary-General to consult the East Timorese people on whether they would accept or reject the proposed constitutional framework for autonomy, the Secretary-General will, subject to the appropriate legislative mandate, begin preparations for the popular consultation by deploying in East Timor such personnel as will be adequate for the purpose of executing the various phases of the consultation process. Preparations for the vote outside East Timor will also begin at locations of major East Timorese concentration outside East Timor.

A. Date for consultation

The ballot will take place on Sunday, 8 August 1999, both inside and outside East Timor.

B. Question to be put before the voters

The question that the Secretary-General will put to the voters is:

"Do you accept the proposed special autonomy for East Timor within the Unitary State of the Republic of Indonesia?	**ACCEPT ☐**

OR

"Do you reject the proposed special autonomy for East Timor, leading to East Timor's separation from Indonesia?"	**REJECT ☐**

The United Nations logo will appear on the ballot papers. The ballot papers will include symbols to facilitate voting by illiterate persons.

C. Entitlement to vote

The following persons, aged 17 years or above, shall be eligible to vote in the popular consultation:

(a) persons born in East Timor,

(b) persons born outside East Timor but with at least one parent having been born in East Timor, and

(c) persons whose spouses fall under either of the two categories above.

D. **Schedule of the consultation process (in overlapping time periods)**

The schedule for the operational stages of the consultation process will be approximately as follows:

Operational planning/Deployment	10 May-15 June
Public information programme/ Voter education	10 May - 5 August
Preparation and Registration	13 June - 17 July
Exhibition of lists and challenges/ Decisions on challenges and complaints	18 July - 23 July
Political Campaign	20 July - 5 August*
Cooling off period	6 August-7 August
Polling Day	8 August

* Subject to revision

E. **Operational Phases**

a) Information Campaign

- The United Nations will make available the text of the main Agreement and the autonomy document to be voted on in the following languages: Tetun, Bahasa Indonesia, Portuguese and English.
- The United Nations will disseminate and explain the content of the main Agreement and the autonomy document in an impartial and factual manner inside and outside East Timor.
- The United Nations will explain to voters the process and procedure of the vote, and the implications of an 'accept' or 'reject' vote.

- The radio stations and the newspapers in East Timor as well as other Indonesian and Portuguese media outlets will be utilized in the dissemination of this information. Other appropriate means of dissemination will be made use of as required.

b) Registration

- Registration inside and outside East Timor will take place for a continuous period of 20 days.
- Two hundred registration centres will be opened in East Timor for this purpose.
- Outside East Timor, special registration centres will be opened in Jakarta, Yogyakarta, Surabaya, Denpasar, Ujung Pandang, Sydney, Darwin, Perth, Melbourne, Lisbon, Maputo, Macau, New York with adjustments to be made as appropriate. The United Nations may utilize the services of the Australian Electoral Commission for the balloting in Australia and of the International Organization for Migration (IOM) in Portugal and elsewhere.
- The registration lists will be exhibited for five days at the end of the registration period at the respective registration centres, regional offices and at Dili headquarters. Challenges to the lists shall be submitted to the regional offices for a final decision by the Electoral Commission prior to polling day.

c) Campaign

- Supporters and opponents of the autonomy proposal will campaign ahead of the vote in a peaceful and democratic manner during the period designated for this purpose.
- There will be a Code of Conduct for the campaign, to be proposed by the United Nations and discussed with the supporters and opponents of the autonomy proposal.
- The United Nations will devise the means to provide equal opportunity for the two sides to disseminate their views to the public.
- Officials of the Governments of Indonesia and Portugal will not participate in the campaign in support of either option.
- East Timorese government officials may campaign in their personal

capacity. All such campaigning will be carried out strictly according to the Code of Conduct without use of public funds and government resources or recourse to pressure of office.

d) Balloting in East Timor

- Voting in East Timor will take place in approximately 700 registration/polling stations located in 200 polling centres.

e) Balloting outside East Timor

- Voting will take place in polling stations set up in the same locations as the registration centres mentioned above.

f) Observers

- Indonesia and Portugal shall be entitled to send an equal number of representatives to observe all the operational phases of the consultation process both inside and outside East Timor.
- International observers will be able to observe the consultation process under terms to be developed by the United Nations to regulate their presence.

F. Funding

The Secretary-General will seek the approval of the Security Council for the operation in order to ensure assessed budgetary funding. Voluntary contributions will be channeled through a Trust Fund established for this purpose.

G. Security

The Indonesian authorities will ensure a secure environment for a free and fair popular consultation process and will be responsible for the security of United Nations personnel. A number of United Nations security guards will be deployed to ensure the security and safety of United Nations personnel and property. A number of international civilian police will be available in East Timor to advise the Indonesian Police during the operational phases of the popular consultation and, at the time of the consultation, to supervise the escort of ballot papers and boxes to and from polling sites.

DONE in New York on this 5th day of May, 1999.

For the Government of Indonesia	For the United Nations	For the Government of Portugal
Ali Alatas	Kofi A. Annan	Jaime Gama
Minister for Foreign Affairs	Secretary-General	Minister for Foreign Affairs

EAST TIMOR POPULAR CONSULTATION

AGREEMENT REGARDING SECURITY

The Governments of Indonesia and Portugal and the Secretary-General of the United Nations,

Agree as follows:

1. A secure environment devoid of violence or other forms of intimidation is a prerequisite for the holding of a free and fair ballot in East Timor. Responsibility to ensure such an environment as well as for the general maintenance of law and order rests with the appropriate Indonesian security authorities. The absolute neutrality of the TNI (Indonesian Armed Forces) and the Indonesian Police is essential in this regard.

2. The Commission on Peace and Stability established in Dili on 21 April 1999 should become operational without delay. The Commission, in cooperation with the United Nations, will elaborate a code of conduct, by which all parties should abide, for the period prior to and following the consultation, ensure the laying down of arms and take the necessary steps to achieve disarmament.

3. Prior to the start of the registration, the Secretary-General shall ascertain, based on the objective evaluation of the UN mission, that the necessary security situation exists for the peaceful implementation of the consultation process.

4. The police will be solely responsible for the maintenance of law and order. The Secretary-General, after obtaining the necessary mandate, will make available a number of civilian police officers to act as advisers to the Indonesian Police in the discharge of their duties and, at the time of the consultation, to supervise the escort of ballot papers and boxes to and from the polling sites.

DONE in New York on this 5th day of May 1999

For the Government of Indonesia	For the United Nations	For the Government of Portugal
Ali Alatas Minister for Foreign Affairs Indonesia	Kofi A. Annan Secretary-General United Nations	Jaime Gama Minister for Foreign Affairs Portugal

Chronology

1974

April 25. The Portuguese military, under General Antonio Spinola, initiates a coup leading to the overthrow of the Caetano Government.

May 16. The Revolutionary Government announces that all overseas colonies of Portugal, including Portuguese Timor, will be accorded democratic rights.

May 28. Col. Fernando Alves Aldela, Governor and Military Commander of East Timor, declares that the people of the territory will be given the opportunity to decide their political future in a referendum to be held on 13 March 1975.

May 11 – 27. Political parties are allowed to be formed. The new political parties thus formed are:

1. Uniao Democratica Timorense (UDT or TimoreseDemocratic Union)
2. Associacao Social Democratica Timor (the ASDT or Timorese Social Democratic Association), later to become the Frente Revolucionara do Timor Leste Independente (FRETILIN).
3. Associacao Popular Democratica Timorense (APODETI or Timorese Popular Democratic Association), which favours integration with Indonesia.

September 21 . Indonesian Foreign Minister Adam Malik and Portuguese Foreign Minister Mario Soares meet in New York to discuss Indonesian-Portuguese relations and the decolonization of Portuguese Timor.

October 14. Lt. General Ali Moertopo, Head of Indonesia's Special Operations Unit (OPSUS) and close confidant of President Suharto, visits Lisbon for talks with President Francisco da Costa Gomes, Prime Minister Vasco Goncalves and other high officials, on East Timor. He reports very positive response.

November 14. Col. Mario Lemos Pires succeeds Fernando Alvez Aldela as Governor of East Timor.

1975

January 22. UDT agrees to form a coalition with the FRETILIN.

March 9. Representatives of the Indonesian and Portuguese Governments meet in London in a follow-up to the Lisbon meeting.

May 26. UDT withdraws from its coalition with the FRETILIN.

June 26 – 27. Representatives of the Portuguese Government and East Timor political parties meet in Macau. The Indonesian Government is allowed to attend on a standby basis in Hong Kong. The FRETILIN boycotts the meeting.

July 17. Constitutional Law 7/75 is promulgated in Lisbon, setting down the regulations on the decolonization process in East Timor. It provides for the election of a People's Assembly in October 1976 and the formation of a transitional Government.

August 11. In an atmosphere of rising tensions and demonstrations against the colonial government, the UDT launches a coup in Dili, which they describe as a "pre-emptive strike" against the FRETILIN.

August 20. Counterstrike by the FRETILIN. Civil war breaks out. Tens of thousands of East Timorese civilians cross the border and flee to

Indonesian West Timor.

August 27. The colonial Governor and his administration abandon Dili and evacuate to the island of Atauro, from where they subsequently withdraw to Australia.

August 28. The Portuguese Government sends former Minister for Interterritorial Affairs, Dr. Almeida Santos, as special envoy to Indonesia and Australia to discuss ways to restore order in the territory. His visit and talks in Indonesia proceed in two stages: the first on 29 August and the second on 11 September 1975, after his return from Australia.

September 7. The UDT, previously known for its pro-Portugal political sentiments, joins two other parties, the KOTA and the Trabalhista, in declaring their desire to integrate with Indonesia. In the town of Batugade, the leaders of these parties sign a petition to President Suharto seeking integration of East Timor with Indonesia.

October 9. Portuguese Foreign Minister Melo Antunes in his speech at the U.N. General Assembly acknowledges the legitimate interest of Indonesia in the peaceful decolonization of East Timor. Back in Portugal, he proposes another round of talks with Indonesia.

November 1-2. The Foreign Ministers of Indonesia and Portugal hold talks in Rome, Italy. Indonesia again acknowledges the fundamental responsibility of Portugal for the decolonization of East Timor and pledges its full support and cooperation.

November 28. The FRETILIN issues a unilateral "Declaration of Independence" of the territory, naming it the "Democratic Republic of Timor Leste".

November 30. In turn, the four allied parties – the UDT, Apodeti, KDTA and Trabalhista – denounce the unilateral act of the FRETILIN and proclaim the independence of East Timor and its simultaneous integration with Indonesia.

Both declarations are rejected by Portugal and Indonesia.

December 7. Indonesian forces enter East Timor at the request of the four allied parties.

December 17. The four parties establish the Provisional Government of East Timor in Dili.

December 22. The U.N. Security Council adopts Resolution 384, lamenting Portugal's failure to fulfill its responsibilities as administering power and calling on Indonesia to withdraw its forces from East Timor.

December 29. U.N. Secretary-General Kurt Waldheim appoints Vittorio Winspeare Guicciardi, Director-General of the U.N. Office in Geneva, as his Special Representative to conduct a fact-finding mission to Indonesia and East Timor.

1976

January 15 – February 12. Guicciardi undertakes his first mission to Indonesia, some parts of East Timor, Australia and Portugal.

April 22. After considering the reports of the U.N. Secretary-General and of Guicciardi on his mission, the U.N. Security Council passes another resolution (Resolution 389) requesting the Special Representative to continue making an on-the-spot assessment of the situation in East Timor. In his report on his first mission, Guicciardi has acknowledged that an accurate assessment of the situation remains elusive. His second mission will not be any more successful.

May 31. The exercise of the right to self-determination in East Timor is carried out by the People's Assembly, during which a formal request is submitted to the Indonesian Government to accept the decision of the people of East Timor to integrate with the Republic of Indonesia.

July 15. After a fact-finding mission to East Timor reports positively on the situation, the Indonesian Parliament passes legislation on integration of East Timor.

July 17. The President of Indonesia signs and promulgates the law on East Timor's integration. East Timor legally becomes the 27th province of Indonesia.

December 1. The U.N. General Assembly adopts the first Resolution on East Timor initiated by Portugal. Every year after that, until 1983, the U.N. General Assembly passes a Resolution on East Timor.

1976 - 1982

The U.N. General Assembly from 1976 to 1982 every year adopts a Resolution calling for Indonesia's withdrawal from East Timor, with the following detailed break down of votes:

Date	Resolution No.	Recorded Vote
December 1, 1976	Resolution 31/53	68 for, 20 against, 49 abstain
November 28, 1977	Resolution 32/34	67 for, 26 against, 47 abstain
December 13, 1978	Resolution 33/39	59 for, 31 against, 44 abstain
November 21, 1979	Resolution 34/40	62 for, 31 against, 45 abstain
November 11, 1980	Resolution 35/27	58 for, 35 against, 46 abstain
November 24, 1981	Resolution 36/50	54 for, 42 against, 46 abstain
November 23, 1982	Resolution 37/30	50 for, 48 against, 50 abstain

1982

December. U.N. Secretary-General Javier Perez de Cuellar, offers his good offices to Indonesia and Portugal in the search for a peaceful solution to the East Timor question.

1983

January. Both sides accept the good offices of the U.N. Secretary-General. For this purpose the Secretary-General appoints Undersecretary-General Rafeeuddin Ahmed as his Special Representative.

March. Preliminary contacts and discussions are made between the two Ambassadors / Permanent Representatives of Indonesia and Portugal to the UN in New York, under the auspices of the Secretary-General.

May 16. Msgr. Costa Lopes, Apostolic Administrator of East Timor resigns and is replaced by Msgr. Carlos Felipe Ximenes Belo.

June 15. A ceasefire is signed by the Indonesian Commander of East Timor, Col. Purwanto, and FRETILIN guerrilla leader, Kay Rala Xanana Gusmao. The ceasefire almost immediately collapses.

1984

October 1. Indonesian Foreign Minister Mochtar Kusuma-Atmadja and Portuguese Foreign Minister Jaime Gama meet in New York. They agree to formalize the tripartite dialogue and focus first on humanitarian issues and clarification of each side's position with regard to developments in East Timor.

1985

September 11. In his annual progress report to the General Assembly, the Secretary-General observes that the substantive talks between Indonesia and Portugal have made progress and that the next phase will be the consideration of the political, civil and other aspects of the problem.

September 23 . Secretary-General Perez de Cuellar meets with the Foreign Ministers of Indonesia and Portugal. Both sides agree to sustain the tripartite talks and tackle the more difficult and sensitive issue of a viable blueprint or plan for a just, comprehensive and internationally acceptable solution to the East Timor problem.

1986

November. As a result of intensive rounds of talks, the outline of a solution takes shape. It is envisaged that the Secretary-General will dispatch a UN team to observe the April 1987 general elections in Indonesia, including in East Timor. The Secretary-General will submit a Report of the team's findings to the General Assembly in 1987.

The report will be will then be freely debated by the entire membership of the General Assembly and there will be a vote on whether the East Timor issue will be removed from its agenda. The verdict will provide a solution acceptable to the international community and an honourable way out for both Portugal and Indonesia.

At the Ambassadorial/Permanent Representative level in New York, the proposed plan is *ad referendum* agreed upon and reported to the respective governments.

1987

March. The Indonesian Government accepts the proposed plan for a peaceful solution. However, at the last minute the Portuguese Government officially states that it cannot accept the Secretary-General's plan.

April 27-29. The Secretary-General visits Lisbon for talks with President Mario Soares, Prime Minister Anibal Cavaco Silva and Foreign Minister Pires de Miranda. Portugal expresses interest in the possibility of a visit to East Timor by members of its Parliament. The Portuguese also agree that the Secretary-General continue his good offices.

September. After further negotiations, both sides agree on a text of the Secretary-General's annual progress report to the General Assembly, stating that the tripartite talks will continue. Both sides express willingness to consider the possibility of a Portuguese Parliamentary Delegation visiting East Timor with a view to obtaining first-hand information on the situation.

October. The Foreign Minister of Portugal, in a message to the Secretary-General, conveys a request for a letter from the Indonesian Parliament to the Portuguese Parliament inviting a delegation from the latter to visit East Timor.

1988

February 4. The letter of invitation from the Chairman of the Indonesian House of Representative, Mr. Karis Suhud, is presented to the Secretary-General for transmittal to the President of the Assembly of Portugal, Mr. Victor Pereira Crespo.

March. Ali Alatas, the Indonesian Permanent Representative to the UN in New York is called back to Jakarta to assume the post of Minister of Foreign Affairs, succeeding Dr. Mochtar Kusuma-Atmadja.

July 28. The Portuguese Parliament accepts the invitation of the Indonesian House of Representatives.

August. The two sides agree in principle that the Portuguese Parliament's delegation will visit East Timor with a view to obtaining first-hand information of the situation, subject to mutually agreed terms of reference.

1989

May 9. A Non-paper by Mr. Rafeeuddin Ahmed on the terms of reference and modalities for the visit of the Portuguese Parliamentary Delegation to East Timor is discussed.

1990

September 4. In the tripartite meeting, the Indonesian Government agrees to the terms of reference and modalities of the visit as proposed in the Non-paper.

1991

May 23. In the tripartite meeting, Portugal suddenly brings up a new matter by proposing to issue a unilateral interpretative statement to be annexed to the agreement on the visit of the Portuguese Parliamentary Delegation to East Timor. The proposed statement is about "freedom of movement and contacts". The tripartite meeting ends inconclusively.

June 27. In a meeting chaired by Secretary-General Perez de Cuellar, Portugal withdraws its proposal to issue an additional unilateral interpretative statement.

July 19. The Portuguese Government agrees to the terms of reference for the visit of a Portuguese Parliamentary Delegation to East Timor.

Sept 30 – Oct 4. An advance team, led by a representative of the Secretary- General with two members from each of the Portuguese and Indonesian Governments, visits East Timor.

October 16. The two sides exchange proposed lists of international journalists to accompany the Portuguese Parliamentary Delegation with the understanding that the lists are subject to clearance by their respective governments.

October 26. Portugal announces to the press in Lisbon its unilateral decision to suspend the visit, blaming Indonesia and accusing it of "a serious violation of the fundamental principles of the right to inform and be informed."

October 28. Two persons die, one of them, Sebastiao Gomes, a pro-independence youth, in a clash between the pro and anti-integration groups in front of the Sao Antonio Church in Motael district of Dili.

October 29. Portugal finally sends a letter to the UN Secretary-General informing him of its decision to suspend the visit.

November 12. Scores are killed when Indonesian troops fire on a large group of East Timorese walking from the Motael Church to the

Santa Cruz cemetery in Dili. The incident is filmed by journalists who have gone to East Timor to cover the aborted visit of the Portuguese Parliamentary Delegation.

November 19. The Government of Indonesia establishes a National Commission of Inquiry to investigate the Santa Cruz incident.

December 26. An initial report on the incident is submitted to President Soeharto.

1992

January. Dr. Boutros Boutros-Ghali assumes office as UN Secretary-General.

January 2. A Military Council of Honour, headed by Major General Feisal Tanjung, is established.

January 13. Portuguese Foreign Minister Joao de Deus Pinheiro, writes to the Secretary-General expressing Portugal's readiness to resume the tripartite talks.

February. Indonesian Foreign Minister Ali Alatas travels to major capitals to explain the policies and measures taken by the Indonesian Government in responding to the incident.

February 9-14. The UN Secretary-General's personal envoy, Mr. Amos Wako, visits Jakarta and East Timor to obtain clarifications on the Santa Cruz tragedy.

March 11. The Portuguese ferry ship "Lusitania Expresso" enters Indonesian waters without permission. On board are 125 persons, including members of international youth groups and NGOs, and journalists who wish to pay tribute to the Santa Cruz incident victims. The ship turns back, however, after it is given bullhorn warnings by the Indonesian navy.

April 13. A full report on the November 12 incident is released for publication.

September 26. Secretary-General Boutros Boutros-Ghali calls for consultations in New York. An agreement is reached to continue the tripartite dialogue under his offices, this time at the level of foreign ministers.

November 20. Xanana Gusmao is apprehended in Dili.

December 17. The first round of tripartite talks is held in New York.

1993

February. Xanana Gusmao is brought to trial.

April 3-8. Mr. Amos Wako makes a second visit to Jakarta and East Timor.

April 21. The second round of tripartite talks is held in Rome.

May 31. Xanana Gusmao is sentenced to 20 years imprisonment.

September 17. The third round of ministerial tripartite talks is held in New York.

December 14-16. A meeting takes place near London between two groups of leading East Timorese personalities both living in East Timor and abroad. This comes to be known as the All-inclusive Intra-East Timorese Dialogue (AIETD).

1994

May 6. The fourth round of tripartite talks is held in Geneva.

October. Foreign Minister Alatas meets with leading East Timorese supporters and opponents of integration and the Portuguese Foreign Minister in Luxemburg and New York.

December 7. Foreign Minister Alatas presents to a limited cabinet session of the political and security ministers a list of possible solutions to the East Timor question. The meeting results in a consensus on the grant of wide-ranging autonomy to East Timor, based on the 1945 Constitution and relevant laws.

December 20. President Suharto, in a letter to the Coordinating Minister for Political and Security Affairs, expresses his views on why the option of wide-ranging autonomy is not feasible.

1995

January 9. The fifth round of the tripartite talks is held in Geneva where the two Foreign Ministers agree to the Secretary-General's intention to facilitate and offer the necessary arrangements for the convening of the All-inclusive Intra-East Timorese Dialogue (AIETD).

June 3-5. The first AIETD is held in Burg Schlaining, Austria, attended by representatives of the UN Secretary-General as observers.

July 8. The sixth round of the tripartite dialogue is held in Geneva.

December 2-7. United Nations High Commissioner on Human Rights visits Indonesia and East Timor.

1996

January 5. Three East Timorese leaders and their families who have lived in Portugal since 1960 return to Indonesia and East Timor following approval by the Indonesian Government of their request to come back.

January 16. The seventh round of tripartite talks is held in London.

February 29. Portuguese Prime Minister Antonio Guterres proposes to President Suharto that Portuguese and Indonesian "Interest

Sections" be established in friendly embassies in each other's capital city.

March 19-20. The second AIETD is held in Austria.

March 22-23. Participants to the AIETD meet with Portuguese Foreign Minister Jaime Gama in Vienna.

June 27. The eighth round of tripartite talks is held in Geneva. The proposal to establish an East Timorese Cultural Centre in Dili and the development of human resources is discussed.

1997

January 1. Kofi Annan begins his tenure as UN Secretary-General.

January 6. Bishop Basilio do Nascimento, a Portuguese national, is ordained by Pope John Paul II as Bishop of the Diocese of Baucau. He is granted citizenship by the Indonesian Government two months later.

February. Dr. Jamsheed Marker is appointed as the Secretary-Generals' Personal Representative for the issue of East Timor.

March 20-31. Ambassador Jamsheed Marker visits Indonesia, including East Timor.

May 29. General elections in Indonesia. In East Timor, 14 civilians are killed and others are wounded by FALINTIL in a bid to prevent the civilians from casting their votes.

May 31. FALINTIL members attack and kill 17 police officers who are on their way back to base after performing security duties at remote polling stations.

June 8. The FALINTIL burns down the market in Dili, causing heavy losses in property and income to hundreds of small-scale East Timorese merchants.

June 19-20. The ninth ministerial tripartite meeting is held in New York under the auspices of Secretary-General Kofi Annan.

July. President Nelson Mandela of South Africa, on a state visit to Indonesia, requests for a meeting with Xanana Gusmao. They meet at the state guest house for a two-hour private talk.

August 4-7. The first tripartite talks at senior officials' level are held in New York under the chairmanship of Ambassador Marker.

July 22. President Mandela writes a letter to President Suharto but the letter inadvertently gets into the hands of the Portuguese Ambassador in Pretoria who opens it and leaks its contents to the Portuguese press. The ambassador is later declared *persona non grata* by the South African government.

October 1-3. The second tripartite senior officials meeting is held in New York.

October 20-23. The third AIETD is held in Krmbach Castle, Vienna.

November 5-7. The third tripartite senior officials' talks are held in New York.

December 16-23. Ambassador Marker visits Indonesia and meets with several personalities involved in the question of East Timor

1998

May 6-8. The fourth tripartite senior officials' talks are held in New York.

May 21. President Soeharto resigns and Vice President B.J. Habibie succeeds him as President.

May 22. Foreign Minister Ali Alatas is reappointed by President Habibie.

June 5. Foreign Minister Alatas submits a proposal to a limited cabinet meeting for a peaceful solution/compromise through the grant of special status with wide-ranging autonomy to East Timor. The proposal is accepted by the meeting.

June 9. The proposal to grant special status with wide-ranging autonomy is approved by the President and the Cabinet.

June 18. Indonesia's proposal for wide-ranging autonomy for East Timor is officially submitted to the UN Secretary-General who promises to immediately convey it to the Government of Portugal.

August 4-5. The tripartite ministerial meeting in New York discusses Indonesia's proposal for special autonomy for East Timor. The meeting agrees to hold technical talks at SOM level and to open "Interest Sections" at the Netherlands's Embassy in Jakarta (for Portugal) and the Thai Embassy in Lisbon for (for Indonesia).

1999

January 25. President Habibie presides over a limited cabinet meeting of Ministers concerned with political affairs and defence and brings up a proposal for a "second option" on East Timor. The second option simply means that if the East Timorese do not accept wide-ranging autonomy, the Government will ask the People's Consultative Assembly to allow the East Timorese to separate themselves from the Republic of Indonesia.

January 27. A plenary cabinet session accepts the "second option" as an alternative solution to the problem of East Timor.

February 5. Foreign Minister Alatas explains the "second option" to the Commission I of the House of Representatives.

March 8. A draft agreement on wide-ranging autonomy for East Timor is reported to a special plenary cabinet session.

April 6. A militia force attacks the church of Liquica, East Timor, where hundreds have taken refuge.

April 17. Manuel Carascallao's residence is attacked by paramilitary elements.

April 21. A peace agreement is signed between the pro and anti integration groups in Dili as proposed by the Indonesian Government. Also agreed is the formation of a Peace and Stability Commission (which is later recognized by the New York agreement.)

May 5. Signing of the New York Agreements on East Timor, with a constitutional framework for special autonomy for East Timor as an annex. The Agreements are:

a. An Agreement regarding the modalities for the popular consultation on the East Timor through a direct ballot.
b. An Agreement concerning security.

May 7. The UN Security Council accepts through a resolution the May 5, 1999 agreements.

May 15-16. The proposal for wide-ranging autonomy for East Timor is explained by Foreign Minister Alatas to representatives of East Timor groups in Bali.

May 18. The President creates a team to oversee the implementation of the agreement on East Timor between Indonesia and Portugal.

June 1. The Task Force to oversee balloting in East Timor starts operations.

June 3. The UNAMET starts operations with the inauguration of its headquarters in Dili.

June 11. The United Nations Assistance Mission in East Timor (UNAMET) opens its office in Dili.

June 16- 18. A second meeting of pro and anti-integration groups is held in Jakarta, resulting in an agreement between the warring groups in East Timor to hand over their weapons to the UNAMET or the Government.

June 29. The UNAMET office in Maliana is attacked.

July 6. The Secretary-General appoints three members of the East Timor electoral commission.

July 12. Foreign Minister Alatas visits East Timor with several other ministers

July 16. Start of registration of voters.

July 28. The UN Secretary-General decides to postpone the date of voting from August 8 to August 30, 1999.

August 3. The UN Security Council extends the mandate of the UNAMET until September 30,1999.

August 7. Foreign Minister Alatas visits East Timor again with several other ministers.

August 14-17. Period of campaigning starts in connection with the voting.

August 27. The UN Security Council again extends the mandate of the UNAMET mandate until November 30, 1999.

August 30. Balloting in East Timor, in Indonesia and abroad.

September 2. The Electoral Commission holds a hearing on complaints of pro-autonomy groups on deviations in the implementation of the voting.

September 3. The UN Secretary-General submits the results of the voting to the UN Security Council:

94,388 votes (21%) pro-autonomy
344,580 votes (78.5%) reject autonomy
7,985 votes declared invalid (Resume here)

September 4. The results of the voting are announced in Dili. The UN Electoral Commission submits its evaluation in a written report addressed to the UN Secretary-General. President Habibie in a special statement accepts the result of the voting.

September 5. Foreign Minister Alatas visits East Timor with the Coordinating Minister for Political Affairs and Security. Coming back, they bring along three members of the UN Electoral Commission and electoral officers of UNAMET to hold a press conference in Jakarta.

September 6. The residence of Archbishop Belo and the ICRC office are attacked.

September 7. Military State of Emergency is declared in East Timor. Major General Kiki Shahnakri is appointed Military Emergency Commander. Xanana Gusmao released from prison.

September 11. A Special UN Security Council mission visits East Timor.

Foreign Minister Alatas leaves for New York to convey Indonesia's agreement on the sending of a UN Multi-National Force to East Timor.

September 15. The UN Security Council adopts a resolution forming and deploying a multinational force by virtue of Chapter VII of the UN Charter. Later known as INTERFET, the force is sent to East Timor.

September 20. The first INTERFET contingent arrives in Dili.

September 21. President Habibie addresses a plenary session of the House of Representatives on the problem of East Timor.

September 27. Major General Kiki Shahnakri transfers powers of operation in East Timor to the commander of INTERFET, Major General Peter Cosgrove.

October 14 and 17 President Habibie delivers his accountability speech before the general session of the People's Consultative

Assembly.

October 19. The People's Consultative Assembly accepts the results of the August 30,1999 voting and voids its decision in 1978 integrating East Timor with the Republic of Indonesia.

October 22. Xanana Gusmao returns to East Timor.

October 25. The UN Security Council adopts a resolution forming the UN Transitional Administration of East Timor (UNTAET). Mr. Sergio Vieira de Mello is appointed Special Representative of the Secretary-General and Transitional Administrator for East Timor.

Index

B

C

D

E

F

G

H

I

N

O

P

Q

R

S

T

U

V

W

X

Y

Bibliography

Department of Foreign Affairs and Trade, Australia. 2000. *Australia and the Indonesian Incorporation of Portuguese Timor 1974 – 1976*

Department of Foreign Affairs and Trade, Australia. 2001. *East Timor in Transition 1998-2000 – An Australian Policy Challenge*

Department of Foreign Affairs, Republic of Indonesia. 1977. *Decolonization in East Timor.* Jakarta.

Department of Foreign Affairs, Republic of Indonesia. 1977. *East Timor after Integration.* Jakarta.

Department of Foreign Affairs, Republic of Indonesia. 1992. *East Timor: Building for the Future.* Jakarta.

Dunn, James. 1983. *Timor – A People Betrayed.* Jacaranda Press.

Fischer, Tim. 2000. *Ballot and Bullets – Seven days in East Timor.* Allen & Unwin.

Greenlees, Don and Robert Garran. 2002. *Deliverance: The Inside Story of East Timor's Fight for Freedom.* Allen & Unwin.

Krieger, Heika, ed. *East Timor and the International Community—Basic Documents.* 1997. Cambridge International Documents Series, Volume 10. Cambrdge: Cambridge University Press.

Lopes Da Cruz, F. X. 1999. *Kesaksian – Aku dan Timor Timur.*

Jakarta:Yayasan Tunas Harapan Timor Lorosae.

Makarim, Zacky Anwar et al. 2003. *Hari-Hari Terakhir Timor-Timur – Sebuah Kesaksian.* Jakarta: P.T. Sportif Media Informasindo.

Martin, Ian. 2001. *Self-Determination in East Timor – The United Nations, the Ballot and International Intervention* in International Peace Academy Occasional Paper Series.

Masker, Jamsheed. 2003. *East Timor – A Memoir of the Negotiations for Indonesia.* Jefferson N. Carolina: McFarland.

Neonbasu Gregor P. 1997. SVD *Peta Politik dan Dinamika Pembangunan Timor Timur.* Jakarta: Yanense Mitra Sejati Publisher.

Singh, Bilveer 1995. *East Timor, Indonesia and the World – Myths and Realities.* Singapore Institute of International Affairs.

Singh, Bilveer. 1999. *The United Nations' Role in the Birth of Independent East Timor – A Blunder?* Singapore: Crescent Design.

Soekanto et. al.1976. *Integrasi – Kebulatan Tekad Rakyat Timor Timur.* Jakarta: Yayasan Parikesit.

Taylor, John G. 1991. *Indonesia's Forgotten War – The hidden history of East Timor*
London: Zed Books.

Tomodok, E. M. 1994. *Hari-Hari Akhir Timor Portugis.* Jakarta: Dunia Pustaka Jaya.

United Nations. 1980-1999. *Progress Reports of the Secretary General on the Question of East Timor.*

Wiranto. 2002. *Pergulatan Menguak Kebenaran.* Jakarta: Institute for Democracy in Indonesia.